3vo

D1024928

A STUDY OF BRITISH GENIUS

A STUDY OF BRITISH GENIUS

BY

HAVELOCK ELLIS

New Edition
Revised and Enlarged

BOSTON AND NEW YORK
HOUGHTON MIFFLIN COMPANY
The Riverside Press Cambridge
1926

COPYRIGHT, 1926, BY HAVELOCK ELLIS

ALL RIGHTS RESERVED

The Riverside Press
CAMBRIDGE · MASSACHUSETTS
PRINTED IN THE U.S.A.

HUNTINGTON
LIBRARY

RELEASED
FROM HEH

PREFACE

For many years past material has been growing under my hands bearing on the psychological and anthropological characters of genius, and from time to time I have examined the data, and reached certain, more or less secure, conclusions. At one time indeed I hoped to set forth these conclusions and a summary of the material on which they are founded in a series of volumes. The present volume was published in 1904 as the first of these studies of genius. It would now appear that it is also likely to be the last. I am well content that this should be so. It deals with a subject which can scarcely fail to be of interest to most of us, even apart from the biological questions involved, and, as it stands, it seems to illustrate by a single concrete example of the first magnitude — the genius of Great Britain — many of the special characteristics of genius. At the same time it also illustrates the method of investigation which to me seems desirable, on one hand avoiding the superficial and casual and unsystematic ways current in the past, and, on the other hand, equally avoiding the attempt to introduce elaborate apparatus of precision which, when we bear in mind the nature of the data, would be worse than supererogatory.

In the past the phenomena of genius have mostly

been approached from two distinct standpoints. In the first place they were dealt with by alienists who, being impressed by the fact that certain men of eminent genius had presented symptoms which may properly be termed insane, became unduly inclined to class with insanity the manifestations of genius generally. On the other hand the subject has more recently been taken up by anthropologists and statisticians who have ignored altogether the psychiatric and even, for the most part, the psychological aspects of genius. Sir Francis Galton was the earliest and most distinguished exponent of this highly important aspect of the study of genius. But in the Prefatory Chapter to the second edition (1892) of *Hereditary Genius*, Galton admitted that it is not the only aspect, stating that some place must be given to the study of genius as a mental anomaly, an 'inborn excitability and peculiarity.'

My own attempt to investigate the phenomena of genius may be said to start from the point where Galton's left off (though my standpoint was reached some years before 1892). My method of approaching the group corresponds, so far as the data allow, with that which in France Dr. Toulouse adopted so brilliantly and thoroughly (notably in his study of Zola) in approaching the individual man of genius. From the purely psychiatric standpoint, from the purely anthropological standpoint, it is alike impossible to interpret the phe-

nomena of genius adequately. The methods which are instructive in the lunatic asylum, as well as those other methods (such as under Dr. Haddon's initiating influence were first carried out by Dr. Browne in the islands of the West of Ireland), which proved fruitful in isolated communities of the normal population, are here both out of place. In a study of genius which is biological in the widest sense of that term, we must ascertain alike the psychological data and the anthropological data, normal and abnormal, and seek to balance these steadily, without swerving unduly either to the right hand or to the left.

The plan of the present book, as originally published in 1904, is simple. The bulk of the volume is taken up with the succinct co-ordination and summation of the data before us, all introduction of foreign matter which might unduly overweight the conclusions at any point being strictly excluded. In small type are inserted the results obtained by previous investigation on somewhat similar bodies of data, together with the results obtained by the study of other mentally abnormal groups; these results are often of the highest significance in enabling us to interpret our conclusions. In the Appendices I have brought together some of the elementary facts on which I have worked; the reader is thus enabled to examine and check my results for himself; he will also, I hope, be able at many points to correct or amplify the original data.

I had purposed to represent the results of this study graphically by means of curves. On consideration, however, it seemed that such a method was unsuited to the nature of the data, and might tend to mislead the reader. In most of the groups of facts here dealt with the data are necessarily incomplete, and although a more thorough sifting of the sources would certainly yield further facts, they would in the end still remain incomplete. It is undesirable to give an air of precision to data which we have, indeed, good reason to consider approximately correct, but which at the same time do not enable us to reach the exact composition of the whole of the groups we are dealing with.

In bringing out this new edition after an interval of more than twenty years I have been seriously concerned as to the degree of revision and enlargement which might be desirable. In looking back at it from this distance of time I see, in the main outlines, no important modifications to make. It was prepared with much care and caution, in part as an essay in the method of studying a genius-group on the basis of the available data, and in part as an attempt to ascertain the special traits of a national group, which might later be compared with other national groups, when such other groups were similarly studied, and I had myself actively begun the study of the German national group, though I was compelled through stress of different work to lay it aside. At every point, so far as I can see, the

conclusions remain as sound to-day as when I worked them out.

It has, indeed, sometimes seemed to me that I might fortify and check these conclusions by embodying in them an examination of the results yielded by the supplementary volumes of the *Dictionary of National Biography* containing lives of all the important persons of British genius who have died in the interval since my book was published. But on consideration this has seemed to me unnecessary or even undesirable. The recent group would be too small to carry much weight taken separately, while to amalgamate the recent group with the main group would involve a complete recalculation of the results, which would not only be unlikely to reveal any significant modification, but also mean a degree of tedious labour hardly worth while to undertake again. The preparation of this book was indeed more laborious than any other work I have ever undertaken. One fails to realise beforehand that even a very crudely statistical study of this nature, with a large number of various units, involves endless possibilities of small errors and confusions, and must be slowly repeated many times to ensure absolute correctness. I still recall weary hours spent on some bench in the Luxembourg Gardens in Paris, near which I chanced then to be living, over these calculations. I am pleased to be able to add that no critic has discovered any errors in the calculations except one (an anthro-

pologist of repute, sad to say, now no more), and his 'discovery' was merely a careless misapprehension of my statements. Moreover, while it might seem that the investigation of recent persons of genius offers special facilities, practically that is not so. Biographers of recent personages may know more, but they tell less, nor is it so easy to estimate the real intellectual stature of our contemporaries as of the men of the past, so that the perspective is likely to be injured. Therefore this study remains, on the whole, much as it was originally prepared.

It is true that in the interval I have been able to change many of the data in small details, to correct some of them and to enlarge others. I have noted a few of these modifications in the text. They could not, however, affect the general conclusions, though they might give them a little more weight. I have also enlarged some of the special discussions and I have referred to the results of various investigations along allied lines made in recent years, for the most part confirming the conclusions I have reached.

It may seem inconsistent if I proceed to say that I have added several new chapters to the volume, and I have in fact only done so with hesitation, almost with reluctance. These additional chapters, four in number, were not written to form part of the book, and therefore, to my eyes, they destroy its symmetry, since, being supplementary chapters,

they follow the 'General Conclusions.' I prefer to think of the book without them. But they are all concerned with special aspects of the problem of genius and for the most part British genius. They do also really help to elucidate some of the points treated in the book, and the better because more discursively. I know also that to many readers they are of considerable interest. On these grounds, therefore, I have sought to overcome my own objection to their inclusion in this volume. As some of them were written nearly thirty years ago, it is scarcely necessary to say that they would have been written differently to-day and that more recent authorities would have been quoted. But in the main I still regard their conclusions as sound; and since the changes made necessary by time will be obvious to the instructed reader, I have preferred to leave them as they were written, save for a few minor modifications and omissions.

HAVELOCK ELLIS

CONTENTS

I. INTRODUCTORY 1

The problem to be investigated — The method of investigation — The *Dictionary of National Biography* — The principle ruling the selection of names — Cattell's method of selection — Reasons for the principles here adopted — Proportion of eminent women to eminent men — The distribution of intellectual ability in the various centuries — The biological data with which the present inquiry is chiefly concerned — Fallacies to be avoided.

II. NATIONALITY AND RACE 18

The determination of place of origin — Birthplaces of grandparents the best available criteria — Relative productiveness in genius of England, Wales, Scotland, and Ireland — The group of mixed British origin — The group of mixed British and foreign origin — Importance of the French element — Origins of eminent British women — The distribution of English genius according to counties — The genius of Kent — The regional distribution of British women of ability — The probable predominance of Norfolk and Suffolk in relative amount of ability — The three great foci of English genius — The East Anglian focus — The apparent poverty of London in aboriginal genius — The southwestern focus — The Welsh Border — The Anglo-Danish district — The psychological characteristics of East Anglian genius — The characteristics of the southwestern focus — The characteristics of the Welsh Border — The significance of the position of Kent — The distribution of genius in Wales — The distribution of genius in Scotland — The distribution of genius in Ireland — The regional distribution of various kinds of ability — The distribution of scientific ability — The regional variations of scientific aptitude — The distribution of eminent soldiers — The distribution of eminent sailors — The distribution of artists — The distribution of dramatic ability — The possible modification of racial factors by environmental conditions.

III. SOCIAL CLASS 66

Status of parents of British men of genius — Upper class — Yeomen and farmers — Clergy — Medicine

— Law — Army — Navy — Miscellaneous professions — Commercial classes — Crafts — Artisans and unskilled — The parentage of artists — The parentage of actors — How far change has taken place in the social composition of the genius-producing class — Comparison of the genius-producing class with the ordinary population.

IV. HEREDITY AND PARENTAGE 81

The tendency to heredity in intellectual ability — Inheritance of ability equally frequent through father and mother — Mental abnormality in the parents — Size of the families to which persons of eminent ability belong — Normal standards of comparison —Genius-producing families tend to be large — Men of ability tend to be the offspring of predominantly boy-producing parents — Women of ability perhaps tend to belong to girl-producing parents — Position in the family of the child of genius — Tendency of men of ability to be youngest and more especially eldest children — The age of the parents of eminent persons at their birth — Tendency to disparity of age in the parents.

V. CHILDHOOD AND YOUTH 118

The frequency of constitutional delicacy in infancy and childhood — Tendency of those who were weak in infancy to become robust later — The prevalence of precocity — University education — The frequency of prolonged residence abroad in early life.

VI. MARRIAGE AND FAMILY 136

Celibacy — Average age at marriage — Tendency to marry late — Age of eminent women at marriage — Apparently a greater tendency to celibacy among persons of ability than among the ordinary population — Fertility of Marriage — Fertility and sterility alike pronounced — Average size of families — Proportion of children of each sex.

VII. DURATION OF LIFE 153

The fallacy involved in estimating the longevity of eminent men — The real bearing of the data — Mortality at different ages.

VIII. PATHOLOGY 159

Relative ill-health — Consumption — The psychology of consumptives — Gout — Its extreme frequency in men of ability — The possible reasons for the association between gout and ability — Other allied diseases — Asthma and angina pectoris — Insanity — The question of its significance — Apparent rarity of grave nervous diseases — Frequency of minor nervous disorders — Stammering — Its significance — High-pitched voice — Spasmodic movements — Illegible handwriting — Short sight — Awkwardness of movement.

IX. STATURE 184

Nature of the data — Tendency of British men of ability to vary from the average in the direction of short and more especially of tall stature — Apparent deficiency of the medium-sized.

X. PIGMENTATION 189

Hair-colour and eye-colour — Method of classification — Sources of data — The index of pigmentation — Its marked variation in the different intellectual groups — Some probable causes for this variation.

XI. OTHER CHARACTERISTICS 196

Personal beauty or the reverse — The eyes —Shyness and timidity — Tendency to melancholy — Persecution by the world.

XII. CONCLUSIONS 203

The characteristics of men of genius probably to a large extent independent of the particular field their ability is shown in — What is the temperament of genius? — In what sense genius is healthy — The probable basis of inaptitude for ordinary life — In what sense genius is a neurosis.

XIII. THE CELTIC SPIRIT IN LITERATURE 213

Definition of the Celtic spirit — Its feeling for the remote — Its decorative sense — Irish and Welsh literature — The Nordic spirit — The *Chanson de Roland* — The blending of Celtic and Nordic spirits in English literature.

XIV. The Evolution of Painting in England 244

The two European centres of painting — Main characteristics of these centres — The position of Great Britain in relation to them — The Traditional School of the West Coast — The Naturalistic School of the East Coast.

XV. Genius and Stature 271

Fallacies of the inquiry — The stature of normal persons — Tall, middle-sized, and short persons of genius — Undue infrequency of the middle-sized — The variational tendency of genius — Some of the problems involved.

XVI. The Comparative Abilities of the Fair and the Dark 289

The hair-colour and eye-colour of the British population — The National Portrait Gallery — Eye-colour the chief criterion — The index of pigmentation — The royal family — The aristocracy — The pigmentary character of different groups — Characteristics of the fair and the dark.

Appendices

A. List of Eminent British Persons of Ability 311

B. Origins of British Persons of Ability 324

C. Occupation or Social Position of Fathers 373

D. Stature 381

E. Pigmentation 382

Index 385

A STUDY OF BRITISH GENIUS

A STUDY OF
BRITISH GENIUS

I

INTRODUCTORY

The problem to be investigated — The method of investigation — The *Dictionary of National Biography* — The principles ruling the selection of names — Cattell's method of selection — — Reasons for the principles here adopted — Proportion of eminent women to eminent men — The distribution of intellectual ability in the various centuries — The biological data with which the present inquiry is chiefly concerned — Fallacies to be avoided.

UNTIL now it has not been possible to obtain any comprehensive view of the men and women who have chiefly built up English civilization. It has not, therefore, been possible to study their personal characteristics as a group. The sixty-six volumes of the *Dictionary of National Biography* (later increased by a second supplement of three volumes) have for the first time enabled us to construct an authoritative and well-balanced scheme of the persons of illustrious genius, in every department, who have appeared in the British Isles from the beginning of history down to the end of the nineteenth century; and, with a certain amount of labour, they assist us to sum up their main traits. It has seemed to me worth while — both for the

sake of ascertaining the composition of those elements of intellectual ability which Great Britain has contributed to the world, and also as a study of the nature of genius generally — to utilize the *Dictionary* to work out these traits. I propose to present here some of the main conclusions which emerge from such a study.

The *Dictionary* contains some record — from a few lines to several dozen pages — of over thirty thousand persons. Now, this is an impracticable and undesirable number to deal with — impracticable because, regarding a large proportion of these persons, very little is here recorded or is even known; undesirable because it must be admitted that the majority, though persons of a certain note in their own day or their own circle, cannot be said to have made any remarkable contribution to civilization or to have displayed any very transcendent degree of native ability. My first task, therefore, was to discover a principle of selection in accordance with which the persons of relatively less distinguished ability and achievement might be eliminated. At the outset one class of individuals, it was fairly obvious, should be omitted altogether in the construction of any group in which the qualities of native intellectual ability are essential: royalty, and members of the royal family, as well as the hereditary nobility. Those eminent persons, the sons of commoners, who have founded noble families, are, of course,

not excluded by this rule, according to which any eminent person whose father, at the time of his birth, had attained the rank of baronet or any higher rank, is necessarily excluded from my list. Certainly the son of a king or a peer may possess a high degree of native ability, but it is practically impossible to estimate how far that ability would have carried him had he been the son of an ordinary citizen; it might be maintained that a successful merchant, ship-owner, schoolmaster or tradesman requires as much sagacity and mental alertness as even the most successful sovereign; by eliminating those individuals in whom the accident of birth counts for so much, we put this insoluble question out of court. I am surprised to find how few persons of obviously pre-eminent ability are excluded by this rule, and many whom, at first, one would imagine it excludes, it really allows to pass, especially in the case of sons born before the father was created a peer. In order to avoid any scandalous omissions, I have thought it well to rule in all those sons of peers whose ability has clearly been of a kind which could not be aided by position and influence; thus I have included the third Earl of Shaftesbury, for it cannot be held that the possession of an earldom tends to aid a man in becoming a philosopher. It has, however, very rarely indeed been necessary to accord this privilege; I have always refrained from according it in the case of soldiers and statesmen.

Having eliminated those whose position in the world has clearly been influenced by the accident of birth, it remained to eliminate those whose place in the world, as well as in the *Dictionary*, was comparatively small. After some consideration I decided that, generally speaking, those persons to whom less than three pages were allotted were evidently not regarded by the editors, and could scarcely be generally regarded, as of the first rank of eminence. Accordingly, I excluded all those individuals to whom less than that amount of space was devoted. When this was done, however, I found it necessary to go through the *Dictionary* again, treating this rule in a somewhat more liberal manner. I had so far obtained some seven hundred names, but I had excluded many persons of undoubtedly very eminent ability and achievement; Hutton, the geologist, and Jane Austen, the novelist, for instance, could scarcely be omitted from a study of British genius. It was evident that persons with eventful lives had a better chance of occupying much space than other persons of equal ability with uneventful lives. Moreover, I found that a somewhat rigid adherence to the rule I had laid down had sometimes resulted in groups that were too small and too ill-balanced to be useful for study. In the case of musical composers, for instance, while those of recent times, of whom much is known, bulk largely in the *Dictionary*, the earlier musicians, of whom little is known, though

their eminence is much greater, were excluded from my list. On the other hand, a certain number of persons had been included because, though of quite ordinary ability (like Bradshaw, the regicide), they happened by accident to have played a considerable part in history. In going through the *Dictionary* a second time, therefore, I modified my list in accordance with a new rule, to the effect that biographies occupying less than three pages should be included if the writers seemed to consider that their subjects had shown intellectual ability of a high order, and that those occupying more space should be excluded if the writers considered that their subjects displayed no high intellectual ability. In this way I eliminated those persons who rank chiefly as villains (like Titus Oates), and have little claim to the possession of any eminent degree of intellectual ability. I likewise felt compelled to exclude women (like Lady Hamilton) whose fame is not due to intellectual ability, but to beauty and to connection with eminent persons. I also omitted one or two persons for the reason that, although their claim to inclusion was unimpeachable, we are not in possession of a single definite biographical fact concerning them; from the present point of view they would merely cumber the ground.

So far as possible, it will be seen, I have sought to subordinate my own private judgment in making the selection. It has been my object to place the list, so far as possible, on an objective basis. At

the same time, it is evident that, while I only reserved to myself a casting vote on doubtful points, there was inevitably a certain proportion of cases where this personal vote had to be given. A purely mechanical method of making selections would necessarily lead to various absurdities, and all that I can claim is that the principles of selection I adopted have involved a minimum of interference on my part. It is certainly true that, even after much consideration and repeated revision, I remain myself still in doubt regarding a certain proportion of people included in my list and a certain proportion omitted. Indeed any reader who finds on going through my list that there are certain omitted names which most certainly ought to have been included, and certain included names which might well be omitted, will have reached precisely the conclusion which I have myself reached. However often I went through the *Dictionary*, I know that I should each time make a few trifling readjustments, and any one else who took the trouble to go over the ground I have traversed would likewise wish to make readjustments. But I am convinced that if my principles of selection are accepted, the margin for such readjustment is narrow.

It will be observed that, by means of a slightly complicated and so far as possible objective method of selection, I have not merely sought to include only individuals of a very high order of intellectual

ability, but have at the same time sought to avoid, so far as possible, the omission of others who may have an equal claim to inclusion on account of their possession of a high degree of intellectual ability. It will at the same time be observed that I do not claim to be absolutely successful either as regards the inclusions or the omissions. I must hasten to add that any failure here very slightly impairs the primary object of this study. It has not been my main object to attain a final list to date of those British men and women who have shown the highest degree of intellectual ability. I wished to ascertain some of the biological characteristics — anthropological and psychological — of persons of the highest intellectual ability produced by Great Britain. For this purpose it was essential that the list should be carefully and impartially obtained; it was not essential that it should be faultless, although that was the ideal I set before myself.

There is some interest in comparing my list with another list, prepared by Professor Cattell, of the 1000 most eminent men that have appeared in the world generally (J. McKeen Cattell: 'A Statistical Study of Eminent Men,' *Popular Science Monthly*, February, 1903). Professor Cattell, in constructing the list, adhered rigidly to the very simple and mechanical method of selection which I had at first proposed to follow, but, as has been above explained, found it desirable in some degree to modify by the adoption of additional rules of selection. He took six biographical dictionaries — Eng-

lish, French, German, and American — and, reducing space to a common standard, selected the 1000 persons who were allowed the greatest average space, inclusion in at least three of the dictionaries being regarded as an essential condition. The list was thus, so far as Professor Cattell was concerned, absolutely objective.

Of Professor Cattell's 1000 most eminent persons, 243, or nearly a quarter, appear to be British or to have flourished in Great Britain. Of these as many as at least 60 are not found in my list. (As the names in Professor Cattell's list appear without dates, the identification is not always quite certain.) Of these 60, 33 were excluded from my list as royal personages, and 20 as belonging to the hereditary aristocracy. There remain 7 who, since they thus figure among the 1000 most eminent persons who ever lived, ought surely to appear in my longer list of purely British persons. One, Jeffreys, was excluded because, although he may not have been without legal ability, the space which he occupies in the minds of men is not due to his ability, but to the scandal which he caused. In a somewhat similar manner, Macpherson, who appears in Professor Cattell's list but not in mine, was excluded because, although he occupies an important position in literary history, his contributions to literature have their main value from the traditions they embody; he is an insignificant character who accidently aroused great controversies, and showed little or no ability in his undoubtedly original literary work. Another, Thomas Brown, is a metaphysician, who, at all events in the *Dictionary*, is regarded as of little importance. Another, Robert Hall, was a Baptist preacher who left a reputation for pulpit oratory. The remaining three — Arbuthnot, Armstrong, and Akenside — are minor literary men whose productions are now unread, though it is possible that one, Armstrong, is undeservedly neglected. I do not consider that the exclusion of these seven persons reveals a very serious defect in my

list, even though it may well be that a few individuals have found their way into my list who showed intellectual ability that was of but little higher order.

An examination of Professor Cattell's list suffices to show how extremely difficult it is to obtain a reliable estimate of intellectual eminence on a simple objective basis. A test which places Napoleon III as the eleventh greatest man that ever lived — before Homer, Newton, and Alexander the Great — and includes some unread minor poets, while it excludes Gilbert, 'the father of experimental science,' is scarcely satisfactory. It is certainly better than a subjective method, but its results seem to justify such an attempt as I have made, however imperfectly, to adopt a more complexly objective method of selection.

In the final result my selection yields 975 British men of a high degree of intellectual eminence. The eminent women number 55, being in proportion to the men about 1 to 18.

A slightly lower standard of ability, it would appear, prevails among the women than among the men. On account of the greater rarity of intellectual ability in women, they have often played a large part in the world on the strength of achievements which would not have allowed a man to play a similarly large part. It seemed, again, impossible to exclude various women of powerful and influential personality, though their achievements were not always considerable. I allude to such persons as Hannah More and Mrs. Montagu. Even Mrs. Somerville, the only feminine representative of science in my list, could scarcely be included were

she not a woman, for she was little more than the accomplished popularizer of scientific results. In one department, and one only, the women seem to be little, if at all, inferior to the men in ability, that is in acting.

Professor Cattell finds the proportion of women in his list of the most eminent persons of history generally to be 3.2 per cent, while in my British list it is higher, being 5.3 per cent. This is a difference which might have been anticipated, since my list refers only to post-classical times, includes persons of a lower degree of eminence, and is concerned with a people among whom the conditions have possibly been more than usually favourable to the development of ability in women.

It may be asked how these 1030 persons of pre-eminent intellectual ability have been distributed through the course of English history. I find that from the fourth to the tenth centuries, inclusive, there are only 11 men of sufficient distinction to appear in my lists, nearly half of these belonging to the seventh century. From that date onwards (reckoning by the date of birth) we find that the eleventh century yields 5, the twelfth yields 11, the thirteenth 9, the fourteenth 16, the fifteenth 32, the sixteenth 161, the seventeenth 191, the eighteenth 372, the nineteenth 223. It is probable that the estimate most nearly corresponds to the actual facts as regards the seventeenth and eighteenth centuries. Before that time our information is too scanty, so that many men of notable ability have passed away without record. In the nineteenth

century, on the other hand, the material has been too copious, and the national biographers have probably tended to become unduly appreciative of every faint manifestation of intellectual ability. The extraordinary productiveness of the eighteenth century is very remarkable. In order to realize the significance of the facts, however, a century is too long a period. Distributing our persons of genius into half-century periods, and omitting the scanty early figures, I find that the following groups are formed:

1101–1150	1151–1200	1201–1250	1251–1300	1301–1350
4	7	2	7	6
1351–1400	1401–1450	1451–1500	1501–1550	1551–1600
10	6	26	49	112
1601–1650	1651–1700	1701–1750	1751–1800	1801–1850
112	79	134	238	219

Only four individuals belong to the second half of the nineteenth century. It is scarcely necessary to remark that the record for the first half of the nineteenth century is still incomplete. Taking the experience of the previous century as a basis, it may be estimated that some 35 per cent of the eminent persons belonging to the first half of the

nineteenth century were still alive at the time when this inquiry terminates. This would raise that half-century to the first place, but it may be pointed out that the increase on the previous half-century would be comparatively small, and also that the result must be discounted by the inevitable tendency to overestimate the men of recent times. We have to accept the perspective by which near things look large and remote things look small, but we must not be duped by it.

When we bear in mind that the activities of the individuals in each of these groups really fall, on the whole, into the succeeding period, certain interesting points are suggested. We note how the waves of Humanism and Reformation, when striking the shores of Britain, have stirred intellectual activity, and have been prolonged and intensified in the delayed English Renaissance. We see how this fermentation has been continued in the political movements of the middle of the seventeenth century, and we note the influence of the European upheaval at the end of the eighteenth century. The extraordinary outburst of intellect in the second half of that century is accentuated by the fact that, taking into account all entries in the *Dictionary*, the gross number of eminent men of the low standard required for inclusion shows little increase in the eighteenth century (5789, as against 5674 in the preceding century, is the editor's estimate); the increase of ability is thus in

quality rather than in quantity. It is curious to note that, throughout these eight centuries, a marked rise in the level of intellectual ability has very frequently, though not invariably, been preceded by a marked fall. It is also noteworthy that in every century, from the eleventh to the eighteenth, with the exception of the seventeenth, the majority of its great men have been born in the latter half. This outburst is very distinct at the beginning of the nineteenth century, and, as we have seen reason to believe, it was probably succeeded by an arrest, if not a decline, in the production of genius.

It is noteworthy that the progress of European ability generally, as illustrated by Professor Cattell's results, has followed very much the same curve as I have found in the case of British genius. 'Following the extraordinary development of the two nations of antiquity,' Professor Cattell writes, summarising his own diagrams, 'we have a decline, not sudden, . . . but the light fails towards the fifth century. The curve shows a rise towards the tenth century, increasing in rapidity as it proceeds. There are three noticeable breaks. Thus in the fourteenth century there was a pause followed by a gradual improvement and an extraordinary fruition at the end of the fifteenth century. . . . There was a pause in progress until a century later. . . . The latter part of the seventeenth century was a sterile period, followed by a revival culminating in the French revolution.' For Europe generally, as for Great Britain, the latter half of the eighteenth century represents the unquestionable climax of genius, 238 individuals belonging to the eighteenth century altogether as against less than one hun-

dred for the previous century. Professor Cattell's curve also shows the same general tendency for genius to become productive towards the end of each century, with the same very marked exception in the case of the seventeenth century, the fall here, Professor Cattell finds, extending to nearly every department of intellectual ability. In England we might have been tempted to attribute the fall to the social disturbance caused by the Civil Wars, but since it was a general European phenomenon (except in Germany, where the eighteenth-century expansion began earliest) this is impossible; it represents a period of rest between the activity of the late sixteenth and early seventeenth centuries, and the still greater intellectual energy of the eighteenth century.

When the list of eminent persons had at last been completed my task had still scarcely begun. It was my object to obtain as large a mass as possible of biological data — anthropological and psychological — so that I could deal with these persons of eminent intellectual ability as a human group and compare them with other human groups, normal and abnormal. I had, somewhat too innocently, assumed that the national biographers would usually be able to furnish the elementary data I required, whenever such data were extant. I soon realised, however, that the biographers were, with a few notable exceptions, literary men, unfamiliar with biological methods, and that they had seldom realised that biography is not a purely literary recreation, and that it demands something more than purely literary aptitudes. Method was, for the most part, conspicuously absent; if, for instance,

one wished to know if an eminent man had or had not been married, it was frequently necessary to read through the whole article to make sure that one had not missed a reference to this point; when found, one was still left frequently in doubt as to whether or not there had been offspring of the marriage, and when no reference to marriage could be found one was left in doubt as to whether this meant that there had been no marriage, or that the point was unknown, or simply that the biographer had forgotten to refer to the matter. This failure of precision in regard to so elementary a biographical fact introduced into the consideration of a very important matter a margin of error which I have had much difficulty in controlling, and it still remains considerable. Again, much trouble has been caused by the persistent vagueness of the biographers in describing the eminent man's position in his father's family. There is distinct interest in knowing the size of the family from which the great man sprang and his precise position in that family; but the biographers, in possibly the majority of cases, use such expressions as 'eldest son,' 'second son,' 'youngest son,' which tell us almost nothing. A brief personal description of the eminent man, once more, is always very instructive for biological purposes, and when the great man lived several centuries ago the biographer is usually careful to reproduce any scrap of information bearing on this point. But no such care is shown

in the case of the more modern persons concerning whom the information obtainable is still copious, and even when the biographer has personally known his subject he omits, almost as a rule, to give any information regarding his personal appearance. These and the like imperfections might easily have been avoided, and the value of the *Dictionary* immensely increased, had the editors adopted the fairly obvious device of issuing a few simple instructions to their fellow-workers on the question of method.

The greatest part of my labour has been due to these defects of the *Dictionary of National Biography* in respect of those biological data which necessarily form the central and most essential part of biography. In order to supplement the information furnished by the *Dictionary* I have consulted over three hundred biographies, as well as many other sources of information in memoirs, personal reminiscences, etc. In regard to some of the more recent persons included I have been able to fill in various facts from my own knowledge. As concerns eye and hair colour I have made a systematic examination of several picture galleries, more especially the National Portrait Gallery.

Having thus explained the nature of the data with which we have to deal, and the methods by which it has been obtained, we may now proceed, without further explanations, to investigate it. We have to study the chief biological characteris-

tics — anthropological and psychological — of the most eminent British men and women of genius, here using that word merely to signify high intellectual ability.

II

NATIONALITY AND RACE

The determination of place of origin — Birthplaces of grandparents the best available criteria — Relative productiveness in genius of England, Wales, Scotland, and Ireland — The group of mixed British origin — The group of mixed British and foreign origin — Importance of the French element — Origins of eminent British women — The distribution of English genius according to counties — The genius of Kent — The regional distribution of English women of ability — The probable predominance of Norfolk and Suffolk in relative amount of ability — The three great foci of English genius — The East Anglian focus — The apparent poverty of London in aboriginal genius — The south-western focus — The Welsh Border — The Anglo-Danish district — The psychological characteristics of East Anglian genius — The characteristics of the south-western focus — The characteristics of the Welsh Border — The significance of the position of Kent — The distribution of genius in Wales — The distribution of genius in Scotland — The distribution of genius in Ireland — The regional distribution of various kinds of ability — The distribution of scientific ability — The regional variations of scientific aptitude — The distribution of eminent soldiers — The distribution of eminent sailors — The distribution of artists — The distribution of dramatic ability — The possible modification of racial factors by environmental conditions.

It is scarcely necessary to remark that nationality and race, when used as distinguishing marks of people who all belong to the British Islands, are not identical terms and are both vague. The races — however we may describe them * — constituting the people of Great Britain are to be found in all the main divisions of the two islands,

* For summary of the position of this question, see Ripley's *Races of Europe*, ch. xii.

and the fact that a man is English or Scotch or Irish tells us nothing positive as to his race. Some indication of race, however, is in many cases furnished if we know the particular district to which a man's ancestors belonged, and this indication is further strengthened if we can ascertain his physical type.

In determining on a large scale the place of origin of men of genius the usual method hitherto has been to adopt the crude plan of noting the birthplace. I have so far as possible discarded this method, for a man's birthplace obviously tells us nothing decisive as to his real place of origin.

It has seemed to me that a man's place of origin can most accurately be determined by considering the districts to which his four grandparents belonged. If we know this we know with considerable certainty in what parts of the country he is really rooted, and in many cases we can thus form an estimate of his probable race. I have expended a very considerable amount of time and trouble over this part of my inquiry; yet so vague, confused, or conflicting is often the available evidence that probably none of my groups of data contain so many slight inaccuracies as this. It is only in a very small proportion of cases (even when the information derived from the *Dictionary* is supplemented) that I have been able to determine the origins of all four grandparents; I have usually

considered myself fortunate when I have been able to tell where the father and mother came from, and have often been well content merely to find out where the father came from. Only in a few cases have I admitted the evidence of birthplace.* London as a birthplace has been ignored altogether. When the facts are available it is nearly always found that the parents had migrated to London; we may reasonably assume that this is probably the case when the facts are not available. It very rarely occurs (as in the case of J. Bentham) that even one grandparent belonged to London.

In order to represent the varying values of this evidence, I have adopted a system of marks. If the four grandparents are of known origin, an eminent man is entitled to four marks, these marks being divided among the counties to which he belongs; when the evidence is less explicit the marks are correspondingly diminished. By this method I am able to give due weight to the very numerous cases in which the parents (or grandparents) belonged to different parts of the kingdom.

Every one of the 1030 persons included in this inquiry may be definitely classed, with at all events a fair degree of probability, in one part or another of the British Islands. When this is done we obtain the following results:

* This evidence varies in value; in the case of an eminent person whose father was a farmer it is fairly acceptable; but if the father was a clergyman it has little or no value.

English	659	Mixed British	97
Welsh	28	Mixed British and foreign	46
Scotch	137		
Irish	63		

Omitting for the moment the individuals of mixed ancestry, we find that 74.2 per cent are English, 3.1 Welsh, 15.4 Scotch and 7.1 Irish. If we take the basis of the present population and regard the proportion of eminent persons produced by England as the standard, Wales has produced slightly less than her share of persons of ability, Ireland still less, and Scotland decidedly more than her share.

As regards Wales we have to bear in mind the difficulty of a different language. As regards Scotland we probably have to recognise that intellectual aptitudes are especially marked among the Scotch, and also that the tendency has been fostered by circumstances, since, as is well known, the lowland Scotch are almost identical in racial composition with the northern English, and there are no artificial barriers of language. On the other hand, the Irish have been seriously hampered by geographical and to some extent by linguistic barriers, as well as by unfortunate political circumstances, in contributing their due share to British civilisation.

Mr. A. H. H. Maclean has shown (*Where We Get Our Best Men*, London, 1900) that of some 2500 British persons of ability belonging to the nineteenth century 70 per cent are English, 18 per cent Scotch, 10 per cent

Irish, and 2 per cent Welsh. We thus find that, by taking a much lower standard of ability and confining ourselves to the most recent period, Scotland stands higher than ever, while Ireland benefits very greatly at the expense of both England and Wales. This is probably not altogether an unexpected result. It is on the whole confirmed by an analysis of British *Men of the Time*, made by Dr. (now Sir) Conan Doyle (*Nineteenth Century*, August, 1888).

Both Mr. Maclean and Sir Conan Doyle adopted the crude test of birthplace. The somewhat higher place which they give to the Irish is, however, really confirmed by the analysis of my results. At an earlier stage of my inquiry, when the standard of ability adopted was higher, and the most recent group of eminent persons (those included in the supplement to the *Dictionary of National Biography*) had not been added, I found that the English contribution was larger, and the Irish smaller, than I now find it. It appears evident that possibly with some lowering of the standard of ability, and certainly with the advent of modern times, the Irish contribution tends to reach a larger proportion.

When we turn to consider the 143 persons who are of mixed British, or mixed foreign and British, race, we find that they may be divided as follows:

English and Irish	33
English and Scotch	30
English and Welsh	25
Mixed British, other than above	9
British and foreign	46

In percentages these results are: English and Irish, 23; English and Scotch, 20.9; English and Welsh, 17.4; other British, 6.2; British and foreign, 32.1. We here reach the interesting result that not-

withstanding the extreme frequency of English-Scotch marriages, and the very high proportion of ability among the unmixed Scotch, the English-Irish group stands, even absolutely, above the English-Scotch group, while the English-Welsh group is still more largely out of proportion with the small pure Welsh group, and is not far behind the English-Scotch group. It would appear that, so far as ability is concerned, the Irish and the Welsh are much better adapted for crossing with the English than are the more closely related Scotch.

There are forty-six persons in whom one or more elements of foreign blood are mingled with one or more British elements. These do not, of course, include all the foreigners who have played a part in English civilisation, since no person of purely foreign blood was taken into account in the preparation of my list. This has, for instance, led to the omission of numerous early Normans (like Becket) some later French Huguenots (like Romilly), and several eminent Jews.

Even though the purely French persons of eminence are omitted, the French elements remain distinctly the most important. At least seventeen of our forty-six individuals of partly foreign origin have had a French parent or grandparent. Some of these were Huguenots. No account has been taken of ancestors beyond the grandparents, but a Huguenot ancestral element seemingly more re-

mote than the grandparents is certainly of very frequent occurrence; I have noted it in seventeen cases, and it certainly occurs much oftener. Other remote Huguenot elements (especially Walloon, Flemish and Dutch) occur with only less frequency. German parents and grandparents only occur ten times; the Dutch and Flemish, occurring eight times, are but little behind, while five of our eminent persons were partly Italian. The exact combinations, with the number of times of their occurrence, are as follows:

English and French	12
English and German	8
English and Dutch	5
English and Italian	3
English and Flemish	2
Scotch and French	2
English, Irish, French and Swiss	2
English and Russian	1
English and Danish	1
English, Irish and German	1
Irish and French	1
Irish and Italian	1
Irish and Spanish	1
English, Irish and Italian	1
Scotch and Dutch	1
Irish and Austrian	1
English, Scotch and German	1
Welsh and Swiss	1
Welsh and Italian	1

There is much interest in considering separately the places of origin of the 55 eminent women on our list. Of these 29 are English, 4 Scotch, 4 Irish, and 18 of mixed origin. The obvious points to note here are the very remarkable prevalence of women

of mixed race (in the proportion of 32 per cent instead of only 13 per cent as in the case of our eminent persons generally), and the rise of Ireland to equality with Scotland. When we analyse the eighteen mixed cases the same prevalence of the Irish element appears in a very much more marked form. The various mixtures are as follows:

English and Irish	8
English and Scotch	2
English and Welsh	2
English and French	2
English and Italian	1
English, Irish and German	1
English, Irish and Italian	1
English, Irish, French and Swiss	1

Here we see that while an English element enters into every combination, in not less than eleven of the eighteen cases it is combined with an Irish element. The Scotch element reaches no higher a level than the Welsh and is even inferior to the French. Among our eminent persons generally not more than one in fifteen is Irish; among the eminent women more than one in four is Irish, while Scotland, which has produced relatively the largest share of eminent men, has produced relatively the smallest share of eminent women.

So far we have been concerned solely with the distribution of our eminent ability in the main divisions of the United Kingdom. There is, however, much interest in determining the distribution of ability within these main divisions. The obvious,

and indeed the inevitable, basis for this part of the inquiry is the division into counties. It is, however, a very awkward and inconvenient basis. The counties are very unequal in size, usually too small, and in most cases they correspond to no ancient boundaries. They have neither the historical significance of the ancient French provinces, nor the practical convenience of the modern French departments. The ancient English dioceses furnish on the whole a better basis and one that for the most part corresponds to real ancient divisions;* but it was obviously inconvenient and inadvisable to fall back on an extinct division of the country. It was necessary to be content with the county basis and to seek so far as possible to minimise its disadvantages.

In the first place the English counties may be presented in accordance with the absolute number of elements of ability which each possesses, with no attempt to show the significance of the numbers. It will, of course, be remembered (and may be clearly seen by reference to Appendix B) that in consequence of the imperfection of our knowledge these elements are of disparate value, so that while one individual may be counted four times (*i.e.*, once for each of his grandparents), another may only be counted once. Most individuals are counted twice.

* See, *e.g.*, G. Hill, *English Dioceses*.

Yorkshire	90	Hampshire	19
Norfolk	67	Buckinghamshire	19
Devon	56	Northamptonshire	18
Kent	51	Hertfordshire	18
Suffolk	50	Herefordshire	17
Lancashire	43	Oxfordshire	16
Lincolnshire	37	Cumberland	16
Somerset	30	Nottinghamshire	16
Cornwall	30	Leicestershire	15
Gloucestershire	28	Cambridgeshire	15
Essex	27	Surrey	14
Warwickshire	26	Westmoreland	11
Shropshire	24	Sussex	10
Staffordshire	24	Durham	8
Wiltshire	24	Bedfordshire	8
Northumberland	20	Berkshire	8
Worcestershire	20	Rutland	6
Derbyshire	19	Middlesex	5
Cheshire	19	Huntingdonshire	5
Dorset	19	Monmouth	3

The significance of these results is not quite obvious to casual inspection. We see that the origins of English ability are to be found all over the country, and we see also, as we should expect, that the large counties have produced much ability and the small counties little. How can we ascertain the real significance of these figures?

There are two methods we may adopt for ascertaining the significance of our figures: we may determine the amount of ability in each county in relation to its area, or we may determine it in relation to its population.

The method of comparison which rests on ascertaining the relative amount of ability per square mile for each county is not so absurd in the case of a country like England as it may possibly seem

at the first glance. To compare the ability per square mile of a county like present-day Lancashire covered with great towns, to an agricultural county like present-day Norfolk or Suffolk, would be obviously unfair to the latter. But we may remember that East Anglia was a populous manufacturing centre for many centuries during which Lancashire resembled modern Cumberland. During the long history of England the various counties have passed through many economic vicissitudes, and while some have doubtless succeeded in remaining throughout at a fairly medium level of populousness, others have at some periods been great centres of population, and at other periods denuded of their inhabitants.* Thus when we put one period against another the differences between the counties in average density of population are probably small, and it is by no means so absurd to ascertain the relative amount of ability per square mile for the whole period as it would be for a single century.

An even approximate determination of the amount of ability in relation to the population is obviously impossible for the whole period; we can only obtain it with certainty for the nineteenth century. I have thought it of some interest, and

* The poll-tax returns for the fourteenth century (as reproduced, *e.g.*, by Edgar Powell, *The Rising in East Anglia in 1381*, Appendix I, pp. 120 *et seq.*) seem to indicate that, absolutely, Yorks, Norfolk, Suffolk, Somerset and Lincoln were at that time the most populous counties.

probably of real significance as an aid to determining the problem before us, to consider separately the eminent persons born during the nineteenth century (nearly all in the first half), and to determine what relation the elements they supply us with bear to the population of the various counties as revealed by the census of 1841.* The basis of comparison seems here to be fairly sound, though unfortunately the numbers for each county are necessarily so small that we cannot consider the results as absolutely conclusive when they are not otherwise confirmed.

It must be added, further, that there is another source of error the existence of which probably might not be suspected. Apart altogether from its rise and fall in population a county may still exhibit a very marked fluctuation in its genius-producing power. A very interesting and decisive example of this is furnished by Kent. On account of its proximity to the continent Kent has from the earliest periods been a highly civilised county, and it has always been a populous one; it remains a populous and flourishing county at the present day. It has also been, as we shall see, very prolific indeed in genius. Yet at the present day its ability-producing powers have almost ceased. It is associated, perhaps more than any other county, with the Renaissance in England; Caxton and Gower belonged

* I selected this census as it was convenient to use Fletcher's statistical analysis of its results.

to Kent; it was the home of Marlowe and Lyly, the two teachers of Shakespeare, as well as of Linacre and Harvey, who represent the English Renaissance on the scientific side; at that period it was prolific in administrators, diplomatists, and soldiers. It was strongly Royalist, and suffered greatly in the cause of Charles I. When Charles fell, Kent fell so far as genius-producing power is concerned,* and however it may continue to flourish in population and general prosperity, it has never regained its power to add largely to English ability. In the sixteenth and seventeenth centuries its contributions to the elements of English ability are represented by the figures 15 and 16 respectively — relatively a very large proportion; but in the eighteenth century, so fertile in ability, Kent is only responsible for the relatively small contribution of eleven elements, and in the nineteenth century its contribution has sunk to four elements, which do not include a single individual who was wholly Kentish. Yet, as we shall see, Kent stands almost, if not quite, at the head of all the English counties in its total contribution to English genius. Although no other county could be found to furnish so remarkable an instance of great intellectual fertility fol-

* It cannot be said that this coincidence adequately explains the phenomenon. Dr. Beddoe suggested to me that the decline of Kent may be largely due to the attraction of London draining away its best stocks, and that we may thus account for the fact that Surrey, Essex, and even Suffolk, stand lower in genius-producing power for the nineteenth century than for the whole period.

lowed by intellectual decadence, without decrease in population and prosperity, this case is enough to show that we can by no means assume that the intellectual fertility of a county in one century is any certain index to its general intellectual fertility.

I now present, side by side, the order of decreasing intellectual fertility into which fall the counties our eminent men belong to when we consider the relative amount of the total ability for the whole period on the basis of area (taken as per 1000 square miles), and also the order into which the elements for the nineteenth century fall on the basis of the population of the counties in 1841. A plus sign after the figures in the first column indicates that as the modern population of the county in question is very decidedly below the average for the country generally, we probably ought to add a few units to the figures given; a minus sign indicates that as the modern population is much above the average for the country generally, we probably ought to subtract a few units to reach a fair estimate; the sign of equality means that the population of the county approximates to the average for the country generally. Those counties which contain a proportion of elements of genius equal to more than 19 to the 1000 square miles, or more than 2 per 100,000 inhabitants, must be considered prolific in genius.

	Amount of ability in ratio per 1000 square miles		Amount of ability during 19th century in ratio per 100,000 inhabitants (1841)
Rutland	40+	Norfolk	5.3
Suffolk	33+	Herefordshire	4.3
Kent	32–	Oxfordshire	4.3
Norfolk	31+	Hertfordshire	3.8
Warwickshire	29–	Worcestershire	3.8
Hertfordshire	28+	Westmoreland	3.6
Worcestershire	27–	Dorsetshire	3.4
Buckinghamshire	25+	Cumberland	3.4
Cornwall	22+	Warwickshire	2.7
Gloucestershire	22=	Cornwall	2.6
Lancashire	22–	Buckinghamshire	2.5
Devonshire	21+	Shropshire	2.5
Oxfordshire	21+	Northumberland	2.4
Herefordshire	20+	Wiltshire	2.3
Staffordshire	20–	Cambridgeshire	2.3
Nottinghamshire	19+	Lincolnshire	2.2
Dorsetshire	19+	Suffolk	2.1
Northamptonshire	18+	Nottinghamshire	2.0
Leicestershire	18+	Berkshire	1.8
Somerset	18+	Devonshire	1.5
Shropshire	18+	Yorkshire	1.5
Cambridgeshire	18+	Derbyshire	1.4
Derbyshire	18=	Cheshire	1.2
Surrey	18–	Gloucestershire	1.2
Cheshire	18–	Hampshire	1.1
Essex	17+	Leicestershire	.9
Wiltshire	17+	Somerset	.9
Bedfordshire	17+	Lancashire	.8
Middlesex	17	Staffordshire	.8
Westmoreland	14+	Essex	.8
Yorkshire	14=	Kent	.7
Huntingdonshire	13+	Sussex	.4
Lincolnshire	13+	Surrey	.3
Berkshire	11+	Durham	.3
Hampshire	11+	Bedfordshire	0
Cumberland	10+	Northamptonshire	0
Northumberland	9+	Huntingdonshire	0
Sussex	7+	Monmouth	0
Durham	7–	Rutland	0
Monmouth	5+	Middlesex, omitted *	

* There are three units to Middlesex, but not having the population for Middlesex in 1841, excluding the metropolis, I have not included this county.

If we consider the eminent women separately we find that eleven English counties have produced more than one unit of ability. The absolute numbers are as follows:

Norfolk	9	Lancashire	2
Suffolk	5	Worcestershire	2
Yorkshire	4	Shropshire	2
Hereford	3	Devonshire	2
Kent	3	Cornwall	2
Northumberland	3		

The numbers are too small to make it worth while to attempt to ascertain the relative value of these figures. It is sufficiently clear that Norfolk stands first and that Suffolk, a much smaller county, follows very closely after.*

Although the estimate of ability on the basis of the area of the counties is obviously only roughly approximate, while the more reliable method of ascertaining the proportion to population during the nineteenth century suffers from the defect that it by no means necessarily indicates the amount of ability in previous centuries, and while both methods are hampered by the very small size of many of the counties, we may still reach certain conclusions by considering the two lists together. The counties that stand high on both lists have probably been highly productive of intellectual

* Conan Doyle in his analysis of *Men of the Time* found that 'Suffolk appears to be pre-eminently the county of famous women.' Macfarlane (*Lady's Realm*, March, 1911) classified all the women in the *Dictionary* according to birthplace, and found that (putting aside London, and Yorkshire for its size) Norfolk comes first, followed by Suffolk and Somerset.

ability; those that stand low in both lists have probably been markedly unproductive. We may probably believe that the counties that have contributed most largely to the making of English men of genius are Norfolk, Suffolk, Hertfordshire, Warwickshire, Worcestershire, Herefordshire, Buckinghamshire, Cornwall, Dorsetshire, Oxfordshire, and Shropshire. To these we must certainly add Kent, since its total output more than compensates for its intellectual decadence during recent centuries; but we are perhaps scarcely justified in including Rutland, which by a curious anomaly appears at the head of the first list, though the smallest and one of the most thinly populated of English counties.

It cannot hastily be assumed that, while these counties rank probably at the head of English counties from the intellectual point of view, there are not others which perhaps on a perfectly sound basis ought not to rank almost on a level with them. This would especially be so if we were to take quality of genius as well as quantity into consideration. It is probable that Somerset, Devonshire, Gloucestershire, Wiltshire and Essex should be included among those of the first rank, although the two associated East Anglian counties of Norfolk and Suffolk have a fairly assured position at the head.

Maclean, who finds that Suffolk is among the six English counties which on the basis of population con-

tributed the largest number of eminent men to the Victorian period, places Ipswich first among the towns (excluding the large cities) which have been prolific in ability. Sir Conan Doyle, investigating *Men of the Time*, finds that Suffolk is among the three English counties that stand first in production of intellectual ability on the basis of population, and remarks that its intellectual productivity is 'quite phenomenal.'

It must be remembered that these inquiries were on the basis of birthplace, and that as East Anglians show a marked tendency to emigrate westwards, and especially to London, in a large number of cases they are credited to other districts.

On the basis of these results, and taking into consideration also the special quality of the individuals (as may be done by studying Appendix B), we come, I believe, to the conclusion that there are two, or, rather, three, great foci of intellectual ability in England: the East Anglian focus, the south-western focus, and the focus of the Welsh Border.

The East Anglian focus may for the present purpose be said to include not only Norfolk and Suffolk, but also the adjoining counties of Essex, Cambridgeshire and Hertfordshire, which, though inferior both in the quantity and the quality of their genius to East Anglia proper, are still high in intellectual ability which is nearly always of distinctively East Anglian type; these five counties form a compact whole. Among the eminent men who, so far as our knowledge, sometimes limited, extends, belong wholly to this region are Bishop

Andrewes, the Bacons, Thomas Cavendish, Chaucer (?), Constable, Cotman, Cowper, Cranmer, Flaxman, John Fletcher, Gainsborough, William Gilbert, Grosseteste, the Lyttons, Nelson, the Newmans, Porson, Pusey, Ray, the Veres, Robert Walpole and Wolsey. Among those who belong in part to this region are Airy, the Arnolds, Barrow, Bradlaugh, Colet, Gresham, Stephen Hales, Charles Lamb, the Martineaus, Sir Thomas More, Pater, Sir Thomas Smith and Walsingham. Ethnologically, it may be remarked, this focus is the most recent of the three. East Anglia is a region very open to invasion; Brythons, Romans, Angles, and Normans all seem to have come here in large numbers; and it differs from every other English district (except to some extent Kent, a county closely allied to it) in continuing to welcome foreigners — Dutch, Flemish, Walloon, French — all through mediæval times, down to the revocation of the Edict of Nantes at the end of the seventeenth century.

Middlesex with London lies on the borders of the East Anglian focus, with which, probably, of all the foci of English genius it is most intimately connected. It can scarcely, however, be included within that focus. The Metropolis itself is excluded from our inquiry, partly because we are not taking the accident of birthplace into account, and partly because it seems impossible to find any eminent person who belongs to London, or even to

Middlesex, through all his grandparents. Middlesex is poor in aboriginal ability, even for a small county, and if we were to class it psychologically at all I believe it would fall in with the predominantly Saxon group of counties which includes Berkshire, Surrey, Sussex and Hampshire — a group which, as we shall see, constitute a district remarkably poor in aboriginal ability.

The marked prevalence of merely native ability in London, and the marked deficiency of really aboriginal ability, are phenomena alike easy of explanation. Among the crowds who drift into every great metropolis there are always many clever and ambitious people; hence the number of able persons who are merely connected with a metropolis by the accident of birth. But a great metropolis swiftly kills those whom it attracts; Cantlie (*Degeneration amongst Londoners*, 1885, p. 19) very properly defined a Londoner as one whose parents and grandparents were born and bred in London; but during the four years in which he investigated this question he was unable to find a single Londoner in this true and definite sense, and even those who were Londoners back to the grandparents on one side only, were usually stunted or feeble, and unlikely to propagate. Dr. Harry Campbell (*Causation of Disease*, p. 245) among 200 London-born children found two or three whose parents and grandparents were born and bred in London, and these children were very delicate.

The south-western focus of English genius is the largest, and although in proportion to the population ability is here less prevalent than in the East Anglian district, in absolute amount, and perhaps even in importance, this region may per-

haps be said to be the most conspicuous centre of English intellectual energy. I regard it as comprising the counties of Wiltshire, Somerset, Dorset, Devon, and Cornwall. These counties, together with part of Hampshire, make up the whole of the south-western promontory of Great Britain. The population of this region is marked by very much darker hair, and therefore a much higher index of nigrescence, than the population of the counties to east of it. The district is defended by Wansdyke and Bokerley Dyke, one of the most important structures of this kind in Europe, and this fact indicates that the region was once arrayed against the rest of Britain. Pitt-Rivers * has shown that this wall is of Roman or post-Roman date, possibly Saxon. This great focus of British genius is, taken altogether, unquestionably the oldest of the three foci which we may detect in England. We may call it the Goidelic-Iberian centre. It is well known that this region was the last stronghold of the early British power in England; when, finally, its power was broken in war the Saxon invaders had become Christianised and settled peacefully side by side with the aboriginal inhabitants. The people of this region were still described by King Alfred as 'Welsh Kin,' and the predominance of the aboriginal element may still be detected in the characteristics of the genius of this region. Among the more eminent

* *Excavations in Cranborne Chase*, vol. 3.

individuals who seem to belong wholly to this region are Roger Bacon, Blackstone, Robert Blake, Saint Boniface, Clifford, Coleridge, Dampier, Drake, Saint Dunstan, Ford, Grocyn, Hawkins, Hobbes, Hooker, John of Salisbury, Keats, Locke, Pym, Raleigh, Reynolds, Rodney, Alfred Stevens, Sydenham, Trevithick, Thomas Young. Among those who belong to it in part are Matthew Arnold, Bradley, Browning, Byron, the Cannings, Fielding, C. J. Fox, Froude, Huxley, the Kingsleys, and the Pitts.

The third focus, that of the Welsh Border, includes the counties of Gloucestershire, Warwickshire, Worcestershire, Herefordshire, Shropshire, and Cheshire. This selection of counties may possibly seem a little arbitrary, but it will be found not to be so on turning to the anthropological map of the British Islands (as given, for instance, in Ripley's *Races of Europe*), founded on Beddoe's observations of the index of nigrescence. These six counties form a dark-haired borderland in western England against Wales, and the eastern enfolding to Warwickshire cannot be disregarded.* Monmouth is properly excluded; its contribution to English genius is extremely minute; it was not

* There is a curious and compact island of very dark-haired peoples in the counties to the north of London, possibly connected with the Warwick enfolding of the Welsh Border; and the Chiltern Hills evidently proved a refuge for the earlier and darker peoples of Britain, like Devon and Cornwall; but any psychological affinity of the inhabitants of these counties with those of the Welsh Border does not seem to be clear, though it is possible.

even nominally English until the time of Henry VIII; it still remains anthropologically Welsh, and the study of its surnames shows, as Guppy states in his *Homes of Family Names*, that it is even more Welsh than Wales. The counties here included in the Welsh Border are all much more thoroughly Anglicised, but Welsh was spoken in most of them until comparatively recent times, even in Gloucestershire, undoubtedly a very mixed county.* The language of Shropshire has been described as 'English spoken as a foreign language.' In Herefordshire Welsh appears to be not quite extinct even yet.† The whole of the district represents the mingling on the one side of Welsh elements, on the other of Saxon and Anglian elements. It is not difficult to account for this mingling; when in the eighth century Offa extended the limits of Mercia westwards, changing the name of the British town of Pengwyrn to Shrewsbury, he adopted the policy of leaving on the land all the Britons who wished to remain; in more recent times there has been a Welsh reflux eastwards, and the result is a fairly thorough assimilation of Welsh and English racial elements. The Welsh elements have been regarded as predominantly Bry-

* 'The Transsabrina is very "aboriginal" and dark-haired,' remarks Dr. Beddoe; 'the Cotswolds are largely Saxon and fair; the Vale lies between in race as in position.'

† Rhys and Brynmor-Jones, *The Welsh People*, p. 526; cf. Southall, *Wales and Her Language*, especially ch. IX, dealing with traces of Welsh in the Marches.

thonic rather than Goidelic, the latter people being mainly confined to the north-west and south-west districts of Wales. It may therefore be said that this Anglo-Brythonic district of the Welsh Border is intermediate in age between the recent East Anglian focus and the ancient south-western focus.

Among the more eminent individuals who belong wholly to the Welsh Border are Alexander of Hales, Samuel Butler, Warren Hastings, Sir Thomas Lawrence, Shakespeare, Purcell, William Tyndale and Wycherley. Among those who belong to it in part are Robert Boyle, John Bright, Sir Thomas Browne, Clive, Charles Darwin, Fielding, Keble, the Herberts, the Kembles, Landor, Macaulay, Map, William Morris, the Penns, Wedgwood, the Wesleys, Wren, Wycherley.

It will be noted that all three of the great foci of English intellect belong mainly to the southern half of the country, the most anciently civilised part, although within recent centuries the least prosperous and the most thinly populated. It must be added that nearly the whole of the northern part of England from Lincolnshire, Nottinghamshire and Derbyshire, through Yorkshire well on into the Lowlands of Scotland, constitutes a large region which, although its intellectual elements are of no great density, presents its own peculiar anthropological characters. It is the predominantly Anglo-Danish part of England, containing the fairest

population of the country.* Its intellectual fertility is greatest in its northern portions, which now form part of Scotland, and at its southern border, where it blends with East Anglia. To this last district belongs Sir Isaac Newton, the supreme representative of Anglo-Danish genius.†

Apart from exact science and from scholarship, the Anglo-Danish district, in proportion to its size, has not produced many men in purely intellectual fields. Its children have usually been more remarkable for force of character than for force of intellect. Their stubborn independent temper involves an aptitude for martyrdom; many religious martyrs come from this region, and the martyrologist Foxe also. East Anglia is productive of great statesmen and great ecclesiastics; it is also

* Leicestershire should doubtless be included in the Anglo-Danish district. On the basis of place-names Taylor finds it to be the most Danish county in England. Beddoe's map of the index of nigrescence, however, shows it to be ethnologically darker than the Anglo-Danish district proper. Psychologically its genius seems to me rather mixed but certainly in large measure Anglo-Danish.

† I was formerly inclined to think that Lincolnshire and Nottinghamshire should be affiliated to the East Anglian focus, but a more careful consideration of the facts leads to the conclusion that, on the whole, both anthropologically and psychologically they belong to the Anglo-Danish district. I still think that the northern portion of Northamptonshire, and still more emphatically Rutland, are mainly East Anglian in the character of their genius. The former county, however, seems to present a very special and vigorous mixture of East Anglian, Anglo-Danish and aboriginal elements. (At the Norman Conquest, also, Fleming and Picard elements were introduced here. *Victoria History of Northamptonshire*, vol. I, p. 289.) It is not easy to fix the exact western limits of the East Anglian district unless we boldly carry it as far as the Welsh Border counties, Warwickshire and Gloucestershire.

a land of great scholars. At the same time nearly half the British musical composers and more than a third of the painters have come from this same region. It has no aptitude for abstract thinking, for metaphysics, but in concrete thinking, in the art of treating science philosophically, it is easily supreme. Its special characters seem to be its humanity, its patience, its grasp of detail, its deliberate flexibility, combined with a profound love of liberty and independence.* The characteristic English love of compromise is rooted in East Anglia. So typically English a statesman as Walpole, with his sound instincts in practical affairs, belonged to Norfolk, and Wolsey belonged to Suffolk. In spite, however, of the marked sanity and self-possession of the East Anglian, it may be added that while East Anglia has produced many of the best Englishmen it has also produced a considerable proportion of the worst.† Those who figure in English history chiefly by virtue of their villainy do not appear in my list, but it is notable that many of the great men who have come down to us with a somewhat flawed reputation

* It may be noted that the founders of New England, both on the political and the religious side, were largely produced by East Anglia. The Washingtons came from the related county of Northamptonshire; the Emersons were from Suffolk, or Saffron Walden in Essex on the borders of Suffolk; Winthrop, who, it has been said, more than any other man moulded Massachusetts which moulded New England, belonged to Central Suffolk.

† It must be added, at the same time, that the records of criminality, at all events during the nineteenth century, by no means show the East Anglian counties among the worst.

belong here; Bacon is a typical example of the first rank.

When we turn to the south-western focus of English genius we find ourselves among people of different mental texture, but of equal mental distinction. In positive intellectual achievement they compare with the slow and patient people of East Anglia, while as brilliant personalities they are in the very first rank. They are sailors rather than scholars, and courtiers, perhaps, rather than statesmen; they are innovators, daring free-thinkers, pioneers in the physical and intellectual worlds. Raleigh, on both sides a Devonshire man, is the complete type of these people. They are, above all, impressive personalities, aggressive, accomplished, irresistible, breaking rather than bending, without the careful foresight of the laborious and self-distrustful people of the east coast. This district alone has furnished a third of the great sailors of Britain, and the most brilliant group, with Drake and Hawkins and Gilbert as well as Raleigh. The expansive Elizabethan age gave the men of these parts their supreme chance, and they availed themselves of it to the utmost. Great Britain's most eminent soldiers have not usually been English, but one of the most famous of all, Marlborough, belongs to this region. In the arts of peace this south-western focus shows especially well in painting. It cannot, indeed, be compared to the East Anglian focus in this respect, but Reynolds belongs to

Devon, and is a typical representative of the qualities of this region on the less aggressive side, just as Raleigh is on the more militant side, both alike charming and accomplished personalities. Both in the material and spiritual worlds there is an imaginative exaltation, an element of dash and daring, in the men of this south-western district, which seems to carry them through safely. The south-western focus is not quite so homogeneous as the eastern group. Somerset, which is the centre of the focus, seems to me to present its real and characteristic kernel, especially on the purely intellectual side. We do not find here the dashing recklessness, the somewhat piratical tendency, nor quite the same brilliant personal qualities as at the western part of the peninsula. The Somerset group of men are superficially more like those of East Anglia, but in reality with a very distinct physiognomy of their own. Like the rest of this region, Somerset is a land of great sailors, but the typical sailor hero of Somerset is Blake, and the difference between Blake and Raleigh is significant of the difference between the men of Somerset and the men of Devon.* Somerset with Wiltshire has pro-

* I now place William Blake also in this region. The patriotic advocacy by Mr. Yeats of Dublin as the ancestral home of William Blake had led me astray; there is no sound basis for this ancestry. On the contrary (it is stated by A. T. Story in his life of Blake) the cousins of William Blake at Southampton had a tradition that the family is descended from the Somerset Blakes of the Admiral's family, through a branch settled in Wiltshire. William Blake would thus be brought into the same south-western

duced the philosophers of this region, Roger Bacon, Hobbes, Locke; and in more recent days Bagehot and Huxley have been typical thinkers of the group. Hooker, the 'judicious,' is among the men of Devon. They are not often scholars (notwithstanding the presence of the 'ever-memorable' Hales), being prone to rely much on their own native qualities. One recalls the remark of Hobbes, when charged with an indifference to books: 'If I read as much as other people I should know as little as other people.' While less concrete than the East Anglians, these eminent thinkers have not the abstract metaphysical tendencies of the North British philosophers; they reveal a certain practical sagacity, a determination to see things clearly, a hatred of cant and shams, a 'positive' tendency, which is one of the notes of purely English thought and may be said to have its headquarters here. The representative scientific man of this region is the brilliant and versatile Thomas Young, whose luminous intelligence and marvellous intuition render him a typical example of genius in its purest form.

It is easy to define the nature of the genius of the Welsh Border. It is artistic in the widest sense, and notably poetic; there is a tendency to literary

focus of English genius as Coleridge, Keats, and other great poets, while it may be added that his characteristics are much in harmony with those of the men of Somerset. If Ireland thus probably loses one of the great figures on my list, she probably gains another in Faraday (p. 57) and the balance is maintained.

and oratorical eloquence, frequently tinged with religious or moral emotion, and among those who belong entirely to this district there are no scientific men of the first order. This region has the honour of claiming Shakespeare; and it may be pointed out that it is difficult to account for Shakespeare without assuming in him the presence of a large though not predominant Celtic element.* Landor, one of the greatest of English masters of prose, comes in part within the Welsh Border, as does Fielding, while Purcell, one of the greatest of English composers, also probably belongs to this district. Sir Thomas Browne, though only a Welsh Borderer on his father's side, is very typical, and Macaulay is characteristic of the Celt as historian. The presence of Mrs. Siddons, although the genius of the Kemble family is attributed mainly to their Irish mother, helps to indicate the characteristics of this region, which although it has produced fewer great personalities than the two main foci of English genius, has certainly had its full share in some of the very greatest. The part of the Welsh Border in Darwin was small, but though he was more characteristically a son of the Anglo-Danish and East Anglian regions, it was probably not without its influence.

It has already been made clear that the county of Kent constitutes a remarkable, though small,

For a discussion of the 'Celtic element' in English genius see a later chapter (pp. 213–43).

centre of English genius. I was formerly inclined to regard this very interesting district as dependent on the important East Anglian focus. I am convinced, however, that this is a mistake. If we carefully contemplate the eminent persons produced by Kent it will be seen that they can be more easily affiliated, on the whole, to the south-western than to the East Anglian focus. Harvey, for instance, the greatest of the Kentish men, resembled the south-western people as much in intellectual temperament, as, by his short stature, dark hair and eyes, choleric constitution, he resembled them anthropologically. This seeming affinity of the genius of Kent to that of the south-western promontory, though it cannot be said to be complete identity, may perhaps be regarded as one of the numerous facts which tend to invalidate the belief, widely prevalent a few years ago under the influence of several eminent historians and ultimately resting on some rhetorical expressions of Gildas,* that the Romano-British inhabitants of Kent were entirely exterminated by the Teutonic invaders.

Undoubtedly, however, the Teutonic element is considerable in all this south-eastern part of England, as far westwards as Wilts. One is indeed

* Professor H. Williams, in his edition of Gildas (*Cymmrodorion Record Soc.* 1899, Part 1), points out that Gildas is not an historian, but a preacher of righteousness who is simply seeking to show how divine anger visits sin. Beddoe finds early elements persisting in the Kentish population.

tempted to ask whether it may serve to explain another psychological phenomenon which is revealed by the distribution of English genius. The Jutes came to Kent; the Saxons occupied the regions to the west of Kent. This district, including (with Kent and Essex) the whole of the light-haired populations of southern England, is occupied by the counties of Sussex, Surrey, Hampshire and Berkshire. Except in so far as Surrey is suburban to London and profits by this proximity, all this region is comparatively bare of aboriginal genius. Mackintosh observed, in his notable study of the psychic characteristics of British peoples, that the unmixed English Saxon, unlike the Angle (and possibly unlike the Jute), is marked by mental mediocrity. One is tempted to ask whether this fact, if it is a fact, may be invoked to explain the result of the present inquiry as regards this region.

I do not propose to consider in detail the distribution of ability in the other parts of the British Islands, for the figures are here too small to yield reliable results. The distribution of ability in Wales, Scotland and Ireland is, however, so definitely confined to certain districts that a mere inspection of the crude figures suffices to give us for each of these countries a fairly close conception of their intellectual geography.

In the case of Wales the elements of ability are distributed as follows:

Glamorganshire	7	Anglesey	3
Denbighshire	7	Cardiganshire	1
Montgomeryshire	6	Pembrokeshire	1
Radnorshire	6	Merionethshire	1
Flintshire	3	Caermarthenshire	0
Carnarvonshire	3		

It is not difficult to understand why a large, fertile and populous district like Glamorganshire — even leaving out of account its commercial and mining activities — should stand high in actual numbers, although it stands lower in proportion to area and very low in relation to population. It is more remarkable that Caermarthenshire, the largest Welsh county, should show no traceable elements of genius. The really productive intellectual region of Wales is comprised in Denbighshire, Montgomeryshire and Radnorshire. This is a fact of some interest when we recall the ethnological history of this region. Wales is a Goidelic country (that is to say, a country inhabited by the earlier Celts mingled with aborigines), which appears to have been subsequently invaded by the Brythonic Ordovices; these formed a wedge in the country reaching to Cardigan Bay, leaving the Goidels in the north-western district and (as we may still observe in the map founded on the index of nigrescence) in the south-western district. But later still — probably soon after the departure of the Romans — a very vigorous stock led by Cuneda and speaking a tongue very closely allied to Gaulish, came from what is now the south of

Scotland, and established themselves in the centre of the Ordovician region, where their leaders became the acknowledged ancestors of the Gwyned Kings and the best known Welsh saints.* Their land comprised Radnorshire, Montgomeryshire and the south-west of Denbighshire, which is precisely the land which we have found to be the focus of Welsh genius. It is very difficult not to see here one at least, and perhaps the chief, of the factors which have caused this comparatively unimportant and thinly peopled region to be so productive in ability.

In accordance with the comparative poverty of Wales in intellectual achievements during the earlier periods of subjection to England is the statement of Rhys and Brynmor-Jones (*The Welsh People*, p. 471) that 'from the people as a whole hardly a voice comes during the centuries from the Norman Conquest to the middle of the eighteenth century. They tilled their land, attended to their flocks and their herds, married and died in complete obscurity, without being in any great degree touched by the intellectual movements of the sixteenth and seventeenth centuries.' These authors have ably expounded the causes of the intellectual decadence of Wales during this long period.

The absolute figures of the ancestral elements of ability in Scotland are as follows:

Midlothian	28	Fife	15
Aberdeenshire	26	Dumfriesshire	14
Ayrshire	21	Forfarshire	12
Lanarkshire	21	Perthshire	9

* J. Rhys and D. Brynmor-Jones, *The Welsh People*, 1900, p. 21.

Haddingtonshire	9	Inverness-shire	2
Ross-shire and Cromartyshire	8	Nairnshire	2
Berwickshire	8	Clackmannanshire	2
Stirlingshire	6	Selkirkshire	2
Argyleshire	5	Wigtonshire	2
Elginshire	4	Banffshire	2
Roxburghshire	4	Kinross-shire	1
Renfrewshire	4	Buteshire	1
Dumbartonshire	3	Caithness	1
Sutherland	2	Linlithgowshire	1
Orkney and Shetland	2	Peeblesshire	0
Kincardineshire	2	Kirkcudbrightshire	0

It will be seen that the genius of Scotland has been mainly produced by the tract between the Cheviots and the Grampians. While, however, the whole of this district is prolific in ability, a narrow central belt has proved pre-eminently able to breed men of intellect. This belt runs from Aberdeen in a south-westerly direction through Forfar, Fife, Midlothian, with the surrounding district, and Lanark (including Glasgow); on reaching Ayr and Dumfries it widens out, not extending beyond the English border westward into Galloway. Aberdeen and Edinburgh have always been the two great centres of Scotch genius. If, however, we were to take into consideration the proportions of genius according to area and population of the various counties this geographical distribution would appear less decisively marked. The upland counties, whether in or out of the Highlands proper, appear poor in genius and the Lowland counties rich. But it must be remembered that the upland counties are also poor in population and the

lowland counties rich. So far as a rough comparison of the total amount of genius with the recent population can be considered as any indication of the true distribution of genius in Scotland it would appear that both Aberdeen and Edinburgh really are very prolific in ability, and that Ayr, Fife, and even Sutherland are little, if at all, inferior in intellectual fertility, while Haddingtonshire, Berwickshire, and Dumfriesshire would appear to stand probably at the head. It would seem that even on a population basis the dark-haired populations show a somewhat less intellectual fertility than the fair-haired populations. This question is obviously complicated by the language question, but it is noteworthy that Sutherland, which is as fair-haired in population as any part of Scotland, would appear to show a fairly high proportion of ability relatively to its population, while Inverness, which is the darkest part of Scotland, stands very low, and Galloway, which is a very dark region, stands very much lower than the border counties, which are very fair. If this tendency prevails in Scotland it is the reverse of the tendency which prevails in England (though not in Wales), where the darker-haired districts seem on the whole to be [illegible]rolific in ability than the fair-haired regions. [illegible]er point about the distribution of genius in [illegible]d which may be noted is that the quantity and quality of its ability tend to go together. Knox, Burns and Scott, the three most famous

Scotchmen — it is unnecessary to say the greatest — all belonged to counties which would appear to be among the most prolific in ability.

Turning to Ireland, we find that, as in Scotland, certain regions appear to be rich in genius, others poor, or even absolutely bare. The distribution is as follows:

Dublin	15	Kerry	2
Cork	10	Galway	2
Antrim	9	Mayo	2
Down	8	Donegal	2
Waterford	6	Armagh	2
Londonderry	6	Cavan	1
Kilkenny	5	Carlow	1
Clare	4	Wicklow	1
Westmeath	4	Queen's County	1
Tyrone	4	Longford	1
Wexford	3	Meath, Louth, King's County, Sligo, Roscommon, Leitrim, Fermanagh, Monaghan	0
Limerick	3		
Kildare	2		
Tipperary	2		

The predominance of Dublin in Ireland, it will be seen, is more decisive than is that of Midlothian in Scotland; it is, however, possible that this is due to a greater ignorance of the ancestry of eminent Irishmen. In any case, however, it will be observed that the region of Ireland chiefly productive in ability is Leinster with the adjoining portion of Munster, and, closely following it, Ulster. Both these districts — for we may consider them as separate though they adjoin, as they are anthropologically distinct, the people of Ulster being much darker — have long been racially mixed. In the first district Goidels and Brythons were both

numerous, and various minor foreign immigrations have taken place here since; in comparatively recent times it was chiefly in Waterford and Dublin that the French Huguenots of Ireland settled. Ulster, as is well known, received a large infusion of English and Scotch blood in the seventeenth century, and this admixture has very largely affected the character of the ability it has produced. It is, however, a mistake to suppose that the temperamental, sometimes rather aggressive, energy of Ulstermen is due solely, or even perhaps mainly, to English and Scotch admixtures, influential as these have been. 'There is neither in Alban nor in Ireland,' we read in Lady Gregory's recension of the great Irish saga, 'an army that can put down the men of Ulster when once their weakness is gone and their anger is kindled.' * Giraldus Cambrensis also bears testimony to the vigour of the aboriginal Ulsterman. The 'Saxon' outsider is sometimes tempted to think that in many respects the modern men of Ulster are more Irish than the Irish themselves, and such an opinion finds support in the fact that, as measured by the index of nigrescence, Ulster anthropologically approaches Connaught. There can be no doubt, however, that English and Scotch elements, however largely admixed with aboriginal elements, play a very large part indeed in the manifestations of Irish genius.

It would be of some interest to classify our

* *Cuchulain of Muirthemne*, p. 256.

eminent persons into groups according to their activities and to note the district in which each group tends to predominate. Appendix B will enable the reader to examine into this matter for himself. As might be expected, politicians, divines, and men of letters abound in all parts of the kingdom. It is curious to note that great lawyers are also scattered over the whole kingdom with notable impartiality. While poets are to be found everywhere, they are distinctly more predominant in the south of England, and to a less extent in Wales and the Welsh Border counties; but when we consider the origins of those English poets who are unanimously recognised to stand first, we find them scattered over the whole country as widely apart as possible, Chaucer in Suffolk, Spenser in Lancashire, Shakespeare in Warwickshire, Milton in Oxfordshire, Wordsworth in Yorkshire, Shelley in Sussex, Keats in Devon or Cornwall.

In science Scotland stands very high, Ireland extremely low. The distribution of scientific men is as follows:

English	84	Scotch-Irish	2
Welsh	2	English-Irish	1
Scotch	21	English-German	1
Irish	1	English-Dutch	1
Scotch-English	7		

In order to realise the extraordinary preponderance of the Scotch over the Irish contingent, it must be remembered that until the present century the population of Ireland has been much larger than

that of Scotland, and it may be noted that the one purely Irish man of science (Tyndall) was of original English origin.*

If we proceed to consider the distribution of English men of science in the four distinct ethnological regions to which reference has already been made, we find that six belong more or less to the East Anglian focus, five to the south-western focus, four to the Welsh Border region, and seven to the large Anglo-Danish district.

It is of interest to compare these results with those obtained by Galton in the case of his modern English men of science (*English Men of Science*, pp. 18, 21). He found that three-fourths were English. Of every ten, there were:

5 Pure English.
1 Anglo-Welsh.
1 Anglo-Irish.
1 Scotch.
1 Included Anglo-Scotch, Scotch-Irish, pure Irish, Welsh, Manx and Channel Islands.
1 Unclassed, including mixture of English, French, German, Creole, Dutch, Swedish, etc.

* I must now add that there is some reason to believe that Faraday was ultimately of Irish origin. His family, which was settled in Yorkshire, had a tradition that they came from Ireland. I disregarded that tradition because I could find no evidence that there are any Faradays in Ireland. Since then two correspondents have furnished me with evidence: Dr. Kiernan of Chicago referred me to Irish pedigree books and stated that 'Faradach' (meaning a dressy man) was an off-shoot of the Irish Kiernans and founder of the Faradays; while from South Wales I was informed that a man, of no education and of undoubted Irish nationality, called Ferriday, was living near Swansea thirty years ago. An Irish origin would certainly help to account for the 'Celtic' quality of Faraday's scientific imagination.

'On an analysis of the scientific status of the men on my list,' he remarks, 'it appeared to me that their ability is higher in proportion to their numbers among those of pure race.'

This may be said to be in agreement with my results, which necessarily deal with men of a higher average order of ability, and which show a very much smaller proportion of individuals of mixed race, though in part this difference may be accounted for by the greater precision of Galton's information in relation to his cases. He further points out that the birthplace of his men of science is usually in towns, away from the coast, and he presents a geographical diagram which shows the distribution. This diagram is of interest, for it shows with great precision the fallacy of birthplace as any true indication of the real distribution of ability. Nearly the whole of both the East Anglian and south-western foci of genius are in this diagram left bare of scientific ability.

'The whole of the Eastern Counties,' Galton remarks, 'and the huge triangle at whose angles Hastings, Worcester, and Exeter, or rather Exmouth, are situated, are very deficient in aboriginal science.' That the deficiency is very far from being 'aboriginal' becomes sufficiently clear when we are careful to ignore the accident of birthplace in determining the origins of men of science.

Psychologically it is not difficult to detect a distinct character in English scientific genius, according as it springs from the Anglo-Danish district or the East Anglian focus or the south-western focus, although I am not aware that this has been pointed out before. The Anglo-Danish district may here be fairly put first, not only on account of the large number of scientific men it has

wholly or in part produced, but also on account of the very high eminence of some among them. The Anglo-Dane appears to possess an aptitude for mathematics which is not shared by the native of any other English district as a whole, and it is in the exact sciences that the Anglo-Dane triumphs.* Newton is the supreme figure of Anglo-Danish science; it will be noted that he belongs to the East Anglian border, and by his mother is claimed by Rutland, a little county which, I am inclined to think, really belongs psychologically and perhaps ethnologically to East Anglia. The combination of the Anglo-Dane and the East Anglian seems highly favourable to scientific aptitude; the abstracting tendency of the Anglo-Dane, and the exaggerated independence of his character, with the difficulty he finds in taking any other point of view than his own, are happily tempered by the more cautious and flexible mind of the East Anglian. Darwin (who also belonged to the Welsh Border) belonged in part, like Newton, to the East Anglian border of the Anglo-Danish district, and also (somewhat remotely) to Norfolk, a county which contains many Danish elements. The science of the Anglo-Danish district is not exclusively mathematical, and geology especially owes much to the Anglo-Dane; it will be remembered that geology was one of the first sciences to attract Darwin.

* The mathematical tendencies of Cambridge are due to the fact that Cambridge drains the ability of nearly the whole Anglo-Danish district.

The East Anglian is in scientific matters drawn to the concrete, and shows little or no mathematical aptitude. He is a natural historian in the widest sense. He delights in the patient collection of facts, and seeks to sift, describe, co-ordinate, and classify them. In his hands science becomes almost an art. Gilbert illustrates East Anglian scientific methods in the inorganic world, Ray in the organic, and Francis Bacon, though he cannot himself be classed among men of science, has in the *Novum Organum* and elsewhere presented a picture of scientific method as it most naturally appears to the East Anglian mind.

It is not easy to see anything specific or definitely Brythonic in the scientific activities of the Welsh Border. At most it may be said that there is some tendency for science here to take on a technological character and to become associated with the artistic crafts. The scientific men found here often belong only in part to the district, and many of them seem to possess the psychological characters of the south-western focus.

The scientific characters of the south-western focus are quite clear, and definitely distinct from those of either the Anglo-Danish district or the East Anglian focus. What we find here is the mechanical impulse, and more especially the physiological temper, the instinct to seek out the driving forces of vital phenomena. It is on this account that Harvey, though of Kentish family, may be said

to belong psychologically to this focus, as also Stephen Hales, though he belonged partly to Kent and partly to East Anglia. The great scientific physicians belong here (the surgeons are largely East Anglian), with Sydenham at the head and Glisson. Huxley, again, is a typical figure. Inventors are numerous, for the scientific men of this region have frequently been enamoured of practical problems, and just as they have been pioneers in the physical world, so in science they have sought rather to make discoveries than to formulate laws. Thus in astronomy we have Adams, and one of the greatest and most typical scientific men of this region was Thomas Young.

When we consider the distribution of great soldiers, we find the following results:

English	22	English-Scotch	4
Welsh	3	English-Irish	2
Irish	4	Scotch-Irish	2
Scotch	13		

Within England seven belong to the Anglo-Danish district, six to the East Anglian focus, five to the south-western focus, and four to the Welsh Border. In England itself, it will be seen, military genius is relatively less pronounced than in any other part of the British Islands, and what absolute numerical preponderance the English element possesses seems to be due exclusively to the earlier periods of English history; the line of great English generals apparently ended with Marlborough. The Scotch

stand easily at the head; the Irish would take a much higher place if we considered the nineteenth century separately.

When, however, we turn to the distribution of great sailors, a very different result is shown, and the position of English ability is more than reasserted. While England has produced as many as 29 great sailors, only two are Scotch, one English-Scotch, one English-Welsh and none Irish. Within England, eleven belong to the south-western focus, ten to the Anglo-Danish district and more especially to its southern border in Lincolnshire, four to the East Anglian focus and four to the Welsh Border.

The distribution of artists (including sculptors and architects as well as painters) is as follows:

English	51	Scotch-Irish	1
Welsh	3	English-French	2
Scotch	10	English-German	2
Irish	5	English-Italian	1
English-Welsh	1	English-Russian	1
English-Scotch	2		

Within England we find that eighteen are scattered over the large Anglo-Danish district, more than a third of these, however, belonging to the small county of Nottinghamshire, twelve are East Anglian, eight belong to the south-west, six to the Welsh Border.

The fertility of Nottinghamshire — a county not otherwise notably productive of genius — in artists is a phenomenon of some interest in view of the fact that Nottinghamshire was a great art-centre in the fourteenth

century, when its 'alabasterers' sent re-tables, screens and figure-panels to all parts of Western Europe. (*Architectural Review*, April, 1903, p. 143.) It would be idle to see here the influences of tradition; we cannot suppose that there was any continuity of this kind between the fourteenth-century alabasterers and nineteenth-century painters, the possibility of such continuity having been absolutely destroyed by the Reformation. The reasonable supposition is that we see here a native bent to art showing itself at one time in one form, at another time in another form.

In a subsequent chapter (p. 266) I have discussed some points in the distribution of British artists, and have shown how the painters of the east coast differ from those of the west.

A very definite case of special distribution of ability, differing markedly from the distribution of ability generally, is furnished by great actors and actresses. So far as it can be traced this distribution is as follows:

English	23*	English-Irish	6
Welsh	1	English-French	1
Irish	6	Irish-French	1
English-Welsh	1	English-Irish-French-Swiss	1
English-Scotch	1	English-Danish	1

It will be seen that the Scotch virtually do not appear at all, and that the relative preponderance of the Irish is enormous. Our knowledge of the ancestry of actors is peculiarly vague and uncertain, and it is highly probable that if our knowledge

* This number is too high. Thus, following the *Dictionary*, it includes L. A. Neilson, who (according to Clement Scott) was really the illegitimate daughter of a Spaniard.

on this point were more precise the preponderance of the Irish element, at the expense of the English element, would be still greater. The distribution of actors within England, so far as we are able to trace it, further illustrates the poverty of the more specifically English districts in dramatic ability of a high order. Four of our great actors and actresses belong more or less to the south-western focus, four to the Welsh Border, three to the East Anglian focus, and only two to the whole Anglo-Danish district.

I do not propose to discuss here the various causes which have led to the special distribution of genius in the British Islands, and to the variations in distribution shown by different kinds of genius. While many of the characters thus revealed are evidently due to racial characteristics, it would be rash to assume that they may all thus be accounted for. We have also to take into account environmental conditions. It is not easy to make an exact comparison on this basis before the nineteenth century. The careful study of the condition of England made by Joseph Fletcher, secretary of the Statistical Society, on the basis of the census of 1841, conveniently enables us to make various comparisons for this period, and we may be fairly certain that the conditions then prevailing had existed during a considerably earlier period.

When, on this basis, we examine the various counties, there would appear to be a tendency to correlation between fertility in genius and (1) amount of real property per head of population; (2) deficiency of persons of independent means; (3) amount of ignorance (Norfolk is among the seven most ignorant counties, while Suffolk

and Hertfordshire are also among the ignorant counties); (4) committals for serious offences against the person (Norfolk is at this period the most criminal county in this respect, being in relation to population 80 per cent above average, while Huntingdonshire, with little genius, has the least criminality, being 63 per cent below average); (5) bastardy (the four counties with largest proportion of illegitimate children being Cumberland, Hereford, Norfolk and Nottinghamshire).

On the other hand there appears to be no tendency to correlation between fertility in genius and (1) offences against property (excluding the 'malicious' group which are included in offences against the person); (2) assaults; (3) improvident marriages; (4) pauperism; (5) density of population; (6) crime (general commitments); (7) amount of deposits in savings banks per head of population.

While such comparisons are at various points of much interest and possibly of real significance, it must be remembered that though it is highly probable that there is a real connection between genius and the conditions prevailing in its environment, we must not here too hastily assume such a connection. It may be added that we should also have to take into consideration the conditions prevailing in the birthplaces of men of genius, which are not always the places of their origin.

III

SOCIAL CLASS

Status of parents of British men of genius — Upper class — Yeomen and farmers — Clergy — Medicine — Law — Army — Navy — Miscellaneous professions — Commercial classes — Crafts — Artisans and unskilled — The parentage of artists — The parentage of actors — How far change has taken place in the social composition of the genius-producing class — Comparison of the genius-producing classes with the ordinary population.

In considering to what social classes the 1030 eminent British men and women on our list belong, we naturally seek to ascertain the position of the fathers. In 201 cases it has not been easy to pronounce definitely on this point, and I have, therefore, omitted these cases as doubtful. The remainder may be classed with a fair degree of certainty. I find that they fall into the following groups:

		Per cent
Upper classes (or 'good family')	154	18.5
Yeomen and farmers	50	6
Church	139	16.7
Law	59	7.1
Army	35	4.2
Navy (and sea generally)	16	1.9
Medicine	30	3.6
Miscellaneous professions	65	7.8
Officials, clerks, etc.	27	3.2
Commercial	156	18.8
Crafts	77	9.2
Artisans and unskilled	21	2.5

In some thirty cases the status of the father is

entered under two heads, but, as a rule, it has seemed sufficient to state what may be presumed to be the father's chief occupation at the time when his eminent child was born.

In the order in which I have placed the groups they may be said to constitute a kind of hierarchy. I place the yeomen and farmers immediately after the upper-class group, although at one end this group includes the peasant-farmer.* Until recent years, the man who lived on the land which had belonged to his family for many centuries, occupied a position not essentially different from that of the more noble families with somewhat larger estates around him. Even at the present day, in remote parts of the country, it is not difficult to meet men who live on the land on farms which have belonged to their ancestors through several centuries. Such aristocrats of the soil, thus belonging to 'old families,' frequently have all the characteristics of fine country gentlemen, and in former days the line of demarcation between them and the 'upper class' must often have been difficult to draw. I have formed my 'upper-class' group in a somewhat exclusive spirit; I have not included in it the very large body of eminent men who are said to

* The yeoman may be defined as an owner-cultivator; the farmer may be only a tenant. The poet Crabbe in 1791 visited his wife's uncle, a Suffolk yeoman, called Tovell, to whom he refers as 'the first-rate yeoman of that period — the yeoman that already began to be styled by courtesy an esquire. Mr. Tovell might possess an estate of some eight hundred pounds per annum, a portion of which he himself cultivated.'

belong to 'old families'; these I have mostly allowed to fall out as 'doubtful,' but there is good reason to believe that a considerable proportion really belong to the class of small country gentlemen on the borderland between the aristocracy in the narrow sense and the yeoman and farmer class. To this class, therefore, must be attributed a very important part in the production of the men who have furnished the characteristics of British civilisation.

The same must be said of the clergy, whom I place next, because they are largely drawn from the same ranks and have on the whole led very similar lives. (With the clergy I have included thirty-two ministers of religion belonging to very various denominations.) The religious movements of the past century have altogether transformed the lives of the clergy, but until recent years the parson was usually simply a country gentleman or farmer somewhat better educated, and more in touch with intellectual tastes and pursuits. The proportion of distinguished men and women contributed from among the families of the clergy can only be described as enormous. In mere number the clergy can seldom have equalled the butchers or bakers in their parishes, yet only two butchers and four bakers are definitely ascertained to have produced eminent children, as against 139 parsons. Even if we compare the Church with the other professions with which it is most usually classed, we find that

the eminent children of the clergy considerably outnumber those of lawyers, doctors and army officers put together. This preponderance is the more remarkable when we remember that (although I have certainly included eminent illegitimate children of priests) it is only within the last three and a half centuries that the clergy have been free to compete in this field.

It is of interest to note that genius is not the only form of mental anomaly which is produced more frequently by the clergy than by any other social class. The clerical profession, as Langdon Down pointed out many years ago, also produces more idiots than any other class.

Law, Medicine, and the Army and Navy furnish contingents which, though very much smaller than that of the Church, are sufficiently important to be grouped separately, but all the remaining professions I have thrown into a single group. These are: artists (painters, sculptors, engravers, architects), 20; actors, etc., 16; musicians, composers, etc., 9; men of letters, 6; schoolmasters, 7; engineers, surveyors and accountants, 4; men of science, 3. Although so few of the fathers of eminent men can be described professionally as men of letters or men of science, it must be added that in a considerable number of cases literary or scientific aptitudes were present in the parents.

We now reach a group of altogether different character, Trade. It is a group of great magnitude, but its size is due to the inevitable inclusion of a

very large number of occupations under a single heading. These occupations range from banking to inn-keeping. The bankers evidently form the aristocracy of the trading class, and a remarkable number, considering the smallness of the class (not less than 12), have been the fathers of eminent sons. Under the rather vague heading of 'merchants' we find 25, and there are at least nine 'manufacturers.' Wine merchants, brewers, vintners, publicans and others connected with the sale or production of alcoholic liquors have yielded as many as 16 distinguished sons, who have often attained a high degree of eminence, from Chaucer to Joule. Tea and coffee are only responsible for one each. There are eight drapers, mercers and hosiers, and six tailors and hatters; grocers and a great number of other shop-keeping trades count at most three or four eminent men each. It is, perhaps, noteworthy that at least four Lord Mayors of London have been the fathers of distinguished sons; only one of them (Gresham) attained fame in business, the others becoming men of letters and scholars. It must be added in regard to this group that in a certain number of cases the particular 'trade' or 'business' of the father is not specified.

The group which I have denominated 'Crafts' is closely related to that of 'Trade,' and in many cases it is difficult or impossible to decide whether an occupation should be entered under one or the

other head. But, speaking generally, there is a very clear distinction between the two groups. For success in the essentially commercial occupations is involved, above all, financial ability; the crafts are essentially manual, and success here involves more of the qualities of the artist than of the tradesman. Just as the banker is the typical representative of commercial transactions, so the carpenter stands at the head of the crafts. There seems to be something peculiar in the life or aptitudes of the carpenter especially favourable to the production of intellectual children, for this association has occurred as many as thirteen times, while there are four builders. No other craft approaches the carpenter in this respect; there are five shoemakers, five cloth-workers, five weavers (all belonging to the early phase of industrial development before factories), five goldsmiths and jewellers, four blacksmiths, while many other handicrafts are mentioned once or twice.

Finally, we reach the group of parents engaged in some unskilled work, and, therefore, belonging to the lowest social class. It is the smallest of all the groups, and, though including some notable persons, it can scarcely be said to be a pre-eminently distinguished group. As many as eight of the parents were common soldiers, the rest mostly agricultural labourers.

It may be interesting to inquire whether our eminent men, when grouped according to the

station and occupations of their fathers, show any marked group-characters; whether, in other words, the occupation of the father exercises an influence on the nature and direction of the intellectual aptitudes of the son. To some extent it does exercise such an influence. It is true that there are eminent men of very various kinds in all of these groups. But there is yet a clearly visible tendency for certain kinds of ability to fall into certain groups. It is not surprising that there should be a tendency for the son to follow the profession of the father. Nor is it surprising that a great number of statesmen should be found in the upper-class group. Men of letters are yielded by every class, perhaps especially by the clergy, but Shakespeare and, it is probable, Milton belonged to the families of yeomen. The sons of lawyers, one notes, even to a greater extent than the eminent men of 'upper-class' birth, eventually find themselves in the House of Lords, and not always as lawyers. The two groups of Army and Medicine are numerically close together, but in other respects very unlike. The sons of army men form a very brilliant and versatile group, and include a large proportion of great soldiers; the sons of doctors do not show a single eminent doctor, and if it were not for the presence of two men of the very first rank — Darwin and Landor — they would constitute a comparatively mediocre group.

Painters and sculptors constitute a group which

appears to be of very distinct interest from the point of view of occupational heredity. In social origin, it may be noted, the group differs strikingly in constitution from the general body, in which the upper class is almost or quite predominant. Of 63 painters and sculptors of definitely known origin, only two can be placed in the aristocratic division. Of the remainder 7 are the sons of artists, 22 the sons of craftsmen, leaving only 32 for all other occupations, which are mainly of lower middle class character, and in many cases trades that are very closely allied to crafts. Even, however, when we omit the trades as well as the cases in which the fathers were artists, we find a very notable predominance of craftsmen in the parentage of painters, to such an extent indeed that while craftsmen only constitute 9.2 per cent among the fathers of our eminent persons generally, they constitute nearly 35 per cent among the fathers of the painters and sculptors. It is difficult to avoid the conclusion that there is a real connection between the father's aptitude for craftsmanship and the son's aptitude for art. To suppose that environment adequately accounts for this relationship is an inadmissible theory. The association between the crafts of builder, carpenter, tanner, jeweller, watchmaker, woodcarver, rope-maker, etc., and the painter's art is small at the best, and in most cases non-existent. Nor, on the other hand, is there any reason whatever to conclude that the fathers

have acquired manual dexterity which the sons have inherited and put to finer use. Without reverting to the hypothesis of the inheritance of acquired characteristics, we may well suppose that among craftsmen there is a natural selection of individuals possessing special dexterity of hand, and this tendency to manual skill would tend to be inherited. Such a supposition would adequately account for the phenomena which meet us in the present investigation. That there is physical selection in occupations we know to be the case, so that, as Beddoe has shown, butchers tend to be fair and shoemakers to be dark.

It may be noted that Arréat (*Psychologie du Peintre*, 1892, ch. 11), in investigating the heredity of 200 eminent European painters, reached results that are closely similar to those I have reached in my smaller purely British group. He found that very few were of upper-class social rank, and these not usually among the most important, while nearly two-thirds of the whole number were found to be the sons either of painters or of workers in some art or craft. He refers to the special frequency of jewellers among the fathers. I may remark that in my list, working jewellers and watchmakers occurred twice, a small number, but relatively large considering that there are only three fathers of this occupation in the total parentage of British men of ability; Kassel, also, in his inquiry on an international basis into heredity (*South Atlantic Quarterly*, April, 1924) found a significant association between painters and a craft parentage.

The group of painters and sculptors differs

widely, as we have seen, so far as the social and occupational status of their fathers is concerned, from the general composition of the whole group of eminent persons. The group of actors and actresses, however, reverses altogether the conclusions we reach from contemplating the entire group. While good social class and leisurely cultivated life among the parents would seem on the whole to be of decided advantage for the production of eminent offspring, among actors and actresses low and obscure birth would seem to be a positive advantage. At least three or four were illegitimate children, while in numerous other cases we are led to infer that this was probably the case. Of the thirty whose origin is known, four and probably more — a very large proportion considering the smallness of the unskilled class — can be set down as the children of unskilled labourers or common soldiers, eleven are the children of actors, while the rest mainly belong to miscellaneous and often somewhat unskilled occupations. Only six can be assigned to the whole group of professions (excluding the actor's profession), and only one can be said to belong to the upper class, Booth being the son of an impoverished squire with aristocratic connections. It is not difficult to account for this state of things. The somewhat unbalanced and excessively impressionable nervous system which is apt to result from illegitimate birth, or birth under abnormally Bohemian

conditions, the poverty, irregularity, and manifold changes of occupation to which so many great actors and actresses have been subjected in early life, usually among varied and often low social strata, the absence of training and education in formal knowledge and conventional conduct, combined with the abundant opportunity of becoming familiar with the most naturally dramatic section of the community — all these and other characteristics which have tended to mark the early lives of great actors and actresses, would tend to fit them for the histrionic profession and to unfit them for any other field in which natural ability may be shown.

There is some interest in considering separately the eminent persons in my list, 81 in number, who died in the period during which the *Dictionary of National Biography* was being produced, and are therefore included in the Supplement. These may be expected to give us some indication as to the direction in which we may now look for our eminent men. So far as can be judged, however, from so small a group, the social composition remains exactly the same. The aristocratic element is still very large. The most notable difference is that Commerce (represented by 18 individuals) has gained on the Church (which is represented by only 11); the Church has fallen to the proportion of less than 14 per cent, the general proportion of the Church for the whole period being 16.7 per cent;

and Commerce has risen to over 22 per cent as against 18.8. Whether the relative ability-producing powers of the clergy and the commercial classes have changed, or whether, as is possible, the clergy now constitute a smaller and the commercial classes a larger element in the general population, is a question I do not undertake to answer. The quota produced by the medical profession has relatively risen, and that produced by the legal profession fallen (being only represented by one individual). More significant is the fact that the crafts instead of producing over nine per cent have not produced one of this latest group of eminent men, while (unless the reticence of the national biographers is at fault) the artisan and unskilled classes have been equally unproductive. It would appear that the ability-producing powers of the community are becoming narrowed on what is mainly a mixed aristocratic and commercial basis.

In order to realise the significance of our results it is necessary to bear in mind the class constitution of the ordinary population in Great Britain. According to the Anthropological Committee of the British Association, this may be stated as follows:

Professional classes	4.46 per cent
Commercial classes	10.36
Industrial classes	10.90
Artisans	26.82
Labourers	47.46

The comparison with the class of ability-producing

persons is interesting. We have two pyramids, but the base of the one corresponds with the apex of the other, the same inverted relationship existing harmoniously throughout. The aristocratic class which forms the foundation of the ability-producing pyramid (though this fact is slightly disguised by the omission from my list of hereditary peers) forms the fine and invisible apex of the pyramid constituted by the ordinary population. The professional class which (often in close association with the aristocratic class) forms the great bulk of the one pyramid still merely appears as the apex of the other. The commercial class also bulks more largely in the ability-producing pyramid, but to a much less extravagant extent. The industrial class (or craftsmen) which comes in the middle furnishes about the same proportion in each case, while the artisans and labourers who form nearly three-quarters of the general population appear among the ability-producing persons as a vanishing point almost as negligible as the aristocratic class is among the general population.

This is not altogether an unexpected result, though it has not before been shown to hold good for the entire field of the intellectual ability of a country. Maclean's statistical study of the origins of British men of ability during the nineteenth century shows that 26 per cent of those of known origin were sons of 'aristocrats, officials, etc.'; 16 per cent were sons of clergymen; 15 per cent sons of farmers, tradesmen, artisans, etc.; 9 per cent of military and naval officers; 9 per cent of business

men; 5 per cent of medical men; 4 per cent of lawyers, etc. The result was almost identical when the 100 men of pre-eminent ability were considered separately. Maclean also finds, as I have, and notes with surprise, that the proportion of men of ability produced by the lower social classes is actually decreasing.

C. H. Cooley (*Annals of American Academy*, May, 1897) investigated the point in regard to a group of distinguished European poets, philosophers, and men of letters, and found that 45 belonged to the upper and upper middle classes, 24 to the lower middle class, and only 2 to the lower class.

Odin, in a laborious though not always very illuminative study of French genius (*Genèse des Grands Hommes*, vol. II, table 31), found that 623 talented people of letters, so far as the position of their parents was known, could be classed as: nobility, 25.5 per cent; magistrature, 30 per cent; liberal professions, 23 per cent; middle class, 11.6 per cent; industrial class, 9.8 per cent.

Galton, among 107 recent English men of science (*English Men of Science*, 1874, p. 22), found, as might be anticipated, that the aristocratic element was smaller, only 8.4 per cent; but the allied professional class (Army, Navy, Civil Service, Church, Medicine, Law, etc.) accounted for as much as 48.5 per cent; while the commercial class furnished nearly all the rest, 40.1.

One is tempted to ask how far the industrial progress of the nineteenth century, the growth of factories, the development of urban life, has altered the conditions affecting the production of eminent men. It seems clear that, taking English history as a whole, the conditions of rural life have, from the present point of view, produced the best stocks.

The minor aristocracy and the clergy — the 'gentlemen' of England — living on the soil in the open air, in a life of independence at once laborious and leisurely, have been able to give their children good opportunities for development, while at the same time they have not been able to dispense them from the necessity of work. Thus, at all events, it has been in the past. How it will be in the future is a question which the data before us in no way help to answer. So far as can be seen, the changing conditions of life have as yet made no change in the conditions required for producing genius. Life in the old towns formerly fertile in intellectual ability — towns like Edinburgh, Norwich, Ipswich and Plymouth — was altogether unlike life in our modern urban centres, and there is yet no sign that the latter will equal the former in genius-producing power. Nor is there any sign that the education of the proletariat will lead to a new development of eminent men; the lowest class in Great Britain, so far as the data before us show, has not exhibited any tendency to a higher yield of genius, and what production it is accountable for remains rural rather than urban.

IV

HEREDITY AND PARENTAGE

The tendency to heredity in intellectual ability — Inheritance of ability equally frequent through father and mother — Mental abnormality in the parents — Size of the families to which persons of eminent ability belong — Normal standards of comparison — Genius-producing families tend to be large — Men of ability tend to be the offspring of predominantly boy-producing parents — Women of ability perhaps tend to belong to girl-producing parents — Position in the family of the child of genius — Tendency of men of ability to be youngest and more especially eldest children — The age of the parents of eminent persons at their birth — Tendency to disparity of age in the parents.

THE heredity of intellectual genius has been very fully discussed, with special reference to eminent persons of British birth, by Francis Galton, especially in his *Hereditary Genius*. With, perhaps, even an excess of zeal — for persons of somewhat minor degrees of ability have sometimes been taken into account — Galton has shown that intellectual ability has frequently tended to run in families.* If this hereditary tendency is by no means omnipresent, the present data prove conclusively that it is a very real factor. Notwithstanding that the effects of hereditary position have

* Ability (or 'talent') is more heritable than genius. See, for instance, W. T. J. Gunn (*Eugenics Review*, April, 1924). It may be doubted, indeed, whether genius in the high and narrow sense is ever inherited, although talent may occasionally exist in its ancestry.

been so far as possible excluded, and that our lists only contain persons of pre-eminent ability, distributed over fifteen centuries, it is yet found that among these 1030 persons there are 41 groups, of two or three individuals in each group, who are closely related. The recognised relationships are father and son (the Arnolds, Bacon with his two sons, the Boyles, the Cannings, the Coleridges, the Copleys, the Grenvilles, the Lyttons, the Mathewses, the Mills, the Penns, the Pitts, the Walpoles, the Wilberforces), brother and brother (the Herberts, the Lawrences, the Napiers, the Nasmyths, the Newmans, the Scotts, the Veres, the Wesleys, the Wordsworths), brother and sister (the Arnes, the Carpenters, the Kembles, the Martineaus, the Rossettis), sister and sister (the Brontës). The relationship between grandchildren and grandparents, and between uncles (or aunts) and nephews (or nieces) is best shown in a table. (See page 83.) It will be observed that Darwin has the unique distinction of possessing, within the narrow degrees of relationship here recognised, both a paternal and a maternal ancestor of the high degree of eminence required for inclusion in my list.

The table is of considerable interest because it helps us to answer the question as to the degree in which genius may be inherited in the female line. A consideration of direct heredity has no bearing on this question; a man inherits genius from his

	Paternal Grandfather	Maternal Grandfather
Jevons		Roscoe
Darwin	E. Darwin	Wedgwood
Donne		J. Heywood
Sidney		Duke of Northumberland
Third Earl of Shaftesbury	First Earl of Shaftesbury	

	Paternal Uncle or Aunt	Maternal Uncle or Aunt
J. Baillie		Hunter
Beddoes		M. Edgeworth
G. Bentham	J. Bentham	
Brougham		Robertson
Burnet		Lord Warriston
W. Hook	T. Hook	
F. A. Kemble J. M. Kemble	S. Siddons J. P. Kemble	
M. Kingsley	C. Kingsley	
C. J. Mathews		F. M. Kelly
Christopher Wordsworth Charles Wordsworth	W. Wordsworth	

father more often than from his mother for the simple reason that genius is rare in women. We reach a juster conclusion if we consider those cases in which the heredity is one degree removed, and then note whether it is transmitted more often in the male or in the female line. All such cases in my list are included in the table just given, and we are thus enabled to see that, considering the smallness of the numbers with which we are dealing, the sexual partition of the heredity is as equal as we could possibly hope to expect. A man is just as likely to inherit ability through his mother as through his father.

It will be noted that in the case of the four poets included in this table (Donne, Sidney, J. Baillie, Beddoes), the heredity was in every case maternal. This would at first sight seem to confirm the conclusion of Möbius that a poet's heredity is from his mother. It must be added, however, that in most of these four cases there was also an unusual degree of ability in the father, while only in one case was the eminent maternal relative a poet.

It is held by some that artistic genius is very rarely inherited in any high degree. Thus Max Müller wrote (*Autobiography*, p. 34), 'It seems almost as if the artistic talent was exhausted by one generation or one individual'; and he specially instances the rarity of eminent musicians who are the children of eminent musicians, the case of the Bachs being no true exception since music before J. S. Bach was usually simply a kind of craft. It it true that not a single eminent musical composer (not a large group, be it noted) occurs in the list of related

persons given above, but there are representatives of other arts, though not to any notably large extent. It is probable that whatever truth lies in the statement that high artistic ability is not inheritable may be reduced to the larger statement that 'talent' is more inheritable than 'genius.' The distinction between 'genius' and 'talent' is, however, one that is extremely difficult to make, and we shall not be concerned with this question in the present volume.

It is scarcely necessary to remark that in a very large number of cases the pre-eminent persons in our list were nearly related to eminent persons who have not reached the degree of distinction entitling them to appear in the list. Here an objective test is less easy to apply. The test I have adopted is the statement of the national biographers in referring to such relationship. The results of an inquiry on this basis distinctly confirm the result already reached as to the equal inheritance of intellectual ability on the paternal and maternal sides. Avoiding any summation of the results until the two lists of eminent relations were finally completed, it was found that the numbers on each side were exactly equal. On the father's side there were forty-four intellectually eminent relations, not including the father himself, and an exactly equal number on the mother's side. It is scarcely necessary to point out that these numbers do not even approximately represent the total number of eminent relations, for relationship to one eminent person often involves relationship to a whole family of eminent persons;

they merely serve to show that when the eminent near relations of an eminent man are impartially noted, such relations are just as often through the mother as through the father.

I have also noted every case in which it is stated or implied that one or other, or both, of the parents possessed an unusual amount of intellectual ability, by no means necessarily involving any degree whatever of 'eminence.' These cases are very numerous, and as such ability may often have been displayed in very unobtrusive ways, it must frequently have escaped the attention of the national biographers. In 150 cases the father showed such ability; in 89 cases the mother is noted as of unusual ability, or else as being closely related to some person of eminent ability presumed to have transmitted an intellectual aptitude, whether or not she showed marked signs of such aptitude herself. In 21 of these cases both the father and the mother probably transmitted intellectual aptitudes. Over 20 per cent of our 1030 eminent persons have certainly inherited intellectual aptitudes. Bearing in mind that in many cases the aptitudes of the parents are unknown or have passed unnoticed, and that in other cases the national biographers have failed to record known facts, it is not improbable that the proportion of cases in which one or other of the parents of our 1030 eminent persons displayed more than average intellectual ability may be at least doubled.

A more probable estimate of the real frequency of heredity may be obtained by considering separately the very recent and better known individuals who appear in the Supplement of the *Dictionary of National Biography*. Of the 81 eminent persons, thus incorporated in my list, who died while the *Dictionary* was in progress, it is found that in the case of 33 the father, the mother, or both are noted as being persons of unusual ability. This is equal to a proportion of about 40 per cent, or the proportion in which, on independent grounds, I have already suggested as representing the probable amount of inherited ability. Even for the modern group, however, we must still suppose the data to be incomplete.

From another point of view the consideration of this modern group is of interest in the light it throws on the question of heredity. I find that among the 38 able parents of the 33 eminent persons who may be supposed to have inherited ability, the sexual division comes out as exactly equal; that is to say, that there are 19 able fathers and 19 able mothers.

This would seem to indicate very clearly that, although that superlative degree of ability which is commonly termed 'genius' is rare in woman, yet a more than average degree of ability in the mother is just as important from the point of view of intellectual heredity as a more than average degree of ability in the father.

Among modern English scientific men Galton (*English Men of Science*, p. 72) has also found that ability is just as likely to be inherited through the female as through the male line. Among 100 scientific men, on the paternal side he found 34 grandfathers and uncles of ability, on the maternal side 37. As in my results, there would seem to be an excess, if any, on the maternal side.

In determining the parents who possessed ability I have taken no note of the cases in which it is merely said that the father or the mother possessed 'poetic tastes,' 'musical tastes,' etc., but only of those cases in which it is clearly stated or implied that there was unusual ability. Such 'ability' in most cases by no means involved recognised 'distinction.' As a matter of fact only one of the 81 had a parent of the same degree of eminence as himself, *i.e.*, sufficiently eminent to be included in my list. So that while the proportion of eminent persons with an 'able' parent approaches one in two, the proportion of eminent persons possessing a parent equally 'distinguished' with themselves is only one in 81. This proportion of eminent parents is shown not to be very far astray by reference to the whole body of individuals on my list, among whom there are fifteen possessing a parent of sufficient eminence to be included in the list, or about one in seventy. If we lowered the standard of distinction demanded in the parents the proportion would of course be raised.

It would be interesting to inquire into the moral and emotional qualities, the 'character,' of the parents. This, however, is extremely difficult and I have not attempted it. In a great many cases the mother was a woman of marked piety, and we are frequently led to infer an unusual degree of character, sometimes on the part of the mother, sometimes of the father. Moral qualities are quite as essential to most kinds of genius as intellectual qualities, and they are, perhaps, more highly transmissible. They form the basis on which intellectual development may take place, and they may be transmitted by a parent in whom such development has never occurred. The very frequent cases in which men of eminent intellectual ability have declared that they owed everything to their mothers * have sometimes been put aside as the expressions of an amiable weakness. It requires some credulity, however, to believe that men of pre-eminent, or even less than pre-eminent, intellectual acuteness are unable to estimate the character of their own parents. The frequent sense of indebtedness to their mothers expressed by eminent men may be taken as largely due to the feeling that the inheritance of moral or temperamental qualities is an even more massive and important inheritance than definite intellectual

* A remark of Huxley's in a letter to the present writer — 'Mentally and physically I am a piece of my mother' — may be taken as typical of such declarations.

aptitudes. Such inheritance coming to intellectual men from their mothers may often be observed where no definite intellectual aptitudes have been transmitted. It is not, however, of a kind which can well be recorded in biographical dictionaries, and I have not, therefore, attempted to estimate its frequency in the group of pre-eminent persons under consideration.

I have, however, attempted to estimate the frequency of one other form of anomaly in the parents besides intellectual ability. The parents of persons of eminent intellectual power may not themselves have been characterised by unusual intellect; but they may have shown mental anomaly by a lack of aptitude for the ordinary social life in which they were placed. In at least fifty-seven cases (or over five per cent) we find that the fathers were extravagant, unsuccessful in business, shiftless, idle, drunken, brutal, or otherwise fell into bad habits and neglected their families. In such cases, we may conclude, the father has transmitted to his eminent child an inaptness to follow the beaten tracks of life, but he has not transmitted any accompanying aptitude to make new individual tracks. This list could easily be enlarged if we included milder degrees of ineffectiveness. A certain degree of inoffensive eccentricity, recalling Parson Adams, seems to be not very uncommon among the fathers of men of eminent ability, and perhaps furnishes a trans-

missible temperament on which genius may develop. It may be noted that six of the ne'er-do-weel fathers (a very large proportion) belonged to eminent women. This may be simply due to the fact that a ne'er-do-weel father, by forcing the daughter to leave home or to provide for the family, furnishes a special stimulus to her latent ability.

In 403 cases I have been able to ascertain with a fair degree of certainty the size of the families to which these persons of eminent ability belong. A more than fair degree of certainty has not been attainable, owing to the loose and inexact way in which the national biographers frequently state the matter. Sometimes we are only told that the subject of the article is 'the child' or 'the son'; this may mean the *only* child, but it is impossible to accept such a statement as evidence regarding the size of the family, and the number of families with only children may possibly thus have been unduly diminished. Again, the biographers in a very large number of cases ignore the daughters, and from this cause again their statements become valueless.

In estimating the natality of the families producing children of ability I have never knowingly reckoned the offspring of previous or subsequent marriages; so far as possible, we are only concerned with the fecundity of the two parents of the eminent persons. So far as possible, also, I

have reckoned the gross fecundity, *i.e.*, the number of children born, not the number of children surviving; in the case of a large number of eminent men this gross fertility is known from the inspection of parish registers; in a certain proportion of cases it is probable, however, that we are only dealing with the surviving children. On the whole, the ascertainable size of the family may almost certainly be said to be under the mark. It is, therefore, the more remarkable that the average size of genius-producing families is found to be larger than that of normal families. The average size of our genius-producing families is 6.5. In order to effect an exact comparison with normal families, I have looked about for some fairly comparable series of figures, and am satisfied that I have found it in the results of an inquiry by Mr. F. Howard Collins concerning 4390 families.* These families furnish an excellent normal standard for comparison; they deal mainly with 'Anglo-Saxon' people (in England and America) of the middle and upper classes; they represent, with probably but very slight errors of record, gross fertility; they are apparently not too recent, and they betray little evidence of the artificial limitation of families. The mean size of Collins's group of fertile families is found by Pearson to be 4.52 children.

* As quoted by Karl Pearson, *The Chances of Death*, vol. I, p. 70. In passing through Mr. Pearson's mathematical hands the 4390 emerge as 4444, and it is on this number that my percentages for normal families are based.

This conclusion as to the abnormally large size of the families from which genius tends to spring may be criticised in two directions. It may be argued that there has been no recognition of the possibly larger size of the normal family in the earlier periods which my list covers. It may be said further that even the size of the modern normal family has been underestimated.

It is unnecessary to speculate concerning the average size of the normal family in former days until definite evidence is brought forward. But I may point out that the large size of genius-producing families holds good even when we only take into account the nineteenth-century persons on my list. If, for instance, we consider separately the 39 individuals from the supplement to the *Dictionary* concerning whom I have definite data, it is found that the average size of the families is 5.7, and nine out of the number belong to families containing from nine to seventeen children. I may add that at an earlier stage in my inquiry (see *Popular Science Monthly*, April, 1901, p. 598) I found that the size of the families from which British men of genius spring was still larger than the present average of 6.5, being nearly 7 (6.96). The reduction in size is due in part, it would seem, to the large number of persons of comparatively minor ability who have since been added, and perhaps in part to a tendency to slightly decreased size among the families from which have sprung the quite recent individuals contained in the *Dictionary of National Biography*.

In regard to the correct estimation of the average size of the normal family, it must be said that while my results for British genius-producing families are, without doubt, distinctly too low on account of the imperfection of the data, yet every estimate of the average size of the normal family, although founded on much more complete data, yields an average decidedly below 6.5. Thus

Ansell found the average size of the family, counting all children born alive, among the English professional classes, to be about 5, or, more precisely, clergy 5.25, legal 5.18, medical 4.82. (C. Ansell, *On the Rate of Mortality and other Statistics of Families*, 1874) Galton found the mean of 204 marriages 4.65 children, Pearson the mean of 378 fertile marriages 4.70 children.

A very interesting table is given in Mrs. Henry Sidgwick's *Health Statistics of Women Students of Cambridge and Oxford and of their Sisters*, 1890. Mrs. Sidgwick found that these students (566 in number) belonged to families of which the average size was as high as 6.8 children. (It must be said that this result is slightly vitiated by the inclusion of 70 half brothers and sisters.) One is inclined to look upon the result as necessarily presenting the normal average for the families of the class from which these students spring. It must, however, be borne in mind that these figures refer largely to the early days of the higher education of women; we may be fairly certain that a considerable proportion of these students were women of unusual intellectual ability, and that in numerous other cases they belonged to families in which the brothers showed high ability. The result therefore represents not the average fertility of the professional and allied classes from which these students spring, but is complicated by the considerable admixture of the special ability-producing group of the population with its high fertility. This interpretation is clearly supported by Mrs. Sidgwick's tables. She has presented separately the results of a large group containing the Honours Students, and we are hereby enabled to discern the notable fact that the Honours Students belong to decidedly larger families than do the students generally. In students generally the 6-children families constitute the largest group; for the Honours division the 8-children group is the largest, while very large

families are relatively much more frequent among the Honours division than among the division of 'other students,' so that, for instance, while among Honours students exactly the same number belong to 11-children families as to 2-children families, among 'other students' more than twice as many belong to 2-children families as to 11-children families. Mrs. Sidgwick's results may, therefore, be said to confirm the results reached in the present investigation.

It may be added that the greater fertility which has been shown to mark the families from which British persons of ability in general have sprung, has already been shown by Galton to mark the special group of families from which modern British men of science spring. Galton found (*English Men of Science*) that the average number of brothers and sisters (excluding, for the most part, those who died in infancy) was 6.3. This indicates, as we should expect, a decidedly higher fertility than in the families producing the women students, though probably not higher than would have been shown by the British ability-producing families generally, had my data been more complete.

Yoder, in studying the early lives of 50 eminent men of various nationalities belonging to the eighteenth and nineteenth centuries (A. H. Yoder, 'Boyhood of Great Men,' *Pedagogical Seminary*, October, 1894), found that the average number of children in the families from which they sprang, excluding half brothers and sisters, was 6+. This approximates to the result here reached as regards British eminent men only.

It will be seen that the high fertility which we have found among ability-producing families stands in opposition to the well-known tendency to small families among the higher human races and to the universal tendency, well marked at the present day, for a falling birth-rate to be associated with a rising level of civilization and

well-being. Within the same nation, also, the families of the poorer classes are larger than those of the richer classes; thus in Holland at the present day, both in town and country, the average number of children per marriage in the poorest class is 5.19, against 4.50 for the rich class.

It would, however, be a mistake to suppose that our results can properly be regarded as unexpected. They are, on the contrary, in harmony with all that we know concerning the fertility of the families producing the nervously abnormal classes, which is on the whole decidedly high. Toulouse (*Causes de la Folie*, 1896, p. 91) has summarised the evidence accumulated by Ball and Régis, as well as by Marandon de Montyel, showing that the size of the families from which the insane spring is decidedly larger than the usual average. Professor Magri ("Le Famiglie dalle quali discendono i Delinquenti," *Arch. di Psichiatria*, 1896, fasc. VI–VII) has further shown that this abnormally great fertility is by no means confined to insanity-producing families, but also characterises the progenitors of numerous other mentally abnormal groups. Thus he found that criminals in the majority of cases spring from large families, and that although the average size of the normal family in Italy is three or four, it was very rarely possible to find a criminal who belonged to a family of only two or three children. Magri also found that hysteria and neurasthenia are notably frequent in large families.

Langdon Down had previously pointed out (*Mental Affections of Childhood*) that imbeciles and weak-minded children tend to belong to large families; he found the average number of living children in the families containing idiots to be as high as 7. In Berlin Cassel (*Was lehrt die Untersuchung der geistig minderwertigen Schulkinder*, 1901) found that the average size of the families from which defective children spring is over 7.

Comparing in more detail the composition of our genius-producing families with the normal average, we obtain the following results:

Size of family	1	2	3	4	5	6	7	8
Normal families...	12.2	14.7	15.3	14.1	11.1	8.6	7.8	6.3
Genius-producing families.....	6.9	9.4	10.6	9.4	10.1	10.4	8.9	6.7

Size of family	9	10	11	12	13	14	Over 14
Normal families...	3.9	2.7	1.4	1.0	.5	.2	.1
Genius-producing families.....	5.7	4.7	4.9	4.4	2.2	1.9	3.4

Unless, as is scarcely probable, the mental eccentricities of biographers lead to very frequent selection on definite lines, it will be seen that in genius-producing families there is an invariable deficiency of families below the average normal size, and a gradually increasing excess of families above that size. In the largest size group (over 14) the excess becomes extravagantly large; this, however, may be partly accounted for; probably the biographers have here less seldom failed to record the size of the family, so this group may have been more carefully recruited from the families of our 1030 eminent persons. Even on this basis, however, it remains extremely large. Ansell found that

in 2000 marriages there was no family of more than 18 children; and in Denmark, it is stated, a family of 22 children only occurs once in 34,000 marriages.*

An interesting point, and one which can scarcely be affected at all by any twist in the biographical mind, is the fact that our men of ability (the women are here excluded) are the offspring of predominantly boy-producing parents. Taking the 180 families in which the number of boys and girls in the family is clearly stated, excluding those (29 in number) which are known to consist only of boys, we find that there are about six boys to five girls, or more exactly 121 boys to 100 girls. The normal proportion of the sexes at birth at the present time in England is about 104 boys to 100 girls. It is in accordance with the predominantly boy-producing tendency of families yielding men of genius that the families yielding women of genius should show a predominantly girl-producing tendency. Here, indeed, our cases are too few to prove much, but the results are definite enough as far as they go. Putting aside the families consisting only

* In our genius-producing group there are four families of more than 19 children. Doddridge was the youngest of 20 children; Popham was the youngest of his mother's 21 children; Colet was the eldest and only surviving child of 22; Dempster was, or stated himself to be, the 24th of 29 children. We cannot be absolutely sure that in every case we are dealing with a single couple. It may be added that much larger families are from time to time recorded as produced by a single couple. I may refer, for instance, to the record (*British Medical Journal*, 12th October, 1901) of a family of 36 children; in such a case there are of course numerous plural births.

of girls, the sexual ratio is almost reversed; there are about six girls to five boys; or, more exactly, the ratio is 79 boys to 100 girls. We find that among the children of parents producing an eminent man there are 55 per cent boys to 45 per cent girls; among the children of parents producing an eminent woman there are only 45 per cent boys to 54 per cent girls. Putting the matter in another way, we may say that, while in every ten families from which men of genius spring, the boys predominate in six families; in the families from which women of genius spring the boys predominate only in about three.

Ansell found in England (as has Geissler in Saxony) that there are normally a larger number of boys in large families than in small families; in families of 1–5 children he found the proportion of males to females 1033 to 1000; in families of 6–10 children, 1075 to 1000; in families of 11 children and over 1083 to 1000. It will be seen, however, that this tendency is by no means sufficiently marked to furnish a sufficing explanation of the large preponderance of boys in the families producing eminent men; nor will it account at all for the apparently large excess of girls — this, however, being based on only a small number of cases — in the families producing eminent women.

I may add that while not an all-sufficing explanation, the tendency pointed out by Ansell is evidently a real factor in this peculiarity among the families producing men of ability. I have found it holds good within the limits of the families producing men of ability. Taking at random 25 families with five or fewer children, I find that the girls are in an absolute and decided majority,

while in another series, taken equally at random, of 25 families containing eight or more children, males are to females in the proportion of 130 to 100.

It is possible that some light is thrown on the prevalence of boys in large families by the facts observed among animals. It is believed by many authorities that excess of maternal nourishment tends to produce females, and it has also been found that mares over 14 years of age tend to produce colts (*Veterinarian*, 1st August, 1895). In large families the maternal nourishment would tend to be decreased by much child-bearing. It is noteworthy — although I have not systematically investigated this point — that the interval between the birth of the eminent person and the previous child is often very short.

Yoder, who especially attended to this point, found that in the 26 cases in which the point could be ascertained, the interval was 22.87 months, while the average time in the family, for 30 cases, was 25.36 months. This suggests that it is possible that the maternal exhaustion which tends to produce males also tends to produce children of eminent ability.

It may be said on the whole that this excessive boy-producing tendency of the families which produce men of genius is really the resultant of the combined action of a number of factors, each of which, occurring separately, tends to produce a slighter but still abnormally large excess of boys. Not only would it appear that large families, and families in which the children follow very rapidly, tend to yield a large excess of boys, but observations on man and on other animals indicate that an undue excess of males is also found when the age of the father is unduly advanced (see, *e.g.*, A. J. Wall, *Lancet*, 1887), when the age of the mother is unusually advanced, when the disparity of age between the parents is unusually great, and when the parents live

in the country and are occupied in country pursuits. All these conditions which favour the production of boys have also — as we have seen or shall see — favoured the production of genius in Great Britain. (For a study of the facts and theories bearing on the excess of male births, see A. Rauber, *Der Ueberschuss an Knabengeburten und seine Biologische Bedeutung*, 1900. See also a more recent study, Hans Günther 'Die Sexualproportionen,' *Zeitschrift für Sexualwissenschaft*, October and November, 1925.)

I have made a tentative effort to ascertain what position in the family the child of genius is most likely to occupy. In a large number of cases we are only told his position as a son, not as a child; these are, of course, excluded. In order to investigate this point I considered the families of at least eight children (and subsequently those of at least seven children) and noted where the genius child came. This showed a very abnormally large proportion of eminent first children, and also abnormally few second and third children. Suspecting that certain peculiarities of the biographical mind (needless to enter into here, since we are not investigating the psychology of biographers) may have somewhat affected this result, I have confined myself to a simple inquiry less likely to be affected by any mental tendencies of the biographers. In families of different sizes, what relation do eldest genius children and youngest genius children bear to genius children of intermediate position? The results are very decisive, and are shown in the following table:

Size of Family	Position of Eminent Child		
	Eldest	Intermediate	Youngest
2	15	0	12
3	15	6	11
4	10	16	3
5	10	18	7
6	8	20	6
7	15	14	5
8	2	17	4
9	8	7	4
10	5	10	3
11	3	12	2
12	1	10	2
13	1	4	2
14	0	5	2
Over 14	1	9	4

It would appear that there is a special liability for eldest and youngest children to be born with intellectual aptitudes, the liability being greater in the case of the eldest than of the youngest, for there are altogether 94 eldest children to 67 youngest children, the intermediate children numbering 148; or 30 per cent are eldest children, 21 per cent youngest children, and 47 per cent intermediate. It will be seen that while the eldest and youngest children of ability absolutely outnumber those of intermediate position, notwithstanding the large average size of the families producing children of ability, and the consequently much greater number of chances possessed by the intermediate children as a group, the chances of the eldest attaining eminence as compared with the chances of the youngest are not the same throughout. In

the small and medium-sized families it is the eldest who most frequently achieves fame; in the large families it is the youngest. It may be added that if we were to take into consideration the survivors of a family only (or the net fertility) the youngest children would occupy a still more conspicuous position.

This predominance of eldest children and youngest children among persons of genius accords with the results reached by Yoder in studying an international group of 50 eminent men (*American Journal of Psychology*, October, 1894, p. 146); he found that youngest sons occurred oftener than intermediate sons and eldest sons oftener than youngest. Galton, in his inquiries as to recent British men of science, reached the same result, finding 36 intermediate sons, 15 youngest sons, and 26 eldest sons. (Galton, *English Men of Science*, pp. 33–34.)

It must be added that this result is absolutely in accordance with what a consideration of other mentally abnormal groups would lead us to expect. Sir Arthur Mitchell appears to have been the first to point out many years ago (*Edinburgh Medical Journal*, January, 1866) that among idiots the youngest born and especially the eldest born largely predominate over the intermediate children; he found that among 433 idiots and imbeciles 31 per cent were first-born children and 20 per cent last-born. It will be seen that the proportion of eldest and youngest children among Mitchell's idiots and imbeciles is almost identical with the proportion found among British persons of genius. Langdon Down (*Mental Affections of Childhood*) confirmed this conclusion, as regards the tendency of both eldest and youngest children to be imbecile, and Shuttleworth (*British Medical Journal*, November 17, 1900, p. 1446)

has confirmed it so far as youngest children are concerned. Criminals have also been found to be in undue proportion first-born children (L. Winter, *States Hospital Bulletin*, 1897, p. 463, as quoted by Näcke), and Dugdale found that the first-born child tends to be a criminal and the last-born a pauper. It would appear (see, *e.g.*, Moll, *Untersuchungen über die Libido Sexualis*. Bd. I, p. 19) that there is some ground for believing that sexual inversion tends especially to appear among eldest and youngest children. It may be added that, according to Sir J. Humphrey, in racing stables opinion is not favourable as regards firstlings.

It is interesting to find that the same points have been brought out as regards normal school children. This question was specially studied in its wider bearings at Professor Starbuck's suggestion by Mr. G. S. Wells, among a large number of children at San José, California. (G. S. Wells, *A Study of the Order of the Birth of Children*, 1901. I am indebted to Professor Starbuck for enabling me to see this study in manuscript.) The children were investigated by trained observers, and their position noted as regards weight, height, weight-discrimination, reaction time, voluntary action, ability, endurance, mental ability, neatness and deportment. In nearly all these respects it was found that eldest children tend to show best, and that youngest children, while inferior to eldest, were superior to intermediate children. Out of numerous curves, fourteen show the first group highest, six the last group highest, only two the intermediate group.

The tendency to nervous abnormality in first-born children would seem to be further indicated by the observations of Miss Carman (*American Journal of Psychology*, April, 1899) that first-born boys are more sensitive, as estimated by the temple algometer, than second or subsequent children. She also found that the first-born boys are strongest with the dynamometer. Macdonald

(*Boston Medical and Surgical Journal*, 1st August, 1901) found that first-born men and women are more sensitive to pain than second-born.

I may remark that I had been impressed twenty-five years ago by the tendency of men of genius to be eldest-born children, although I was not then acquainted with Galton's investigations. It appears to be a popular belief (H. Campbell, *Causation of Disease*, p. 262, combats this belief) that the first-born child is inferior. Shandy said that the eldest son is the blockhead of the family. On the other hand, there are popular beliefs in the other direction. Thus in Northern Iceland (*Zeitschrift für Ethnologie*, 1900, heft 2 and 3, p. 74) it is believed that the first-born child, whether boy or girl, surpasses the others in strength, stature, beauty, wisdom, virtue, and good fortune, and in olden times the eldest child possessed certain privileges not accorded to the others. These conflicting popular beliefs are fully accounted for by the actual facts. The eldest-born represents the point of greatest variation in the family, and the variations thus produced may be in either direction, useful or useless, good or bad.

More recently, the distinguished Italian sociological statistician, Gini, also concludes that the early born children are the most variable (*Revista Italiana di Sociologia*, March–April, 1914), and so also the Editor of the *Journal of Heredity*, September, 1916), who shows that the long-lived tend in a disproportionate number of cases to be the eldest born. W. C. Rivers (*Lancet*, 7th October, 1911), dealing primarily with the excess of deaths from consumption among the first-borns, likewise discusses the multiform abnormality of the first-born, bringing together various facts and references.

Whenever it has been possible, I have noted the age of the father at the birth of his eminent child.

It has been possible to ascertain this in 299 cases, and the data thus obtained may be considered as fairly free from fallacy, so far as the biographical mind is concerned, though we may be sure that the biographers would not neglect to mention the two or three known cases in which that age was extremely youthful or advanced. The range of age is considerable, from sixteen, the age of Napier of Merchiston's father at his son's birth, to seventy-nine, the age of Charles Leslie's father, the period of potency in the case of the fathers of persons of eminent ability thus ranging over sixty-three years. The 299 cases may be grouped in five-year age-periods as follows:

Age of Fathers	Under 20	20–24	25–29	30–34	35–39
Number of fathers.	2	9	45	81	59
Percentages.....	6	3	15	27	19

Age of Fathers	40–44	45–49	50–54	55–59	60 and over
Number of fathers.	44	30	13	8	8
Percentages.....	14	10	4	2	2

It will be seen that the most frequent age of fatherhood is from 30 to 34, but there are two separate years of maximum frequency, 34 and 36,

each with 19 cases. A prevalence of elderly fathers seems indicated by the fact that the general average falls later than this maximum, being 37.1 years. For one father who begets an eminent child before the age of maximum paternity — which is also, we may assume, the age of maximum general vigour — there are nearly three who beget an eminent child when that age is past. This result is the more significant when we remember that we are chiefly dealing with the upper social classes (for it is in their cases that these facts are most easily ascertained), and that we must probably exclude the recent tendency to retardation of the age of marriage.

I have thought that it may be of interest to separate from the main body the one hundred most recent of the eminent persons on my list (all born in the nineteenth century) and to consider how the ages of their fathers are distributed. The result is as follows:

Age	20—	25—	30—	35—	40—	45—	50—	55—
Number....	1	18	30	18	14	14	4	1

The most frequent age is 34, but the average age is 37, being almost equal to the average for the fathers of the whole group, so that this factor in the biological constitution of the genius group would appear to be fairly uniform throughout and

independent of social and economic changes, except that the age of the fathers has perhaps tended in the course of time to become slightly lower. Although this decrease in age is very trifling, it appears to be confirmed by the results yielded if we make a separate group of the 71 individuals born before the eighteenth century the age of whose fathers I have been able to determine. The distribution is as follows:

Under 20	20—	25—	30—	35—	40—	45—	50—	55—	60 and over
2	3	13	13	14	10	7	2	4	3

The most frequent age here, taking the years separately, is as low as 25, but on the other hand, the average age is slightly higher than that for the general group, being 37.2. It is possible that this slightly higher age — very trifling as it is — indicates a real tendency. The further we go back the higher becomes the intellectual average of the individuals we are dealing with, and there is some reason to suppose that with such high average intellectual level, the average age of the fathers is also higher, and the range of variation is greater. Such trifling fluctuations would be negligible if they did not all point in one direction.

I may refer to another indication which helps to confirm the conclusion that when we are dealing with a group of men of very high intellectual

eminence the average age of their fathers is slightly higher than when we are dealing with a group of lower eminence. On separating into a distinct group all those eminent men on my list who are also included in the first three hundred (*i.e.*, the most eminent section) of Professor Cattell's one thousand most eminent persons in history (see *ante*, p. 8), we obtain a group of 37 individuals who are without doubt of a higher level of intellectual ability than the general average of the British group. The age of the fathers of the pre-eminent men in this special group is as high as 37.7 years.

The ages of the fathers of Galton's recent British men of science in 100 cases were distributed as follows:

20—	25—	30—	35—	40—	45—	50—
1	15	34	22	17	7	4

The average was 36. These results as regards this group may very fairly be compared with the results reached concerning the contemporaneous group of 100 from my list which has been separately calculated. It will be seen that in the more mixed and more eminent British group, as might be anticipated, the variations are greater; there are a larger proportion alike of younger and of elderly fathers. In Yoder's group of 39 fathers of men of various nationalities whose average eminence was of higher degree than mine and much higher than Galton's, the numbers are too small to bear much

weight; they were distributed as follows, with an average age of 37.78 years:

20—	25—	30—	35—	40—	45—	50—	55—	60—
1	2	10	13	7	3	2	0	1

The most notable point here, as compared with either Galton's results or mine, is the marked deficiency of fathers under 30. It will be noticed that the average age of the fathers in Galton's, mine, and Yoder's groups rises progressively (36, 37.1, 37.78) with the intellectual eminence of the group. It may well be that this is not a casual coincidence. The tendency for the fathers of men of genius to be elderly had, as Yoder points out, already been noted by Lombroso (*Man of Genius*, p. 149).

According to Ansell (*On the Rate of Mortality*, etc., 1874), the average age of fathers of the professional and allied classes (estimated as the length of a generation, *i.e.*, the difference between the age of father and son) is 36.6. An average tells us nothing concerning the range of variation, but it may be observed that this normal average approximates to that obtained in the most nearly normal of the groups of ability we are here able to compare. I have no other data concerning the normal ages of the fathers of the professional and upper classes in modern England, and in any case we could not be sure how far such data could be comparable with that presented by our group of eminent persons which is spread over many centuries. The influence of the age of the fathers in various normal and abnormal groups of the population has been most carefully and elaborately studied by Marro in North Italy (in his *Caratteri dei Delinquenti*, and more recently in *La Pubertà*). Marro regards fathers below the age of twenty-six as belonging to the period of immaturity; the period of maturity is

from twenty-six to forty, and the period of decadence from forty-one onwards. He found, among the normal population, that 9 per cent fathers belonged to the first period, 66 per cent to the second, and 25 per cent to the third. Among the fathers of criminals there was an increase both of immature and of decadent fathers at the expense of the mature, while among the insane fathers there was a similar but more marked increase of immature and decadent fathers. In studying the age of the fathers of school children, Marro found that while children of good intelligence are mostly the offspring of young fathers, those of the highest grade of intelligence are mostly the children of middle-aged and elderly fathers. He found also that the highest proportion of very defectively intelligent children belonged to elderly fathers. Aristotle had long before said that the children of very young or very old people are imperfect in mind or body. We may slightly modify that ancient dictum by saying that the children of such people tend to be abnormal.

I have been able to ascertain the age of the mother in only 86 instances. In these cases it is distributed as follows:

Age of Mother	Under 20	20–24	25–29	30–34	35–39	40–44	45–49	50
Number of cases.....	1	14	22	23	13	11	1	1
Per cent.....	1.1	16	25	26	15	12	1.1	1.1

The average age of the mothers is 31.2 years. Taking the years separately we find that there are only three mothers at the age of 25 and only two

at 26, when there is a sudden rise to ten at the age of 27, representing the chief maximum; there is, however, a secondary maximum (of eight cases) at 30, and again (also of eight cases) at 33. On the whole, it will be seen, the ages of the mothers exhibit the same tendency to late parenthood which marks the fathers. Instead of falling earlier, as we should expect, the age of maximum frequency for the mothers falls within the same five years as for the fathers, and the number of mothers who have reached the sexually advanced age of 40 is nearly as large as the number of those below the age of 25. This is the more remarkable since the predominant tendency of our men of ability to be first-born children would lead us to expect a corresponding predominance of young women among their mothers.

In Galton's 100 cases of mothers of modern British men of science the average age was thirty, and the distribution was as follows:

Under 20	20—	25—	30—	35—	40—	45—
2	20	26	34	12	5	1

It will be seen that in my list of mothers of British persons of ability, the intellectual eminence being greater than in Galton's, there is a comparative deficiency of young mothers (indeed, for all ages under 35), and a very marked excess of elderly mothers, while the average age also is higher than in Galton's. Yoder found

the average age of the mothers in his group to be 29.8, but he is only able to bring forward twenty cases. Vaerting (*Nue Generation*, September and November, 1914) finds that in the parentage of genius the mothers tend to be elderly, in one third of the ascertainable cases older than the father.

Marro in his study of the ages of the mothers of North Italian criminals, insane, school children, etc., found that the relations that existed between the different groups were very much the same as in the cases of the fathers.

The influence of the age of the parents on the children as regards various kinds of mental and nervous ability has been investigated in California by Mr. R. S. Holway, and I am indebted to Professor Starbuck for enabling me to see Mr. Holway's study in manuscript (*The Age of Parents: Its Effects upon Children*, a thesis presented to the Department of Education, Leland Stanford Junior University, 1901). It was found that, while in most physical qualities the children of mature parents tend to come out best, in mental ability the children of young parents show best at an early age, but rapidly lose their precocity; the elder children who show best tend to be the parents of mature and old parents; the exceptionally brilliant children show a tendency to be the offspring of old parents; the children of elderly mothers show a tendency to superiority throughout.

Ansell found that the normal age of mothers in British professional and allied class (estimated as length of a generation) is as high as 32.3 years, but in the absence of information as to distribution we cannot determine the significance of this result. Among the general population of poor class, Collins (*Practical Treatise of Midwifery*) found that the most frequent age of maternity in Ireland (where early marriages are common) was between 25 and 29, the average age being 27. In Edin-

burgh and Glasgow, however, Matthews Duncan (*Fecundity, Fertility, Sterility, and Allied Topics*, 2nd ed., 1871) found the average age in a similar class of the population to be above 29, the distribution being as follows:

Age	Below 20	20—	25—	30—	35—	40—	45—	50—
Per cent	2.30	22.62	30.89	23.61	14.76	5.15	.58	.03

It will be seen that this distribution closely corresponds with that of the mothers of Galton's men of science, but shows much fewer cases at the higher ages than does my group.

The conclusion that among the parents of our men of genius there is an abnormally large proportion of elderly mothers is confirmed by the normal data furnished by Roberton (J. Roberton, *Essays and Notes on the Physiology and Diseases of Women*, 1851, p. 183). He found that among 10,000 pregnant women in Manchester, only 4.3 per cent were over 40, *i.e.*, were at least in their forty-first year.

From a consideration of these various groups of data, among the mothers of highly intellectual children there would certainly appear to be some deficiency of very young mothers, and there is a decided excess of elderly mothers. If, as we may conclude from the marked prevalence of first-born children among our British people of ability, this tendency to a somewhat advanced age of the parents is associated with late marriages, we perhaps have here one of the factors in the prevalence of an excess of boys in the families producing eminent men, since, as Ahlfeld has shown (*Arch. f. Gynäk*, 1876, Bd. IX, p. 448), there is a gradual though not altogether regular increase with age in the proportion of boys among *primiparæ* between the ages of 28 and 36, so that while

at the earlier age there were at Leipzig 110 boys to 100 girls, at the later age there were 190 boys to 100 girls. R. J. Ewart in England also found (*Public Health*, May, 1912) that the older the mother at birth of child the greater the proportion of boys.

It may be noted that in at least 44 cases the mother was a second or third wife. This group is a somewhat distinguished one, including F. Bacon, R. Boyle, Bunyan, Byron, Chaucer, S. T. Coleridge, and Raleigh. The list is certainly very incomplete. In at least nine cases the father was a second husband.

It is instructive to compare the ages of the parents and to ascertain the degree of disparity. I have only been able to do this in 71 cases. There is a marked tendency to disparity which ranges up to 49 years.* In 55 cases the father was older.

The distribution of the various degrees of disparity may be seen in the following table:

Amount of Disparity	None	1–4 yrs.	5–9 yrs.	10–14 yrs.	15–19 yrs.	Over 20 yrs.
Number of cases	4	24	24	13	3	3

The average amount of disparity for the whole of the 71 cases is as high at 7.7 years. It will be seen that the number of cases in which the dis-

* This very exceptional case was that of the father (an eminent bishop) of Charles Leslie, the nonjuring divine. In this case the father was 79, the mother 30.

parity was at least ten years is equal to a proportion of over 26 per cent.

According to Ansell, the mean difference in ages of husband and wife among the professional classes in England during the nineteenth century was 4.16 years; before 1840 it was only 3.89 years, rising to 4.42 years after 1840. This rise is doubtless connected with the accompanying rise in the age of marriage. It will be seen that the degree of disparity in the case of the parents of eminent British persons is nearly double that of the normal average before 1840, with which only it can be compared. The distribution of the different degrees of disparity is not seen from Ansell's tables, but the frequency of high degrees of disparity in age among the parents of eminent British persons is evidently extreme. In Buda-Pesth a table given by Körösi (though not strictly comparable with the present data) shows that if we take men at ages between 26 and 30, covering the most frequent normal age of marriage, in only 3 per cent cases is the discrepancy of age as much as ten years.

A similar tendency to unusual disparity of age in the parents is found among other nervously abnormal groups. It is so, for instance, among idiots. Many years ago, the late Dr. Langdon Down, at my suggestion, kindly went through the notes of one thousand cases of idiots who had been under his care, and found that in 23 per cent cases there was a disparity of age of more than ten years in the parents of the idiot child, the disparity in many cases being more than twenty-five years.

Disparity of age in the parents is also, as Marro has found (*La Pubertà*, p. 259), unusually prevalent among criminals. Among the parents of North Italian school children he found that the normal proportion of parents both belonging to the same stage of development (immature, mature, or decadent) is 70 per cent; among the

parents of North Italian criminals it is only 63 per cent.

It has occurred to me as possible that the tendency to disparity of age may be one of the factors in the marked prevalence of boys. As, however, it has only happened that in a comparatively small proportion of cases I have exact data regarding the respective numbers of boys and girls in the families of parents in whom the exact amount of disparity is known, it has not been possible to test this point with any certainty. So far as figures give any indication, they indicate that if disparity is a factor in the sexual proportion of the offspring it can only be so in a very slight degree.

On the whole it would appear, so far as the evidence goes, that the fathers of our eminent persons have been predominantly middle-aged and to a marked extent elderly at the time of the distinguished child's birth; while the mothers have been predominantly at the period of greatest vigour and maturity, and to a somewhat unusual extent elderly. There has been a notable deficiency of young fathers, and, still more notably, of young mothers.

V

CHILDHOOD AND YOUTH

The frequency of constitutional delicacy in infancy and childhood — Tendency of those who were weak in infancy to become robust later — The prevalence of precocity — University education — The frequency of prolonged residence abroad in early life.

THE first significant fact we encounter in studying the life-histories of these eminent persons is the frequency with which they have shown marked constitutional delicacy in infancy and early life. A group of at least six — Joanna Baillie, Hobbes, Keats, Newton, Smart, Charles Wesley, with perhaps Locke and Sterne — were seven-months children, or, at all events, notably premature in birth; it is a group of very varied and pre-eminent ability (to which among eminent men of later date Lord Rayleigh must be added). Not including the above (who were necessarily weakly), at least fourteen are noted as having been very weak at birth, and not expected to live — even given up as dead; in several cases they were, on account of supposed imminent death, baptised on the same day. Altogether as many as 110 are mentioned as being extremely delicate during infancy or childhood, and the real number is certainly much greater, for this is a point which must frequently be unknown to the biographers, or be ignored by them.

In addition to these, we are told of 103 others (10 per cent) of our eminent British persons that their health was delicate throughout life, so that we may reasonably assume that in most cases their feeble constitutions were congenital. Thus at the lowest estimate 213 of the individuals on our list — a very large proportion of those for whom we have data on this question — were congenitally of notably feeble physical constitution.

Professor A. H. Yoder encountered this fact in the course of his interesting study of the early life of a small group of men of genius (*Pedagogical Seminary*, October, 1894), but failed to realise its significance. He put it aside as due to a desire on the part of biographers to magnify the mental at the expense of the physical qualities of their subjects. There is no evidence whatever in support of this assumption.

The significance of such early delicacy has, however, already been recognised by other writers. Thus Sir W. G. Simpson (*Journal of Mental Science*, October, 1893) points out that illness in children is followed by increased mental development.

It may be noted that a tendency to die at birth is also noted among idiots, who often require resuscitation (Matthews Duncan, *Sterility in Women*, p. 61).

Although it may fairly be concluded that this proportion, at least, of our eminent persons showed signs of physical inferiority at the beginning of life, it must not be assumed that in all cases such inferiority was marked throughout life. The reverse of this is notably the case in many instances. This is not indeed absolutely proved by longevity, fre-

quently noted in such cases, for men of genius have sometimes lived to an advanced age though all their lives suffering from feeble health. But there is a large group of cases (probably much larger than actually appears) in which the delicate infant develops into a youth or a man of quite exceptional physical health and vigor. Bruce, the traveller, is a typical example. Very delicate in early life, he developed into a man of huge proportions, athletic power and iron constitution. Jeremy Bentham, very weak and delicate in childhood, became healthy and robust and lived to 84; Burke, weak and always ailing in early life, was tall and vigorous at 27; Constable, not expected to live at birth, became a strong and healthy boy; Dickens, a puny and sickly child, was full of strength and energy at the age of 12; Galt, a delicate and sensitive child, developed Herculean proportions and energy; Hobbes, very weak in early life, went on gaining strength throughout life and died at 81; Lord Stowell, with a very feeble constitution in early life, became robust and died at 91. It would be easy to multiply examples, though the early feebleness of the future man of robust constitution must often have been forgotten or ignored, and it is probable that this course of development is not without significance.

I have noted that in a very large number of cases one or both parents died soon after the birth of their eminent child. One small but eminent

group — including Blackstone, Chatterton, Cowley, Newton, Adam Smith, and Swift — had lost their fathers before birth. We may trace here the frequent presence of inherited delicacy of constitution.

The chief feature in the childhood of persons of eminent intellectual ability brought out by the present data is their precocity. This has indeed been emphasized by previous inquirers into the psychology of genius, but its prevalence is very clearly shown by the present investigation. It has certainly to be said that the definition of 'precocity' requires a little more careful consideration than it sometimes receives at the hands of those who have inquired into it, and that when we have carefully defined what we mean by 'precocity' it is its absence rather than its presence which ought to astonish us in men of genius.* Judging from the data before us, there are at least three courses open to a child who is destined eventually to display pre-eminent intellectual ability. He may (1) show extraordinary aptitude for acquiring the ordinary subjects of school study; he may (2), on the other hand, show only average, and even much less than average, aptitude for ordinary school studies, but

* For a summary of investigations into the precocity of genius, see A. F. Chamberlain, *The Child*, pp. 42–46. Cf. also an article by Professor Sully on 'Genius and Precocity,' in the *Nineteenth Century*, June, 1886, and another by Professor J. Jastrow (*Journal of Education*, July, 1888) showing that precocity is more marked among persons of transcendent genius than among the merely eminent.

be at the same time engrossed in following up his own preferred lines of study or thinking; he may, once more (3), be marked in early life solely by physical energy, by his activity in games or mischief, or even by his brutality, the physical energy being sooner or later transformed into intellectual energy.

It is those of the first group, those who display an extraordinary aptitude for ordinary school learning, who create most astonishment and are chiefly referred to as proving the 'precocity' of genius. There can be no doubt whatever that even in the very highest genius such extraordinary aptitude at a very early age is not infrequently observed. It must also be said that it occurs in children who, after school or college life is over, or even earlier, display no independent intellectual energy whatever. It is probable that here we really have two classes of cases simulating uniformity. In one class we have an exquisitely organized and sensitive mental mechanism which assimilates whatever is presented to it, and with development ever seeks more complicated problems to grapple with. In the other class we merely have a sponge-like mental receptivity, without any corresponding degree of aptitude for intellectual organization, so that when the period of mental receptivity is over no further development takes place.

The second group, comprising those children who are mostly indifferent to ordinary school

learning but are absorbed in their own lines of thought, certainly contains a very large number of individuals destined to attain intellectual eminence. They by no means impress people by their 'precocity'; Scott, occupied in building up romances, was a 'dunce'; Hume, the youthful thinker, was described by his mother as 'uncommon weak-minded.' Yet the individuals of this group are often in reality far more 'precocious,' further advanced along the line of their future activities, than the children of the first group. It is true that they may be divided into two classes, those who from the first have divined the line of their later advance, and those who are only restlessly searching and exploring; but both alike have really entered on the path of their future progress.

The third group, including those children who are only noted for their physical energy, is the smallest. In these cases some powerful external impression — a severe illness, an emotional shock, contact with some person of intellectual eminence — serves to divert the physical energy into mental channels. In those fields of eminence in which moral qualities and force of character count for much, such as statesmanship and generalship, this course of development seems to be a favourable one, but in more purely intellectual fields it scarcely seems to lead very often to the finest results.

On the whole, it is evident that 'precocity' is not a very valuable or precise conception as applied to

persons of intellectual eminence. The conception of physical precocity is fairly exact and definite. It indicates an earlier than average attainment of the ultimate growth of maturity. But we are by no means warranted in asserting that the man of intellectual ability reaches his full growth and maturity earlier than the average man. And even when as a child he is compared with other children, his marked superiority along certain lines may be more than balanced by his apparent inferiority along other lines. It is no doubt true that, in a vague use of the word, genius is very often indeed 'precocious'; but it is evident that this statement is almost meaningless unless we use the word 'precocity' in a carefully defined manner. It would be better if we asserted that genius is in a large number of cases mentally abnormal from the first, and if we were to seek to inquire precisely wherein that mental abnormality consisted. With these preliminary remarks we may proceed to note the prevalence among British persons of genius of the undefined conditions commonly termed 'precocity.'

It is certainly very considerable. Although we have to make allowance for ignorance in a large proportion of cases, and for neglect to mention the fact in many more cases, the national biographers note that 292 of the 1030 eminent persons on our list may in one sense or another be termed precocious, and only 44 are mentioned as not precocious. Many of the latter belong to the second

group, as defined above — those who are already absorbed in their own lines of mental activity — and are really just as 'precocious' as the others; thus Cardinal Wiseman as a boy was 'dull and stupid, always reading and thinking'; Byron showed no aptitude for school work, but was absorbed in romance, and Landor, though not regarded as precocious, was already preparing for his future literary career. In a small but interesting group of cases, which must be mentioned separately, the mental development is first retarded and then accelerated; thus Chatterton up to the age of six and a half was, said his mother, 'little better than an absolute fool,' then he fell in love with the illuminated capitals of an old folio, at seven was remarkable for brightness, and at ten was writing poems; Goldsmith, again, was a stupid child, but before he could write legibly he was fond of poetry and rhyming, and a little later he was regarded as a clever boy; while Fanny Burney did not know her letters at eight, but at ten was writing stories and poems.

Probably the greatest prodigies of infant precocity among these eminent persons were Cowley, Sir W. R. Hamilton, Wren, and Thomas Young, all of these, it will be seen, being men of a high order of genius. J. Barry, Mill, and Thirlwall were also notable prodigies, and it would be easy to name a large number of others whose youthful proficiency in learning was of extremely unusual

character. While, however, this is undoubtedly the case, it scarcely appears that any actual achievements of note date from early youth. It is only in mathematics, and to some extent in poetry, that originality may be attained at an early age, but even then it is very rare (Newton and Keats are examples), and is not notable until adolescence is completed.

The marked prevalence of an early bent towards those lines of achievement in which success is eventually to be won is indicated by the fact that in those fields in which such bent is most easily perceived it is most frequently found. It is marked among the musicians, and would doubtless be still more evident if it were not that our knowledge concerning British composers is very incomplete. It is specially notable in the case of artists. It is reported of not less than 40 out of 64 that in art they were 'precocious'; only four are noted as not being specially precocious.

A certain proportion of the eminent persons on our list have followed the third course of early development as defined above, that is to say, they have been merely noted for physical energy in youth. Sir Joseph Banks was very fond of play till 14, when he was suddenly struck by the beauty of a lane; Isaac Barrow was chiefly noted for fighting at school; Chalmers was full of physical activity, but his intellect awoke late; Thomas Cromwell was a ruffian in youth; Thurlow, even at college,

was idle and insubordinate; Murchison was a mischievous boy, full of animal spirits, and was not interested in science till the age of 32; Perkins was reckless and drunken till his conversion. It can scarcely be said that any of these remarkable men, not even Barrow, achieved very great original distinction in purely intellectual fields. In order to go far, it is evidently desirable to start early.

The influence of education on men of genius is an interesting subject for investigation. It is, however, best studied by considering in detail the history of individual cases; generalized statements cannot be expected to throw much light on it. I have made no exact notes concerning the school education of the eminent persons at present under consideration; it is evident that as a rule they received the ordinary school education of children of their class, and very few were, on account of poverty or social class, shut out from school education. A small but notable proportion were educated at home, being debarred from school-life by feeble health; a few, also (like J. S. Mill), were specially educated by an intellectual father or mother.

The fact of university education has been very carefully noted by the national biographers, and it is possible to form a fairly exact notion of the proportion of eminent British men who have enjoyed this advantage. This proportion is decidedly large. The majority (53 per cent) have,

in fact, been at some university. Oxford stands easily at the head; 41 per cent of those who have had a university education received it at Oxford, and only 33 per cent at Cambridge. An interesting point is observed here; the respective influences of Oxford and Cambridge are due to geographical considerations; there is a kind of educational watershed between Oxford and Cambridge, running north and south, and so placed that Northamptonshire is on the eastern side. Cambridge drains the east coast, including the important East Anglian district and the greater part of Yorkshire, whilst Oxford drains the whole of the rest of England as well as Wales. This at once accounts both for the greater number of eminent men who have been at Oxford and for the special characteristics of the two universities, due to the districts that have fed them, the more literary character of Oxford, the more scientific character of Cambridge. The Scotch universities are responsible for 14 per cent of our eminent men. Trinity College, Dublin, shows 5 per cent. The remaining 4 per cent have studied at one or more foreign universities. Paris (the Sorbonne) stands at the head of the foreign universities, having attracted as many English students as all the other European universities put together. This is doubtless mainly due to the fact that Paris was the unquestioned intellectual centre of Europe throughout the long period of the Middle Ages, though the intimate relations be-

tween England and France may also have had their influence. With the revival of learning Italian universities became attractive, and Padua long retained its pre-eminence as a centre of medical study. During the seventeenth century the Dutch universities, Leyden and Utrecht, began to attract English students, and continued to do so to some extent throughout the greater part of the eighteenth century. It was not until the nineteenth century that English students sought out the German universities. Douai might perhaps have been included in the list as the chief substitute for university education for the eminent English Catholics who have appeared since the Reformation.

Stated somewhat more precisely, it may be said that of our 975 eminent men, 217 were at Oxford (232 if we include those who had also been at some other university); 177 were at Cambridge (191 if we include those who had also been elsewhere); 76 came from Scotch universities (Edinburgh 28, Glasgow 21, St. Andrews 16, Aberdeen 11); from Trinity College, Dublin, have come 27 men; 23 (or 47 if we include those who had previously been at some British university) have been to one or more foreign universities (Paris 23, Leyden 9, Padua 6, Utrecht 3, Louvain 3, Göttingen 2, Bonn 2, Heidelberg 2, etc.).

It may be interesting to compare these results with those obtained by Maclean in his study of nineteenth-

century British men of ability. He found that among some 3000 eminent men, 1132, or 37 per cent, are recorded as having had an English, Scotch or Irish university education. Of these 1132, 37 per cent were at Oxford, 33 per cent at Cambridge, 21 per cent at Scotch universities, 7 per cent at Dublin, and the small remainder were scattered among various modern institutions. It will be seen that university education plays a comparatively small part in this group. This may be in part due to the lower standard of eminence, but it may also be due to the wide dissemination of the sources of knowledge. In no previous century would so encyclopædic a thinker as Herbert Spencer have been able to ignore absolutely the advantages of university centres.

In America also, as might be expected, a college education has not been received by the majority of able men. Thus Professor E. Dexter ('High Grade Men in College and Out,' *Popular Science Monthly*, March, 1903) shows that not more than 3237 out of 8602 eminent Americans of the nineteenth century (or 37 per cent, exactly the same proportion as Maclean found in Great Britain) are college graduates; those who reach a high grade of scholarship are, however, more likely to become eminent than those of low grade.

While the fact of university education is easily ascertained, it is less easy to define its precise significance. The majority of our men of pre-eminent intellectual ability have been at a university; but it would be surprising were it otherwise, considering that the majority of these men belong to the class which in ordinary course receives a university education. It would be more to the point if we knew exactly what influence the universities had exerted, but on this our present investiga-

tion throws little light. In a considerable number of cases, at least, the university exerted no favourable influence whatever, the eminent man subsequently declaring that the years he spent there were the most unprofitable of his life; this was so even in the case of Gibbon, whose residence at Oxford might have been supposed to be very beneficial, for at the age of 14 he had already been drawn toward the subject of his life task. In a large number of cases, again, the eminent man left the university without a degree, and in not a few cases he was expelled. It is evident, however, on the whole, that university life has not been unfavourable to the development of intellectual ability, and that while our eminent men do not appear to have been usually subjected to any severe educational discipline they have been in a good position to enjoy the best educational advantages of their land and time.

Professor Sully in a study of the influence of education on genius, with special reference to men and women of letters ('The Education of Genius,' *English Illustrated Magazine*, January, 1891), had already reached conclusions in harmony with those here set forth: 'It cannot be said that the boys who afterwards proved themselves to have been the most highly gifted shone with much lustre at school, or found themselves in happy harmony with their school environment. The record of the doings of genius at college is not greatly different. No doubt a number of the ablest men have won university distinctions. In a few cases, indeed, a thoroughly original man has carried everything before

him. At the same time it may safely be said that a very small proportion of the men of genius who have visited our universities have presaged their after fame by high academic distinction. Thus it has been computed that, though Cambridge has been rich in poets, only four appear in her honours lists. (See article on 'Senior Wranglers,' *Cornhill Magazine*, vol. 45, p. 225.) . . . In many cases we have too clear signs of a disposition to rebel against the discipline and routine of college life. . . . We find further that more than one distinguished man has expressed in later life his low estimate of university training. The conclusion that seems to be forced on us by the study of the lives of men of letters is that they owe a remarkably small proportion of their learning to the established machinery of instruction.'

If this is not a very decisive result to reach, there is another less recognised method of educational development which occurs so frequently that I am disposed to attach very decided significance to it. I refer to residence in a foreign country during early life. The eminent persons under consideration have indeed spent a very large portion of their whole lives abroad, whether from inclination, duty, or necessity (persecution or exile), and it might be interesting to ascertain the average period of life spent by a British man of genius in his own country. I have not attempted to do this, but I have invariably noted the cases in which a lengthened stay abroad has occurred during the formative years of childhood or youth. I have seldom knowingly included any period of less than a year; in a few cases I have included lengthened stays abroad

which were made about the age of thirty, but in these cases those periods of foreign residence exerted an unquestionable formative influence. I have excluded soldiers and sailors altogether (as well as explorers), for in their case absence from England at a youthful age has been an almost invariable and inevitable incident in their lives, and has not always been of a kind conducive to intellectual development. Nor have I included the numerous cases in which transference from one part of the British Islands to another has sufficed to exert a stimulating influence of the greatest importance. With these exceptions, we find that as many as 371 of the eminent persons on our list (nearly as large a proportion as received a university education), during early life, and in all but a few cases before the age of thirty, have spent abroad periods which range from about a year, and in very many cases have extended over seven years, up to extreme cases, like that of Caxton, who went to Bruges in early life and stayed there for thirty years; or Buchanan, who went to France at the age of fourteen and was abroad for nearly forty years. It is natural that France should be the country most frequently mentioned as the place of residence, but France is closely followed by other countries, and a familiarity with many lands, including even very remote and scarcely accessible countries, is often indicated. It may further be noted that this tendency to an association be-

tween high intellectual ability and early familiarity with foreign lands is by no means a comparatively recent tendency. It exists from the first; the earliest personage on our list, Saint Patrick, was kidnapped in Scotland at the age of sixteen, and conveyed over to Ireland; it seems, indeed, that in the nineteenth century the tendency became less marked, yielding to the average modern Englishman's hasty and unprofitable method of travelling. In any case, however, it is evident that there has been a marked tendency among these men of preeminent ability to familiarise themselves in the most serious spirit with every aspect of nature and life. It is equally marked among the men of every group, among poets and statesmen, artists and divines. It is not least marked in the case of men of science from the days of Ray onwards; if it had not been for the five years on the *Beagle* we should scarcely have had a Darwin, and Lyell's work was avowedly founded on his constant foreign tours. In a notable number of cases this element comes in at the earliest period of life, the eminent person having been born abroad and spent his childhood there.* The presence of so large a number of our eminent men at a university may be in considerable measure merely the accident of their social position. The persistence with which men of the first

* It may be noted that at least twelve of our eminent persons — seemingly a large proportion — belonged on one side or the other to West Indian families, whether or not they were born in the West Indies.

order of intellect have sought out and studied unfamiliar aspects of life and nature, or have profited by such aspects when presented by circumstances, indicates a more active and personal factor in the evolution of genius.

VI

MARRIAGE AND FAMILY

Celibacy — Average age at marriage — Tendency to marry late — Age of eminent women at marriage — Apparently a greater tendency to celibacy among persons of ability than among the ordinary population — Fertility of marriage — Fertility and sterility of eminent persons alike pronounced — Average size of families — Proportion of children of each sex.

We have some information concerning the status as regards marriage of 988 of the eminent persons on our list. Of these, 79, being Catholic priests or monks (twelve of them since the Reformation), were vowed celibates.* Of the others, 177 never married. We thus find that 25.9 per cent never married, or, if we exclude the vowed celibates, 19.4 per cent. It must of course be remembered that a certain though not considerable proportion of the unmarried were under fifty at death, and some of these would certainly have married had they survived. It may be added that of the women considered separately, about two-thirds were married, though several of them (especially actresses) who were unmarried formed *liaisons* of a more or less public character and in a few cases had several children.

It must not be supposed that all these eminent

* One or two priests who belonged to the early centuries before the celibacy of ecclesiastics was firmly established and who consequently married, are not of course included.

men who lived long lives in celibacy were always so absorbed in intellectual pursuits that the idea of matrimony never occurred to them. This was not the case. Thus we are told of Dalton, that the idea had crossed his mind, but he put it aside because, he said, he 'never had time.' In several cases, as in that of Cowley, the eminent man appears really to have been in love, but was too shy to avow this fact to the object of his affections. Reynolds is supposed only once to have been in love, with Angelica Kauffmann; the lady waited long and patiently for a declaration, but none arrived, and she finally married another; Reynolds does not appear to have been overmuch distressed, and they remained good friends. These cases seem to be fairly typical of a certain group of the celibates in our list; a passionate devotion to intellectual pursuits seems often to be associated with a lack of passion in the ordinary relationships of life, while excessive shyness really betrays also a feebleness of the emotional impulse. In the case of many poets who have adored their mistresses with passionate fervour in verse it would appear that there has often been no accompanying fervour in the love-making of real life. Sir Philip Sidney, even though he was counted the paragon of his time, with all his sweet sonnets never shook the virtue of his Stella (Lady Penelope Rich), who yet eloped some years later with another man who was not a poet. Even in many cases in which marriage

occurs, it is easy to see that the relationship was rooted in the man's intellectual passion.

The average age at marriage among the 503 men on the list concerning whom I have information on this point is 31.1 years, the most frequent age being 26 years. The distribution is as follows:

Age	Under 20	20—	25—	30—	35—	40—	45—	50—	55—
No. of cases..	16	88	139	110	66	43	28	9	.4
Per cent.....	3	17	27	22	15	8	5	1.7	7

I have ascertained the ages at marriage of the fathers of the eminent persons on my list (not including the fathers who are themselves of sufficient eminence to be included in the list) in 73 cases; they are distributed as follows:

Under 20	20—	25—	30—	35—	40—	45—	50—
3	7	30	18	9	4	1	1

The most frequent age of marriage of the fathers is 25, but the average is 30 years. It would thus appear that while both British men of genius and their fathers tend to marry at an abnormally late period, the former marry, if anything, even later than their fathers.

If, however, in the 54 cases in which data are

forthcoming we compare the age at marriage of the individual man of genius with that of his (not eminent or less eminent) father the results are not quite concordant. It is found that five married at the same age as their fathers; while 29 were younger and only 20 older. The deviations from the paternal example are often very considerable in either direction, and it can scarcely be said that the data before us suffice for the conclusion that our British men of genius have married later than their fathers.

If we compare the distribution of the frequency of the marriage-age among British men of genius and their fathers with the general population, the contrast is very striking. In England generally 57 per cent of the men who marry before the age of 30 marry between the ages of 20 and 25, a larger proportion than in any other European country. The curve for the British men of genius much more nearly resembles that for the general population in Sweden or in France, where of all European countries marriage is latest. It is, however, of more significance to compare British men of genius with the professional classes of their own land, avoiding also the fallacy of including second or subsequent marriages. Ansell found that the average age of marriage for clerical, legal and medical bachelors in the nineteenth century before 1840 was about 28 years. There is thus a small but distinct delay in the age of marriage among men of genius, a delay which would be still more marked if we can assume that the gradual tendency, noted by Ansell as in progress during the nineteenth century, for marriage to take place later among the professional classes, may be pushed back to the previous century. It

would be further marked, if the comparison were made more strictly between professional class men of genius and ordinary professional class men, by omitting from the men of genius those of the aristocratic and plebeian classes, among both of whom I find that marriage has frequently taken place very early.

While not disputing the statement of Ansell that during the nineteenth century there was a progressive tendency among the professional classes for marriage to take place at a later age, I am by no means convinced that we can push this tendency back and assert that in earlier centuries marriage among the same classes took place very early. This seems highly improbable. It is much more likely that while there have been fluctuations from time to time, the age of marriage has not on the whole greatly changed, so far as the professional classes are concerned, for many centuries past. I am confirmed in this opinion by an examination of the age of marriage which prevailed in various branches of my own ancestry (belonging to the middle and upper middle class) during the seventeenth and eighteenth centuries; the general average was 29, and taking the seventeenth-century figures separately (though here the numbers are few) it was decidedly higher. The average age, it will be seen, lies between that which I have found for the fathers of our eminent British persons and that found by Ansell for the British professional classes generally before 1840.

I find in the marriage 'allegations' of the Archdeacon of Essex for the years 1791–97, where the age 'about' is given, that the average for 20 bachelors is 26 years. The exact social class is not, however, obvious.

It remains probable that when we take a sufficiently high standard of intellectual eminence the age of marriage is somewhat later than that of the professional classes generally, but it would scarcely appear that the difference is considerable.

The married women among the British people of intellectual eminence concerning whom we have definite information, form but a small group of 26 persons, a group too small to generalise about. Their average age at marriage was 28 years, and the most frequent ages of marriage were 22 and 40. The distribution is as follows:

Age	Under 20	20—	25—	30—	35—	40—
Number of persons.....	3	9	4	3	3	4

Although the numbers are so small, it is probably not an accident that the most frequent ages of marriage should be 22 and 40 years. If we take into account the ages before 30 only, we note a marked tendency to early marriage, more marked than among English women of the professional classes, more marked even than among the general population. But after the age of 24 there is a sudden and extraordinary fall, the ages of 26 and 27 are unrepresented altogether, and, still more remarkable, the slight rise which eventually takes place is postponed to the ages of 40 and 41, towards the end of sexual life.

The interpretation of this curious curve is, however, fairly obvious. The claims of the reproductive and domestic life are in women too preponderant and imperious to be easily conciliated with the

claims of a life of intellectual labour. The women who marry at the period of greatest general and sexual activity, between 25 and 30, tend either to have their intellectual activities stifled, or else to be seriously handicapped in attaining eminence. The women, on the other hand, who have either married very early and then escaped from, or found a *modus vivendi* with, domestic and procreative claims, or else have been able to postpone the sexual life and its dominating claims until comparatively late in life, enjoy a very great advantage in attaining intellectual eminence.

Thus it is that among British women of genius very few marriages take place during the period of great reproductive energy; the large majority of such marriages fall outside the period between 23 and 34 years of age. In the majority of cases marriage took place before this period, the relationship, from one reason or another, being very often dissolved not long afterwards; but in a very considerable proportion of cases, marriage never took place until after this period. Thus, Fanny Burney married at 41, Mrs. Browning at 40, Charlotte Brontë at 38, while George Eliot's relationship with Lewes was formed at about the age of 36; these names include the most eminent English women of letters. It would thus appear that there is a tendency for the years of greatest reproductive activity to be reserved for intellectual development, by accelerating or retarding the disturbing emo-

tional and practical influences of real life. This tendency might still be beneficial, even when the best work was not actually accomplished until after a late marriage.

Ansell found the age of marriage of English spinsters belonging to the professional classes, previous to 1840, to be 24.75 years, while after 1840 it was 25.53. Mrs. Sidgwick found the age of marriage of the sisters of Oxford and Cambridge women students, in exact agreement with Ansell, to be 25.53 years, while the age of marriage of the students themselves was 26.70. Among the general population in England the chief age of marriage for women is between 20 and 25. At the end of the eighteenth century the average age ('about') of 19 spinsters in the marriage allegations of the court of the Archdeacon of Essex was 23.5 years.

We have now to consider more minutely the status as regards marriage of our British men and women of eminent intellectual ability. When we eliminate the 79 individuals who had taken vows of celibacy and the 177 others who are definitely known not to have married, we have 774. Of these, 732 are definitely known to have married, while the remaining 42 are doubtful. It is probable that the doubtful may be equally divided between the married and the unmarried. We cannot assume that the same proportion of married and unmarried prevails among them as among the known group, for it would appear that in many cases the omission of the mention of marriage is to be regarded as a tacit statement on the bio-

grapher's part that the subject was not married. If this is admitted we must conclude that in the whole body of 1030 persons, including the vowed celibates, 277 never married, that is to say, a proportion of 26.8 per cent. If we omit the vowed celibates, the proportion is reduced to 20 per cent. If we leave out of account alike the vowed celibate group and the small dubious group, and consider only those remaining persons, 909 in number, of whom we have definite knowledge, the percentage of those who never married is found to be 19.4. If we consider separately the most recent group, *i.e.*, those whose names are contained in the Supplement to the *Dictionary of National Biography*, the results are not widely different; the proportion of the unmarried being in the ratio of nearly 18 per cent.

It is natural to ask the question whether the tendency to remain unmarried is greater among our men of ability than among the general population. It is, however, obviously difficult to answer the question with any precision, because we must of course compare the men of ability with normal persons not only of the same class but the same period. A consideration of the results seems to suggest that there is a somewhat greater tendency to celibacy among men belonging to the very highest class of genius than there is among the rank and file of able men, but that so far as the latter are concerned the tendency to celibacy is not notably greater than among the ordinary population of the same social class. We see that the most recent group of our eminent British persons, which probably shows a somewhat

lower general level of eminence, also shows a somewhat slighter tendency to celibacy. It is probable that among men of eminent ability the tendency to celibacy has always been slightly, but only slightly, greater than among the general population of the same social class.

This conclusion is confirmed by an inquiry made by Professor E. L. Thorndike ('Marriage among Eminent Men,' *Popular Science Monthly*, August, 1902). He sought to ascertain the proportion of married individuals among the 1000 most eminent men in a biographical compilation of contemporary Americans entitled *Who's Who in America*. The standard of ability here demanded is necessarily very much lower than that of the persons in my list. It was found that of those who had reached the age of 40, 12 per cent were celibate, as against 15 per cent for the most recent group (excluding the women) on my list, nearly all of whom had far passed the age of 40. For the whole male population over the age of 40, in the United States, Professor Thorndike states, the proportion of celibates is from 11 to 7 per cent, decreasing with age.

Of the 753 persons whom we may reasonably suppose to have married, 548 are definitely stated to have had children, 112 are definitely stated to have been childless, the remaining 93 are doubtful. If we assume that two-thirds of this doubtful remainder may be included among the fertile group, we may say that 19 per cent of eminent British men and women who married have remained sterile. If, however, we only take into consideration those cases concerning which we have definite information, we find that the proportion of the sterile is about 17 per cent. This is certainly less

than the real proportion for the whole married group, for there can be little doubt that in a large number of cases the biographers have made no mention of children simply because there were no children to mention. In many cases, I have been able to verify this statement that the merely negative absence of information meant a positive absence of children, though this is not invariably the case. We may assume that the real proportion of individuals whose marriages were sterile, for the whole of our married group, is more nearly 19 than 17 per cent.

If we consider the 55 women separately, we find that one was a vowed celibate, and 19 others remained unmarried, while of the 35 who were married, 14 certainly had children and 21 apparently had no children. A few of the actresses occupy an uncertain borderland between the married and the unmarried. They have here, however (according to the same rule as has been adopted with the men), been regarded as unmarried, even though they had a recognised family, whenever they were not generally recognised as married.

The number of sterile persons (like the number of unmarried persons) among our eminent men and women must be regarded as, in all probability, an abnormally large proportion in comparison with the general population of the same period and class. It must be borne in mind that the figures which have been given do not represent the proportion of fertile and sterile marriages, but the proportion of *persons* who have proved fertile

and sterile in marriage. As many of our eminent persons entered into two or more marriages during life and frequently only proved fertile in one or in none, it is evident that if we were to consider the ratio of fertile and sterile marriages, instead of the ratio of fertile and sterile persons in marriage, the prevalence of sterility would be much more marked.

Simpson found that the proportion of sterile marriages in two Scotch seafaring and agricultural villages was about 10 per cent, while in the British peerage he found that it was about 16 per cent. (J. Y. Simpson, *Obstetric Works*, vol. 1, pp. 323 *et seq.*)

Professor Karl Pearson, manipulating the data furnished by Howard Collins, has found that during the early part of the past century among the middle and upper classes chiefly of British race, or belonging to the United States — a class fairly comparable to those in the present group — the total sterility was about 12 or 13 per cent, rather less than half of this (*i.e.*, about 6 per cent) being due to what may be termed 'natural sterility,' while the remainder (*i.e.*, 6 or 7 per cent) must be set down to artificial restraints on reproduction. At the present day in the United States sterility has greatly increased, and Dr. Engelmann finds it to exist in 20 per cent of marriages in Saint Louis and Boston in dispensary practice, and in 23 per cent among the higher classes in private practice, although among the foreign elements in the population the proportion is very much lower. In New Zealand also, at the other side of the world, sterility is at the present day very marked. Here the methods of registration enable us to form an approximate estimate of the proportion of childless marriages among a population of somewhat mixed British race with a high standard of living, and the proportion of marriages in which there is no surviving child at the father's death is about 16 per cent; but it must be borne

in mind that we have to allow for the early death of the children in some cases, as well as for the early death of the father. We have also to remember that this increase of sterility is a modern phenomenon, and that the artificial restraint of reproduction to which it is in large part, if not mainly, due is of recent development. All the indications point to the conclusion that the sterility of our eminent men is greater than that of their contemporaries of the same social class.

I may add that among the 62 eminent married men on my list who appear in the Supplement to the *Dictionary of National Biography* and therefore constitute the most recent group, the proportion who are sterile appears to be in about the ratio of nearly 20 per cent, which very closely approximates to the general average.

In Galton's group of modern British men of science the proportion of sterile marriages was higher; there were no children in one out of every three cases.

It is somewhat remarkable that, although the number of infertile marriages is so large, the average fertility of those marriages which were not barren is by no means small. We have fairly adequate information in the case of 281 of these eminent men. I have not included those cases in which the biographer is only able to say that there were 'at least' so many children, nor have I knowingly included the offspring of second or subsequent marriages. Whether the number of children represents gross or net fertility, it is, unfortunately, in a very large proportion of instances, quite impossible to say. It is probable that in a certain proportion of cases only the net fertility,

i.e., the number of children who survived infancy and childhood, has been recorded. It is therefore probable that the average number of children in these fertile families, which is 4.8, must be considered as slightly below the real gross fertility. The average reached is not far from the normal average, and very decidedly below that of the families from which the men of genius spring.

With regard to the distribution of families of different sizes, the results, as compared with the figures already given, are as follows:

Size of Family	1	2	3	4	5	6	7	8
Normal families	12.2	14.7	15.3	14.1	11.1	8.6	7.8	6.3
Genius-producing families	6.9	9.4	10.6	9.4	10.1	10.4	8.9	6.7
Families of men of genius	14.2	16.7	10.3	12	11.3	7.4	8.5	4.6

Size of Family	9	10	11	12	13	14	Over 14
Normal families	3.9	2.7	1.4	1.0	.5	.2	.1
Genius-producing families	5.7	4.7	4.9	4.4	2.2	1.9	3.4
Families of men of genius	5.3	2.1	2.1	.7	2.1	1.0	1.0

Allowing for certain irregularities due to the insufficient number of cases, the interesting point

that emerges is the return towards the proportions that prevail in normal families; it will be seen that in all but a few cases the families of men of genius differ from genius-producing families by approximating to normal families. It must be remembered that in neither of our groups are the data absolutely perfect, but as they stand they confirm the conclusion already suggested that men of genius belong to families in which there is a high birth-rate, a flaring up of procreative activity, which in the men of genius themselves subsides towards normal proportions. The families of the men of genius seem to differ chiefly from normal families in showing a greater tendency to variation; there are more very small families, there are more very large families.

It will be noticed that the families of sizes ranging between three and six, both inclusive, are unduly few. It might be supposed that this is due to the artificial limitation of families, more especially since, in Professor Pearson's opinion, the normal families themselves show a deficiency in those groups probably due to this cause. I am, however, inclined to doubt whether that is so in the case of families of men of genius, although to a small extent it may be so. It is possible that from the present point of view the group may not be homogeneous, but made up in part of men with feeble vitality and a tendency to sterility, and in part of men with a tendency towards unusual fecundity, thus leading to a deficiency of medium-sized families.

The relationship which has been found to exist between our British genius-producing families, and the families which the men of genius themselves produce (*i.e.*, the increased fertility followed in the next generation by diminished fertility), does not represent a novel result. It had already been found by Galton (*English Men of Science*, p. 38) in his group of modern British men of science. Eliminating sterile marriages he found that the average size of the families of the men of science was 4.7 children, almost exactly the same size as we have found for the whole group of British men of genius. Galton, however, only took living children into account.

There would appear to be a considerable resemblance between the fertility of genius families and of insane families. We see that our eminent British persons belong to families of probably more than average fertility, that they themselves produce families of probably not more than average size, and with an abnormal prevalence of sterility. In France, Ball and Régis, confirmed by Marandon de Montyel, appear to have found reason for a similar conclusion regarding the insane. They state that natality is greater among the ascendants of the insane than in normal families, but afterwards it is the same as in normal families, while they also note the prevalence of sterility in the families of the insane. The question, however, needs further investigation (Toulouse, *Causes de la Folie*, p. 91).

In the case of 278 families of our British men of genius it has been possible to ascertain the number of children of each sex. This is found to be over 105 boys to 100 girls, a somewhat higher proportion of boys than has prevailed in Great Britain during the past century, but, in accordance with the results we have reached concerning the size of the

families of our men of genius, very much closer to the normal average than are the sexual proportions prevailing among the families from which the men of genius spring. If, however, I am right in supposing that in a certain proportion of our cases the biographers have stated not the gross fertility, but only the net fertility (or the surviving children), we are not entitled to expect so close an approximation to the proportions at birth, since the preponderance of boys begins to vanish immediately after birth. The figures thus suggest that the families of men of genius show the same tendency to excess of boys which we have already seen to be clearly marked in the case of the families producing men of genius. The data are too few to indicate whether there is any corresponding excess of girls in the families of women of genius.

VII

DURATION OF LIFE

The fallacy involved in estimating the longevity of eminent men — The real bearing of the data — Mortality at different ages.

It has long been a favourite amusement of popular writers on genius to estimate the ages at which famous men have died, to dilate on their tendency to longevity, and to conclude, or assume, that longevity is the natural result of a life devoted to intellectual occupations. The average age for different groups, found by a number of different inquirers, varies between 64 and 71 years. One writer, who finds this latter age for certain groups of eminent men of the nineteenth century, argues that here we have a test from which there is no appeal, proving the pre-eminence of the nineteenth century over previous centuries, and its freedom from 'degeneration.' It did not occur to this inquirer to ask at what age the famous men of earlier centuries died. I have done so in the case of a small group of ten eminent men on my list, dying between the fourth and the end of the thirteenth centuries — including, I believe, nearly all those in my list of whose dates we have fairly definite information during this period — and I find that their average age is exactly 74 years. So that, if this test means anything at all, the freedom of the

nineteenth century from 'degeneration' is by no means proved.

In reality, however, it means nothing. If genius were recognisable at birth there would be some interest in tracing the course of its death-rate. But it must always be remembered that when we are dealing with men of genius, we are really dealing with *famous* men of genius, and that though genius may be born, fame is made — in most fields very slowly made. Among poets, it has generally been found, longevity is less marked than among other groups of eminent men, and the reason is simple. The qualities that the poet requires often develop early; his art is a comparatively easy one to acquire and exercise, while its products are imperishable and of so widely appreciated a character that even a few lines may serve to gain immortality. The case of the poet is, therefore, somewhat exceptional, though even among poets only a few attain perfection at an early age. In nearly every other field the man of genius must necessarily take a long period to acquire the full possession of his powers, and a still longer period to impress his fellow-men with the sense of his powers, thus attaining eminence. In the case of the lawyer, for instance, the path of success is hemmed in by tradition and routine, every triumph is only witnessed by a small number of persons, and passes away without adequate record; only by a long succession of achievements through many years can the lawyer hope to

acquire the fame necessary for supreme eminence, and it is not surprising that of the eminent lawyers on my list only five were under sixty at death. Much the same is true, though in a slightly less marked degree, of statesmen, divines and actors.

It is, therefore, somewhat an idle task to pile up records of the longevity of eminent men of genius. They live a long time for the excellent reason that they must live a long time or they will never become eminent. It is doubtless true that men of genius — mostly belonging to the well-to-do classes, and possessing the energy and usually the opportunities necessary to follow intellectual ends of a comparatively impersonal and disinterested character — are in a far more favourable position for living to an advanced age than the crowds who struggle more or less desperately for the gratification of personal greeds and ambitions, which neither in the pursuit nor the attainment are conducive to peaceful and wholesome living. This may well be believed, but it is hardly demonstrated by the longevity of eminent men.

At the same time it is of some interest to note the ages of the eminent persons on our list at death. Though the facts may have little significance in themselves, they have a bearing on many of the other data here recorded. Excluding women, and including only those men whose dates are considered by the national biographers to be un-

questionable, the ages of eminent British men at death range from Chatterton the poet, at seventeen, to Sir A. T. Cotton the man of science, at ninety-six. They are distributed as follows in five-year age-periods:

Age at death..	under 20	20–24	25–29	30–34	35–39	40–44
Men of genius.	1	2	6	14	15	32

Age at death..	45–49	50–54	55–59	60–64	65–69	70–74
Men of genius.	50	55	76	90	130	139

Age at death..	75–79	80–84	85–89	90 and over
Men of genius.	100	65	46	20

If we consider the number for each year separately, certain points emerge which are disguised by the five-year age-period, though the irregularities become frequently marked and inexplicable. A certain order, however, seems to be maintained. There is scarcely any rise from 27 to 38, and even at 45 only 3 individuals died; but, on the whole, there is a slow rise after 38, leading to the first climax at 49, when 16 individuals died; this climax is maintained at a lower level to 53, when there follows a fall to a level scarcely higher than that

which prevailed ten and more years earlier. This lasts for three years; then there is a sudden rise from 7 deaths at 56, to 25 deaths at 57, and this second climax is again maintained at a somewhat lower level to the age of 67, when the highest climax is attained, with 34 deaths. Thereafter the decline is extremely slow but steady, not becoming accelerated until after 80. Each climax is sudden, and preceded by a fall.

A noteworthy point here seems to be the very low mortality between the ages of 53 and 57. It seems to confirm Galton's conclusion, based on somewhat similar data, that a group of men of genius is in part made up of persons of unusually feeble constitutions and in part of persons of unusually vigorous constitutions. After the first climax at 49 the feeble have mostly died out. The vigorous are then in possession of their best powers and working at full pressure; 57 appears to be a critical age at which exhaustion and collapse are specially liable to occur. The presence of these two classes — the abnormally weak and the abnormally vigorous — would be in harmony with the explanation I have already ventured to offer of the deficiency of medium-sized families left by our men of genius.

The age of the women at death is ascertainable in 51 cases. The average is slightly over 62 years. As among the men, there would seem to be among them a small group tending to die early. The age-

distribution arranged in periods of five years is as follows:

Age at death.....	30–34	35–39	40–44	45–49	50–54
Women of genius..	2	4	2	2	2

Age at death.....	55–59	60–64	65–69	70–74	75–79
Women of genius..	5	4	7	4	4

Age at death.....	80–84	85–89	90 and over
Women of genius ..	8	4	3

VIII

PATHOLOGY

Relative ill-health — Consumption — The psychology of consumptives — Gout — Its extreme frequency in men of ability — The possible reasons for the association between gout and ability — Other allied diseases — Asthma and angina pectoris — Insanity — The question of its significance — Apparent rarity of grave nervous diseases — Frequency of minor nervous disorders — Stammering — Its significance — High-pitched voice — Spasmodic movements — Illegible handwriting — Short sight — Awkwardness of movement.

It has already been noted (p. 118) that at least 10 per cent of our eminent British persons suffered from a marked degree of ill-health, amounting to more than minor discomfort, during the years of their active lives. It is of some interest to observe how these persons are distributed among the various chief classes of ability. This distribution appears to be as follows:

Soldiers and sailors	3 per cent
Statesmen, etc.	7 " "
Men of science	11 " "
Lawyers	13 " "
Men of letters	15 " "
Artists	16 " "
Poets	16 " "
Divines	17 " "

This marked prevalence of ill-health among divines had already been noted by Galton (*Hereditary Genius*, pp. 255 *et seq.*). He analysed the 196 biographies contained in Middleton's *Biographia Evangelica*, and came to the conclusion that there is 'a frequent correlation

between an unusually devout disposition and a weak constitution.' He found that over 13 per cent at least were 'certainly invalids,' while a large number of the others were ailing. He found also that of the 12 or 13 who were alone stated to be decidedly robust, 5 or 6 were irregular in their youth, while on the other hand only 3 or 4 divines are stated to have been irregular in their youth who were not also men of notably robust constitutions.

In a large proportion of cases no reference is made by the national biographers to the diseases from which their subjects suffered, nor to the general state of health. This, however, we could scarcely expect to find, except in those cases in which the state of health had an obvious influence on the life and work of the eminent person. In most of these exceptional cases it is probable that the biographers have duly called attention to the facts, and though the information thus attained is not always precise — in part owing to the imperfection of the knowledge transmitted, in part to the medical ignorance of the biographers,* and in part to the deliberate vagueness of their reference to a 'painful malady,' etc. — it enables us to reach some very instructive conclusions concerning the pathological conditions to which men of genius are most liable.

Putting aside the cases of delicate health in

* Thus one of the national biographers informs us that a recent Archbishop of Canterbury had an attack of catalepsy, which is a rare and severe form of hysteria; he probably meant apoplexy.

childhood, with which I have already dealt in a previous section, the national biographers state the cause of death, or mention serious diseased conditions during life, in some 400 cases.

It is natural to find that certain diseased conditions which are very common among the ordinary population are also very common among men of pre-eminent intellectual ability. Thus, a lesion of the vessels in the brain (the condition commonly described as paralysis, apoplexy, effusion on the brain, etc.) is a very common cause of death among the general population, and we also find that it is mentioned 44 times by the national biographers.

Consumption, also so prevalent among the general population, occurred in at least 40 cases. While many of the consumptive men of genius lived to past middle age, or even reached a fairly advanced age, the disease is responsible for the early death of most of the more eminent of those men of genius who died young — of Keats in poetry, of Bonington and Girtin and Beardsley in art, of Purcell (probably) in music. Some appear to have struggled with consumptive tendencies during a fairly long life; these have usually been men of letters, and have sometimes shown a feverish literary activity, their intellectual output being perhaps as remarkable for quantity as for quality, as we may observe in Baxter and in J. A. Symonds. But Sterne in literature, and Black, Priestley, Clifford and other eminent men of science are to be

found among the consumptives. It is evident that the disease by no means stands in the way of the highest intellectual attainments, even if it is not indeed actually favourable to mental activity.*

There is, however, a pathological condition which occurs so often, in such extreme forms, and in men of such pre-eminent intellectual ability, that it is impossible not to regard it as having a real association with such ability. I refer to gout. This is by no means a common disease, at all events at the present day. In ordinary English medical practice at the present time, it may safely be said that cases of typical gout seldom form more than one per cent of the chronic disorders met with. Yet gout is of all diseases that most commonly mentioned by the national biographers; it is noted as occurring in 53 cases, often in very severe forms. We have, indeed, to bear in mind that gout has been recognised for a long time, and that it is moreover a disease of good reputation. Yet, even if we assume that it has been noted in every case in which it occurs among our 1030 eminent persons (an altogether absurd assumption to make), we

* The psychology of the consumptive — marked by mental exaltation, hyper-excitability, the tendency to form vast plans and to exert feverish activity in carrying them out, with, at all events in the later stages, egoism, indifference, neurasthenia — has been studied by Maurice Letulle (*Archives Générales de Médecine*, 1901); a summary of his study will be found in the *British Medical Journal*, 4th May, 1901. An interesting symposium on the mental state of the consumptive will also be found in the *Archives de Neurologie*, January, 1903.

should still have to recognise its presence in five per cent cases. Moreover, the eminence of these gouty subjects is as notable as their number. They include Milton, Harvey, Sydenham, Newton, Gibbon, Fielding, Hunter, Johnson, Congreve, the Pitts, J. Wesley, Landor, W. R. Hamilton and C. Darwin, while the Bacons were a gouty family. It would probably be impossible to match the group of gouty men of genius, for varied and pre-eminent intellectual ability, by any combination of non-gouty individuals on our list. It may be added that these gouty men of genius have frequently been eccentric, often very irascible — 'choleric' is the term applied by their contemporaries — and occasionally insane. As a group, they are certainly very unlike the group of eminent consumptives. These latter, with their febrile activities, their restless versatility, their quick sensitiveness to impressions, often appear the very type of genius, but it is a somewhat feminine order of genius. The genius of the gouty group is emphatically masculine, profoundly original; these men show a massive and patient energy which proceeds 'without rest,' it may be, but also 'without haste,' until it has dominated its task and solved its problem.

Sydenham, the greatest of English physicians, who suffered from gout for thirty-four years, and wrote an unsurpassed description of its symptoms, said in his treatise, *De Podagra*, that 'it may be some consolation to those sufferers from the disease who, like myself and

others, are only modestly endowed with fortune and intellectual gifts, to know that great kings, princes, generals, admirals, philosophers and many more of like eminence have suffered from the same complaint, and ultimately died of it. In a word, gout, unlike any other disease, kills more rich men than poor, more wise than simple.' And another ancient writer, the Jesuit, Father Balde, who in 1661 wrote a work which he called *Solatium Podagricorum*, called gout *Dominus morborum et morbus dominorum.*

I may remark that a much earlier ancient, Aretæus, indicates the superior intelligence of the gouty in his statement that they are specially skilful in the knowledge of the drugs that suit them. In more recent times a long series of physicians have testified to the intellectual eminence of their gouty patients. Cullen said that gout especially affected 'men of large heads'; Watson stated that gout is 'peculiarly incidental to men of cultivated mind and intellectual distinction.' Sir Spencer Wells believed that, in the absence of hereditary predisposition, gout is not easy to produce except 'in men endowed with a highly organised condition of the nervous system,' and again remarks (*Practical Observations on Gout*, 1856, p. 23), in reference to statesmen, 'those who are known to be subject to gout are among the most distinguished for an ancestry rendered illustrious by "high thoughts and noble deeds," for their own keen intelligence, for the assistance that they have afforded to improvements in arts, science and agriculture, and for the manner in which they have led the spirit of the age. . . . I never met with a real case of gout, in other classes of the community, in a person not remarkable for mental activity, unless the tendency to gout was clearly inherited.'

This association of ability and gout cannot be a fortuitous coincidence. I have elsewhere suggested

(*Popular Science Monthly*, July, 1901) that the secret of the association may possibly to some extent lie in the special pathological peculiarities of gout. It is liable to occur in robust, well-nourished individuals. It acts in such a way that the poison is sometimes in the blood, and sometimes in the joints. Thus not only is the poison itself probably an irritant and stimulant to the nervous system, but even its fluctuations may be mentally beneficial. When it is in the victim's blood his brain becomes abnormally overclouded, if not intoxicated; when it is in his joints his mind becomes abnormally clear and vigorous. There is thus a well-marked mental periodicity; the man liable to attacks of gout is able to view the world from two entirely different points of view; he has, as it were, two brains at his disposal; in the transition from one state to another he is constantly receiving new inspirations, and constantly forced to gloomy and severe self-criticism. His mind thus attains a greater mental vigour and acuteness than the more equable mind of the non-gouty subject, though the latter is doubtless much more useful for the ordinary purposes of life, for the gouty subject is too much the victim of his own constitutional state to be always a reliable guide in the conduct of affairs.

It is, however, possible only to speak tentatively of the nature of the pathological relationship between genius and gout, because the true nature of gout itself is not yet definitely known. Some years ago the theory that gout is caused by uric acid was very vigorously promulgated by Garrod and others, and very widely accepted; this theory, however, no longer receives such wide acceptance, and there is a tendency to regard the uric acid produced in gout as a symptom rather than a cause. According to another view which has been maintained by Woods Hutchinson in a very able discussion of this question ('The Meaning of Uric Acid

and the Urates,' *Lancet*, 31st January, 1903), gout is certainly a toxæmia, but chiefly of intestinal origin (the uric acid produced by the disease being comparatively harmless), whence it is that the drugs good in gout are such as either prevent intestinal fermentation or absorb its products. This theory does not, however, clearly answer the question why it is that some persons and not others are liable to gout. A theory which has been upheld by a long series of distinguished clinical physicians regards gout as primarily and pre-eminently a neurosis; this was the belief of Stahl, Cullen, Laycock, Dyce Duckworth (Dyce Duckworth, 'A Plea for the Neurotic Theory of Gout,' *Brain*, April, 1880). I should be going beyond my proper province if I were to state that the facts here brought forward may be regarded as an argument in favour of the existence of a neurotic element in the factors producing gout. That, however, my data confirm the belief in the prevalence of gout among men of high intellectual ability can scarcely be doubted.

I have sometimes found that physicians who readily accept a special association between intellectual ability and gout, are inclined to account for it easily by an unduly sedentary life probably associated with excesses in eating and drinking. This explanation cannot be accepted. Many of the most gouty persons on my list have been temperate in eating and drinking to an extreme degree, and while it is true that the gouty have often written much, the general energy, physical and mental, of the gouty may almost be said to be notorious. Sir Spencer Wells, in questioning the influence of sedentary habits, referred to the remarkable activity of gouty statesmen, and Dr. Burney Yeo remarks (*British Medical Journal*, 15th June, 1901): 'The gouty patients that I have seen have, I should say, in the majority of instances, been extremely active and energetic people,

and it is often difficult to get them to take sufficient rest.' I may note that in a much earlier age Aretæus speaks of a gouty person who, in an interval of the disease, won the race in the Olympic games.

It may be of interest to point out in relation to the connection between genius and gouty conditions, that Marro (*La Pubertà*, p. 256) has observed a very constant relation between advanced age of parents at conception and lithiasis in the child. We have already seen that there is a marked tendency among some of our men of genius for the parents to be of advanced age at the eminent child's conception; and it is possible that the connection between gout and genius may thus be in part due to a tendency of some of the gout-producing influences to be identical with some of the genius-producing influences. If this is so we might probably expect to find that the age of the parents of those of our men of genius who belonged pathologically to the lithiasis group would be higher than the general average. I find that the average age of 19 fathers of eminent gouty men is 37.4, and of seven mothers 33.2 years, while the average age of the fathers of eight eminent men who suffered from stone or gravel is 37.2. These averages are slightly, but very slightly indeed, higher than those for our men of genius generally. It must of course be remembered that the general averages are higher than those for the normal population.

It must not, in any case, be supposed that in thus suggesting a real connection between gout and genius it is thereby assumed that the latter is in any sense a product of the former. It is easy enough to find severe gout in individuals who are neither rich nor wise, but merely hard-working manual labourers of the most ordinary intelligence. It may well be, however, that, given a highly endowed and robust organism, the gouty poison acts as a real stimulus to intellectual energy, and a real

aid to intellectual achievement. Gout is thus merely one of perhaps many exciting causes acting on a fundamental predisposition. If the man of genius is all the better for a slight ferment of disease, we must not forget that if he is to accomplish much hard work he also requires a robust constitution.

It may be added that the other diseases usually described as of the uric acid group are common among our men of genius. Rheumatism, indeed, is not mentioned a large number of times (11), considering its prevalence among the ordinary population. But stone, and closely allied conditions, are mentioned 25 times (sometimes in association with gout), and as we may be quite sure that this is a very decided underestimate it is certain that the condition has been remarkably common.

There are two disorders, allied to gout and at the same time distinctly neurotic in character, which are decidedly common among our eminent persons, and we must, I believe, regard them as of considerable significance. I refer to spasmodic asthma and angina pectoris. Asthma is distinctly connected with gouty conditions, and occasionally also it alternates with insanity; it is a disorder common in individuals of high nervous temperament.* I have noted it in 14 cases, often as beginning in early life. Angina occurred in about nine cases, certainly a large proportion considering that

* I may refer to the slightly analogous respiratory defect in horses called 'roaring' (due to laryngeal hemiplegia), a neurotic disturbance apt to occur in very highly bred horses.

the disease is one which has only been recognised in quite recent times. It is probable that one or two cases were not true angina but that simulated angina which sometimes occurs in neurotic individuals; on the other hand several of the cases mentioned as heart disease would certainly, had they been more definitely described, be set down as angina.*

One other grave pathological state remains to be noticed in this connection — insanity. To the relationship of insanity with genius great importance has by some writers been attached. That such a relationship is apt to occur cannot be doubted, but it is far from being either so frequent or so significant as is assumed by some writers, who rake together cases of insane men of genius without considering what proportion they bear to sane men of genius, nor what relation their insanity bears to their genius. The interest felt in this question is so general that we may be fairly certain that the national biographers have rarely failed to record the facts bearing on it, although in some cases

* The data do not enable us to form any opinion as to the frequency of diabetes, which is, moreover, a disease only recognised clearly toward the end of the seventeenth century. (In 1714 Ford wrote to Swift that Dr. Garth had told him Marlborough was going to Bristol 'to drink the waters for a diabetes.') It is rarely mentioned in the *Dictionary*, but is associated, and seemingly with increasing frequency, with intellectual pursuits. Thus, in France Worms finds (*Bulletin de l'Académie de Médecine*, 23 July, 1895) that in any series of 100 scientists, artists, doctors, lawyers, etc., between the ages of 40 and 60, there will be 10 diabetics.

these facts are dubious and obscure. They may often have passed over gout without mention, but they have seldom failed to mention insanity whenever they knew of its occurrence. It is, therefore, possible to ascertain the prevalence of insanity among the persons on our list with a fair degree of approximation to the truth, as it was known to the eminent man's contemporaries. We thus find that thirteen were, during a considerable portion of their active or early lives, thoroughly and unquestionably insane, in most cases with a clearly morbid heredity which frequently showed itself in early life; in most cases also they died insane. These were J. Barry, Clare, William Collins, Cowper, Denham, Fergusson, Gillray, Lee, Paterson, Pugin, Ritson, Romney, Smart. We further find a second group consisting of individuals who may be said, with a fair degree of certainty, to have been once insane, but whose insanity was either slight, of brief duration, or quickly terminated by death, sometimes by suicide. These were Borrow (?), Chatham (?), Cotman (?), O. Cromwell (?), G. Fox, J. Harrington, Haydon (?), Mrs. Jordan, Kean (?), Lamb, Landseer, Lever, Rodney (?), D. G. Rossetti, Ruskin (?), Tillotson, Sir H. Trollope, Whitbread, Sir C. H. Williams. A third group consists of men who were perfectly sane during the greater part of long lives filled with strenuous intellectual activity, although in two or three cases there was morbid mental heredity or eccentricity

in earlier life, but became insane towards the end of life. These cases, twelve in number, which may usually be fairly regarded as senile dementia, are H. Cavendish, Colman, Marsh, Newton (?), J. Pearson, Sabine, Southey, Stephen, Swift, Warburton, S. Ward, T. Wright. It would be possible to add a fourth group of borderland cases in which the existence of actual insanity was in most cases dubious, but marked eccentricity not amounting to insanity was unquestionable. Such were Boswell and R. Browne and Laurence Oliphant. William Blake clearly lived on the borderland of insanity, and Dr. Maudsley indeed declared many years ago that if the story of his sitting naked with his wife in his summer house is to be believed, he was certainly insane; this, however, one may be permitted to doubt. Blake had strong opinions regarding the action of the sun on the skin, and in a day in which sun baths are regarded as beneficial we may view more intelligently the action of a man who was in many respects a pioneer. I leave this group out of account. Nor are the cases of suicide, at least ten in number, necessarily to be regarded as cases of insanity.

If we count every case of probable insanity which may be inferred from the data supplied by the national biographers, and even if we include that decay of the mental faculties which in predisposed subjects is liable to occur before death in extreme old age, we find that the ascertainable

number of cases of insanity is 44, so that the incidence of insanity among our 1030 eminent persons is 4.2 per cent.

It is probably a high proportion. I do not know the number of cases among persons of the educated classes living to a high average age in which it can be said that insanity has occurred at least once during life, but it is stated that among the general population there are only from 1 to 2 per cent cases of insanity. It may be lower, but at the same time it can scarcely be so very much lower that we are entitled to say that there is a special and peculiar connection between genius and insanity. The association of genius with insanity is not, I believe, without significance, but in face of the fact that its occurrence is only demonstrable in less than 5 per cent cases, we must put out of court any theory as to genius being a form of insanity.

It may be said that although the proportion of insane men of genius is so small, a different result would be attained if we took account of those who sprang from insane stocks, or showed their neuropathic unsoundness by producing insane stocks. 'It is no exaggeration to say,' Dr. Maudsley once boldly wrote, 'that there is hardly ever a man of genius who has not insanity or nervous disorder of some form in his family.' * It is many years since that statement was made, yet neither Dr. Maudsley

* H. Maudsley, 'Heredity in Health and Disease,' *Fortnightly Review*, May, 1886.

nor anyone else has ever brought forward any sound evidence in support of it. So far as the present inquiry bears on the point, it may be said that the number of those men of genius who are noted as having a father or mother who became insane, or children who became insane, is very small indeed, the cases of insanity in the descendants being about equal to those of insanity in the ascendants. Less than two per cent of our eminent persons are stated to have had either insane parents or insane children. We may certainly believe that the records are incomplete, but there is clearly no ground for believing that an insane heredity is eminently productive of intellectual ability. The notion sometimes put forward that in discouraging the marriages of persons belonging to mentally unsound stocks we are limiting the production of genius is without support.

While I cannot compare with any precision the liability of persons of genius to insanity with the similar liability of corresponding normal classes, there is one comparison which it is interesting to make. We may compare the liability of persons of genius to insanity with the similar liability of their wives or husbands. It is noted by the national biographers that in sixteen cases the wives or husband (there is only one case of the latter *) became

* This was Mrs. Barbauld's husband; it may be added that the man to whom Harriet Martineau was engaged became insane, and that Hannah More's marriage was prevented by what seems the morbid eccentricity of the man.

insane. We may be fairly certain that this is a decided underestimate, for while the biographers would hold themselves bound to report the insanity of their subjects, they would not consider themselves equally bound to give similar information concerning the wives, while in other cases it may well be that the record of the fact has been lost. If now, in order to make the comparison reasonably fair, we omit the second group of slight cases of insanity and only admit the first and third groups, we find that the proportion of cases of insanity among the persons of genius is 2.4 per cent. Among the conjugal partners, on the other hand (I have not made any allowance for second marriages), it is 2.2 Thus we see that on a roughly fair estimate the difference between the incidence of insanity on British persons of genius and on their wives or husbands is a negligible difference; it is scarcely hazardous to assert that British men of genius have probably not been more liable to insanity than their wives.

At the first glance it might seem that this may be taken to indicate that the liability of genius to insanity is exactly the normal liability. That, however, would be a very rash conclusion. If the wives of men of genius were chosen at random from the general population it would hold good. But there is a well-recognised tendency — observed among all the mentally abnormal classes — for abnormal persons to be sexually attracted to

each other. That this tendency prevails largely among persons of eminent intellectual ability many of us may have had occasion to observe. What we see, therefore, is not so much the conjunction of an abnormal and a normal class of persons, but the presence of two abnormal classes.

With regard to the significance of insanity, it must be pointed out that even if there is a slightly unusual liability to insanity among men of genius, there is no general tendency for genius and insanity, even when occurring in the same individual, to be concomitant. Just as it is rare to find anything truly resembling genius in an asylum, so it is rare to find any true insanity in a man of genius when engaged on his best work. The simulation of it may occur — either the 'divine mania' of the artistic creator, or a very high degree of eccentricity — but not true and definite insanity. There seem to be very few certain cases — mostly poets — in which the best work was done during the actual period of insanity. Christopher Smart's one masterpiece may be said to be actually inspired by insanity, and much of Cowper's best work was written under the influence of insanity. Periods of insanity may alternate with periods of high intellectual achievement, just as gout may alternate with various neurotic conditions, but the two states are not concomitant, and genius cannot be accurately defined as a disease.

It must also be pointed out, in estimating the

significance of the relationship between genius and insanity, that the insane group is on the whole not one of commanding intellectual pre-eminence. It cannot compare in this respect with the gouty group, which is not much larger, and the individuals of greatest eminence are usually the slightest or the most doubtful cases. Among poets and men of letters, of an order below the highest, insanity has been somewhat apt to occur; marked eccentricity almost or quite amounting to insanity has been prevalent among antiquarians, but the intellectual eminence of antiquarians is often so dubious that the question of their inclusion in my list has been a frequent source of embarrassment.

If we turn from insanity to other grave nervous diseases, we are struck by their rarity. It is true that many serious nervous diseases have only been accurately distinguished during the past century, and we could not expect to find much trace of them in the *Dictionary*. But that cannot be said of epilepsy, which has always been recognised, and in a well-developed form cannot easily be ignored. Yet epilepsy is only mentioned twice by the national biographers — once as occurring in early life (Lord Herbert of Cherbury), once in old age (Sir W. R. Hamilton). Even these two cases, however, cannot be admitted. In Lord Herbert of Cherbury's case the national biographer has simply misunderstood a passage in Lord Herbert's *Autobiography*, in which he tells us how, as he believed,

he escaped the epilepsy which he says is common in his family by acquiring a minor disorder in childhood, a 'defluxion of the ears' which 'purged his system'; in Sir W. R. Hamilton's case the epileptoid fits occurring in old age most certainly cannot be regarded as true epilepsy. There appears to be nothing whatever in the records of British genius favourable to Lombroso's favourite theory, that genius tends to occur on an epileptoid basis.

While, however, grave nervous diseases of definite type seem to be rare rather than common among the eminent persons with whom we are dealing, there is ample evidence to show that nervous symptoms of vaguer and more atypical character are extremely common. The prevalence of eccentricity I have already mentioned. That irritable condition of the nervous system which, in its Protean forms, is now commonly called neurasthenia, is evidently very widespread among them, and probably a large majority have been subject to it. Various definite forms of minor nervous derangement are also common.

Among the minor forms of nervous derangement stammering is of very great significance. I have ascertained that at least thirteen of the eminent persons on my list (twelve men and one woman) stammered. These were Bagehot (?), R. Boyle, Curran, Croker, Erasmus Darwin, Dodgson, Mrs. Inchbald, C. Kingsley, Lamb, Maginn, Priestley,

Sheil, Sidgwick. Seven others are noted as having defects of speech which are sometimes stated not to amount to a stammer, but in other cases were doubtless ordinary stammering. When it is remembered that the normal occurrence of stammering among adults is much below one per cent and also that my record is certainly very incomplete, it will be seen that there can be no doubt whatever as to the abnormal prevalence of stammering among British persons of ability. It may be added that twenty-five persons are described as having a high, shrill, feminine, small or weak voice; this also is certainly very decidedly less than the real number.

Stammering may be defined as a functional disturbance of the central nervous system, congenital or acquired, characterised by involuntary, disorderly spasms in certain muscles concerned in vocal utterance. In other words, it is a spastic neurosis of muscular coordination. E. M. Hartwell ('Report of the Director of Physical Training,' Boston *School Document*, no. 8, 1894), following Marshall Hall, describes it as a Saint Vitus's dance of the finer, more peripheral muscles of speech. Stammering is frequently distinguished from stuttering, but it is unnecessary to observe any distinction here, as our knowledge of the precise nature of the voice defects found among our men of genius is often imperfect. We may with Wyllie regard 'stammering' as the general term. Clouston, in his *Neuroses of Development*, regards stammering as specially associated with rapid brain growth, and as most likely to occur between birth and the seventh year. In his careful investigation among Boston school children Hartwell

found that stammering became more prevalent at the beginning of accelerated growth, just before or just after such growth culminates, and again after its cessation, and he concludes that the irritability of the nervous system of which stammering is an expression, is correlated with the most marked upward and downward fluctuations of the power of the organism to resist lethal influences. Stammering is much less common in adults than in children and is three to four times more frequent in men. Among male adults its frequency has been most carefully investigated in recruits, and its prevalence found to be, according to the standard adopted, 3 to 6 per thousand in France (Chervin), as well as among French recruits in the American War of Secession (Baxter), 1.2 per thousand among native American recruits during the same war (Baxter), and exactly the same in Russia (Ssikorski).

In persons of neuropathic inheritance, stammering is specially liable to occur. 'Even in the very intelligent,' Wyllie remarks (*Disorders of Speech*, p. 22), 'it may be found associated with nervousness and excitability as well as sometimes with more distinct irritability of the nervous system.'

Among the nervously abnormal classes stammering and allied speech defects occur with especial frequency. This is notably the case among mental defectives. Thus in Berlin, Cassel found that 33.5 per cent of defective children showed infirmities of speech, and Dr. Eichholz, a London School Inspector, states ('The Treatment of Feeble-Minded Children,' *British Medical Journal*, 6th September, 1902) that 'quite 75 per cent of defective children speak imperfectly, ranging from complete aphasia to a mere indistinct thickening, including stammering, halting, lisping, word-clipping, mispronunciation, and the mainly purely vocal imperfections.' Most of the minor speech defects mentioned would seem

to have been specially prevalent among our British men of genius.

The tendency to very high-pitched voice which is so remarkably common in men of intellectual ability may possibly be due to a slight paralysis of the vocal cords, such as is apt to occur in more marked degrees in general paralysis (as observed by Permewan, *British Medical Journal*, 24th November, 1894), unless it is caused by a general arrest of laryngeal development.

Involuntary spasmodic twitching movements, or tic, of the smaller muscles, especially of the face, would appear to occur with very unusual frequency among our British men of genius, although I have no figures of the prevalence of such convulsive movements among the ordinary population. I have noted the prevalence of this nervous disorder in seven cases: Brougham, W. Hook, Dr. Johnson, C. Kingsley, Marshall, J. S. Mill, and Paley.

In another form a tendency to nervous incoordination is shown, by no means necessarily by any actual tremours, in the tendency to bad handwriting. Illegible handwriting is mentioned in nine cases which certainly need to be largely increased.

A tendency to scrawling or illegible handwriting has been frequently noted among the men of genius of many countries and is by no means due to too much writing, for it is often traceable at an early age. It must be remembered that the handwriting is a very delicate indication of the nervous balance, and as such has been carefully studied during recent years by Kraepelin and his pupils, while alienists have long been accustomed to attribute significance to the remarkable changes in

handwriting which often occur under the influence of insanity. As Goodhart has truly remarked (*Lancet*, 6th July, 1889), 'illegibility is a disease'; and he compares it to the defects of speech.

Writer's cramp, to which illegible handwriting is occasionally due, is also, it must be remarked, not the mere result of excessive writing, for, as Féré points out ('Professional Neuroses,' *Twentieth Century Practice of Medicine*, vol. x, p. 707), it occurs more frequently in high officials than in their subordinates who write more, and is associated with mental overwork and neurasthenic and neuropathic conditions.

Short sight, another condition frequently occurring on a basis of hereditary nervous defect, is noted as existing in an extreme degree sixteen times, and in twelve cases some other sense was defective or absent.

A condition to which I am inclined to attribute considerable significance from the present point of view is clumsiness in the use of the hands and awkwardness in walking. A singular degree of clumsiness or awkwardness is noted many times by the national biographers, although they have certainly regarded it merely as a curious trait, and can scarcely have realised its profound significance as an index to the unbalanced make-up of the nervous system. This peculiarity is very frequently noted as occurring in persons who are tall, healthy, robust, full of energy. As boys they are sometimes not attracted to games, and cannot, if they try, succeed in acquiring skill in games; as they grow

up all sorts of physical exercise present unusual difficulties to them; they cannot, for instance, learn to ride; even if fond of shooting, they may be unable to hit anything; in walking they totter and shuffle unsteadily; they are always meeting with accidents. Priestley, though great in experiment, was too awkward to handle a tool; Macaulay could not wield a razor or even tie his own neck cloth; Shelley, though lithe and active, was always tumbling upstairs or tripping on smooth lawns. It would be easy to fill many pages with similar examples. It is noted of at least fifty-five eminent men and women on our list that they displayed one or more such inaptitudes to acquire properly the muscular co-ordinations needed for various simple actions of life. In numerous cases this clumsiness was combined with voice defect.

Digital clumsiness, Sir J. Bland Sutton remarks (*British Medical Journal*, 7th November, 1925), referring to its unfortunate occurrence sometimes in surgeons, is 'as much a defect as colour-blindness.'

The reality of the connection between clumsiness of muscular co-ordination and mental anomaly is clearly shown by the fact that in idiocy, the most extreme form of mental anomaly, this clumsiness is seen at its maximum. 'In general,' remarks Dr. W. W. Ireland (*The Mental Affections of Children*, 1898, p. 319), 'idiots or imbecile children are awkward in their motions and slow at learning to walk. . . . No doubt the cause of this lateness in learning to walk is in some cases owing to weakness, in others to nervous diseases; but there are still cases where the child always appeared strong and healthy.

. . . Their gait, too, is awkward. Idiots in general have a bad balance. . . . The same awkwardness applies to the hand.' The awkwardness in the case of idiots is doubtless largely due to absence of mental power. In genius the same result is brought about not by absence of mental power, but by the streaming — not only functionally, it is probable, but organically — of the mental energy into other channels. A cause which we may even consider opposite, leads to a like defect in the muscular machinery.

It is noteworthy that the men of genius who spring from the lower social classes tend to be abnormally tall. The lower social classes are always shorter on the average than the upper classes.* But it is remarkable that among the very small number of our British men of genius who have sprung from the lower social strata a considerable proportion are not only tall, but excessively tall. Of the seventeen British men of genius who are known to have been six feet one inch or over in height, at least seven sprang from the peasantry or a lower than middle-class social group; these include Cook, Cobbett, Trevithick and Borrow. It would appear — although I do not propose to discuss this question here — that the organic impulse to intellectual predominance, most clearly seen in those individuals on our list whose social environment has been against their development, tends in some degree to be associated with a corresponding energy in physical growth. There may well be in men of genius a tendency to physical variation in both directions, to deficiency as well as to excess, but it is predominantly in the direction of excess.†

* The evidence on this point has been brought together by H. de Varigny, art. 'Croissance,' Richet's *Dictionnaire de Physiologie*, vol. IV.

† The results here reached concerning British men of genius accord with the results reached on a somewhat wider basis in a subsequent chapter ('Genius and Stature') in which I have discussed some of the problems involved. (See pp. 271–88.)

The average height of Cambridge students is nearly five feet nine inches (cm. 174.8). Nearly all other classes of the community in England are below this height.

Porter among Saint Louis children (*Publications, American Statistical Society*, 1894) found that superior intellectual capacity is associated with superior stature, and inferior intellectual capacity with inferior stature, Christopher (*Journal, American Medical Association*, 15th September, 1900) found the same result among Chicago school children. This result has been severely criticised and cannot be accepted without qualification. Gilbert at Iowa found no such correlation but rather the reverse. It must be remembered that there are various kinds and degrees of ability and various ways of testing it. Nor can it be assumed that results that hold good of average school children — even when we have definitely ascertained what those results are — necessarily hold good also of men of genius, who are an extremely exceptional class.

Papillault (*Bulletin Société d'Anthropologie de Paris*, 1899, p. 446) has found that giantism is sometimes associated with infantilism (more or less glabrous condition of body, defective pigmentation, more or less under-development of sexual organs and impulse, etc.), although infantile persons have no necessary tendency to become giants. He believes that there is some deep underlying but yet undetermined connection between the giantism and the infantilism. This is interesting in view of the frequent association of some degree of infantilism with some degree of giantism in men of extraordinary intellectual ability.

Ewart found that children born in the first quarter of the year are the tallest and heaviest. Combe stated that individuals born in summer tend to be taller than those born in winter. Although the numbers are far too small for any decisive statement, our British men of genius

possibly show such a tendency. Unless we take the extremely low heights, there is not indeed an absolute majority of winter-born (October — March) over summer-born (April — September) among the short. But it certainly appears that while among those whose height is below five feet five inches there are as many as four winter-born to six summer-born, among those who are over six feet one inch there is only one winter-born to six summer-born.

It was found by Arthur MacDonald that in America first-born children of school age tend to be larger than later children. This is not in accordance with the results found at birth, nor can it be said to hold good as regards the very meagre data furnished by the British men of genius on my list. A strict comparison is not possible, but it may at all events be said that the preponderance of eldest children among British men of genius below five feet seven inches in height is somewhat greater — if indeed there can be said to be any real difference — than among those who are over five feet ten inches. This may possibly be explained by the results of Ewart's inquiry among children of the ordinary population in England. He found that at the age of six the eldest child is the tallest and heaviest, but he attributes this to the absence of a sufficient interval between births, and when a due interval occurs he finds that stature and weight tend to reach a maximum with the third child.

X

PIGMENTATION

Hair-colour and eye-colour — Method of classification — Sources of data — The index of pigmentation — Its marked variation in the different intellectual groups — Some probable causes for this variation.

If we turn to a further anthropological character, pigmentation, or the colour of the hair and eyes, I am able to bring forward a larger body of evidence, and it is not difficult to supplement the data furnished by the *Dictionary* with the help of portraits, more especially those in the National Portrait Gallery.* I have information on this point concerning 424 of the eminent persons on our list. In classifying by pigmentation I have relied in the first place on the eye-colour, but have allowed hair-colour a certain influence in modifying the class in those cases in which there was marked divergence between the two in lightness and darkness. I have sorted the eminent persons into three classes, according as their eyes were unpigmented (blue),

* The determination of the pigmentation of portraits has been in nearly all cases by personal inspection. The only exception is in the case of several eminent Scotch personages whose portraits were exhibited at the Edinburgh Loan Exhibition of Scottish National Portraits, in 1884. Dr. Beddoe was kind enough to lend me his own carefully annotated catalogue of this Exhibition, with permission to make use of his notes. I availed myself of this permission when necessary, with, I need scarcely say, entire confidence.

highly pigmented (brown), or occupying an intermediate position (combinations of blue with yellow, orange or brown).* This intermediate class has necessarily been large, and I have comprised within it three subdivisions: a fair medium, a dark medium, and, between these two, a doubtful medium.

I found that the 424 individuals might be thus classed as regards eye-colour: unpigmented, 71; light medium, 99; doubtful medium, 54; dark medium, 85; fully pigmented, 115. The question arose as to how the results thus obtained might be conveniently formulated, so as to enable us to compare the different groups of eminent persons. I finally decided to proceed with each of these groups as follows: The doubtful medium persons in each of these classes were divided equally between the fair medium and the dark medium; then two-thirds of the fair medium persons were added to the fair class, the remaining third to the dark class, and, likewise, two-thirds of the dark medium

* The chief terms used, popularly and in literature, to describe eye-colour are (besides blue, which is frequently applied to eyes by no means purely blue), grey, hazel and black. 'Grey' is applied to light mixed eyes, *i.e.*, those which show blue with some admixture of yellow or orange; 'hazel,' to dark mixed or greenish brown, and sometimes to fully pigmented brown eyes; 'black' eyes do not really exist at all. It seems to me that the terms 'grey,' 'hazel,' and 'black,' should never be used when we are attempting to define eye-colour with any degree of precision — a somewhat difficult matter at the best. I may add that my division of eyes into these main classes is substantially the same as Dr. Beddoe's.

were added to the dark class, the remaining third to the fair class; the five classes were thus reduced to two, and, on multiplying the fair by 100 and dividing by the dark, we obtain what may be called an index of pigmentation. This method of notation is really simple, and is quite sufficiently accurate for the nature of the data dealt with; it will be seen that by its use an index of 100 means that fair and dark people are equally numerous in a group, while indices over 100 mean an excess of fair persons, and indices under 100 an excess of dark persons.

I may remark concerning this index of pigmentation that, while it yields results which are strictly comparable among themselves in the hands of a single observer, proceeding in a uniform manner, it is doubtful whether two observers would carry it out in a strictly identical manner. Beddoe's index of nigrescence, founded on hair-colour and applied directly to living subjects, is a convenient formula for indicating the degree of pigmentation. But in my observations, largely made on portraits (in which the hair was often whitened by age, absent, concealed beneath a wig, or obscured by the darkening of the paint), it was necessary to accept eye-colour as the primary basis of classification.

I have been able to obtain the index of pigmentation in the case of fourteen groups. I present them with their index of pigmentation in the order

of decreasing fairness, noting also the number of individuals in each group. Some individuals, I may remark, are included in more than one group, while various miscellaneous persons are not included at all.

Group, with Number of Individuals		Index of Pigmentation
Social and political reformers	(6)	400
Scholars	(7)	200
Lawyers	(15)	114
Soldiers	(23)	110
Men of science	(45)	109
Sailors	(13)	100
Philosophers	(12)	100
Painters, sculptors and architects	(38)	94
Poets	(58)	90
Men and women of letters	(98)	79
Statesmen	(49)	78
Explorers	(7)	66
Divines	(44)	48
Actors and actresses	(18)	30

Although the numbers are for some groups few, and we must not regard the index as giving results which are quite invariable, we may accept the general results with some confidence. It may be regarded as fairly certain that the first six groups do really tend to be unusually fair, and the last three groups unusually dark. The average index of pigmentation for the British population generally probably lies between eighty and one hundred, but it varies greatly if we take separate districts, being very high in many parts of Scotland and very low in many parts of the West of England. It is fairly obvious that this fact furnishes, to some extent, a

key to the position of the various groups in reference to this index. Sailors, who tend to be fair, come largely from the coast, and the inhabitants of the coast are usually fairer than people from inland districts.* Men of science come largely from regions where the population is fair. Artists tend to be fair, both in England and France, and it is at first a little surprising to find that they do not appear higher upon the list. It may be pointed out, however, that a large proportion of our most eminent painters come from East Anglia, a region in which, though the hair is not very dark, the eye-colour is very frequently brown.† Actors come largely from regions where the population is dark. But this factor, though it accounts for much, will not account for everything, nor will it explain the decisiveness of the results. Divines come from all parts of the United Kingdom, yet they tend to be distinctly dark.‡ The darkness of eminent actors is very marked, whatever their place of origin; only one of the eighteen on my list, Munden, falls in the unpigmented group, and he is certainly not an actor

* It has, I believe, been stated by Beyer that there is a preponderance of blonds among the Naval Cadets of the United States.

† During a walk from Sudbury to Hadleigh, in Central Suffolk, I noted the eye-colour of the children and adults I passed, and found that the proportion of brownish eyes to bluish eyes was about 70 per cent to 30 per cent. On the following day I found myself in Colchester, Essex, on Market day; here the proportions were reversed; there were about 70 per cent bluish eyes to about 30 per cent brownish.

‡ This result has also been reached by Dr. Beddoe.

of the highest rank. The extreme fairness of political agitators and social reformers (religious reformers, who tend to be decidedly dark, not being included) is peculiar. The darkness of travellers and explorers may be explained by a kind of natural selection, fair persons speedily succumbing to the effects of tropical climates; it may be remarked that this group would have been still darker if it had not been for the presence of two or three individuals, of so-called Celtic type, who are fairly pigmented on the whole, though their eyes are not dark. It would, however, be out of place here to discuss fully the very interesting question of the significance of pigment in relation to intellectual ability.*

I may say that I regard the results of my observations in the National Portrait Gallery (though some of the data are common to both series of observations) as distinctly more trustworthy in the light they throw on the relationship of pigmentation to intellectual occupation, not only because the numbers are larger but also because the standard of ability is much lower, so that the influences of predilection in the direction of the intellectual ability is less complicated by the possibly disturbing factor of very high and versatile intellectual ability. Thus in the small group of very eminent sailors we have several exceptional men like Cook and Dampier, who were notably dark; the large number of

* I have briefly discussed it in 'The Comparative Abilities of the Fair and the Dark,' a subsequent chapter, based on an investigation of pigmentation in the National Portrait Gallery, independent of the *Dictionary*.

more typical but less eminent sailors in the National Portrait Gallery give us a higher index, which is doubtless nearer to the truth. (I should add, however, that the index of pigmentation was here obtained in a way that at one point slightly differed from that adopted in the later series, *i.e.*, in the National Portrait Gallery groups I simply divided all the medium persons in each group equally between the unpigmented and the fully pigmented sections.)

XI

OTHER CHARACTERISTICS

Personal beauty or the reverse — The eyes — Shyness and timidity — Tendency to melancholy — Persecution by the world.

A PHYSICAL characteristic to which the national biographers frequently allude, though I do not propose to attempt to give it any numerical values, is personal beauty or the absence of it. A very large proportion of persons are referred to as notably handsome, comely, imposing; a very considerable, but smaller, proportion are spoken of as showing some disproportion or asymmetry of feature, body or limbs, as notably peculiar or even ludicrous in appearance. A not uncommon type is that of the stunted giant, with massive head and robust body, but short legs.

There is one feature, however, which is noted as striking and beautiful in a very large number of cases, even in persons who are otherwise wholly without physical attractions. That is the eyes. It is frequently found that descriptions of the personal appearance of men of genius, however widely they may differ in other respects, agree in noting an unusual brilliancy of the eyes. Thus the eyes of Burns were said by one observer to be like 'coals of living fire,' and Scott writes that they

'literally glowed'; while of Chatterton's eyes it was said that there was 'fire rolling at the bottom of them.' It is significant that both of these instances, chosen almost at random, were poets. While, however, the phenomenon seems to be noted more frequently and with more emphasis in poets, it is found among men of genius of all classes. One may suppose it to be connected with an unusual degree of activity of the cerebral circulation.

In regard to the mental and emotional disposition of British persons of genius, the national biographers enable us to trace the prevalence of one or two tendencies. One of these is shyness, bashfulness, or timidity. This is noted in sixty-eight cases, while fifty are described as very sensitive, nervous, or emotional, and, although this is not equivalent to a large percentage, it must of course be remembered that the real number of such cases is certainly very much larger, and also that the characteristic is in many cases extremely well marked. Some had to abandon the profession they had chosen on account of their nervous shyness at appearing in public; others were too bashful to declare their love to the women they were attracted to; Sir Thomas Browne, one of the greatest masters of English prose, was so modest that he was always blushing causelessly; Hooker, one of the chief luminaries of the English Church, could never look any one in the face; Dryden, the recognised prince of the literary men of his time, was, said Congreve,

the most easily put out of countenance of any man he had ever met. It is not difficult to see why the timid temperament — which is very far from involving lack of courage * — should be especially associated with intellectual aptitudes. It causes a distaste for social contact and so favours those forms of activity which may be exerted in solitude, these latter, again, reacting to produce increased awkwardness in social relations. Moreover, the mental state of timidity, which may be regarded as a mild form of *folie du doute*, a perpetual self-questioning and uncertainty, however unpleasant it may be from the social point of view, is by no means an unsatisfactory attitude in the face of intellectual problems, for it involves that unceasing self-criticism which is an essential element of all good intellectual work, and has marked more or less clearly the greatest men of scientific genius. Fundamentally, no doubt, timidity is a minor congenital defect of the nervous mechanism, fairly comparable to stammering. It may be noted that the opposite characteristic of over-self-confidence, with more or less tendency to arrogance and insolence, is also noted, but with much less frequency, and usually in men whose eminence is not due to purely intellectual qualities. In some cases, it would seem, the two opposite tendencies are com-

* 'None are so bold as the timid when they are fairly roused,' wrote Mrs. Browning in her *Letters*. The same point has been brought out by Dugas in his essay on timidity.

bined, the timid man seeking refuge from his own timidity in the assumption of arrogance.

In a certain number of cases information is given as to the general emotional disposition, whether to melancholy and depression, or of a gay, cheerful and genial character. In eighty-five cases the disposition is noted as melancholy, in twenty as cheerful or jovial; in seven cases both dispositions are noted as occurring, in varying association, in the same person.*

This marked tendency to melancholy among persons of intellectual aptitude is no new observation, but was indeed one of the very earliest points noted concerning men of genius. According to a saying attributed to Aristotle, all men of ability are melancholy, and Reveillé-Parise, one of the first and still one of the most sagacious of the modern writers on genius, devoted a chapter to the point. It is not altogether difficult to account for this phenomenon. Melancholy children, as Marro found, are in large proportion the offspring of elderly fathers, as we have also found our persons of intellectual eminence to be. A tendency to melancholy, again, even though it may always fall short of insane melancholia, is allied to those neurotic and abnormal conditions which we have found to be not infrequent. Moreover, it certainly has a stimulating influence on intellectual work. The more normal man of cheerful disposition instinctively seeks the consolations of society. The melancholy man, like the shy man, is ill-adapted to society, and more naturally seeks his consolations in a non-social field, such as that of the intellect,

* We are here brought to the rather hazardous problem of temperament which has in recents years been suggestively studied by Kretschmer, *Physique and Character* (English translation), 1925.

often plunging more deeply into intellectual work the more profound his melancholy becomes. Wagner said that his best work was done at times of melancholy, and among the eminent men on our list several writers are mentioned who turned to authorship as a relief to personal depression. It may also be said that not only is melancholy a favourable condition for intellectual work, but that the sedentary and nerve-exhausting nature of nearly all forms of intellectual work in turn reacts to emphasize or produce moods of depression.

Another cause that serves largely to accentuate the tendency of men of genius to melancholy is the attitude of the world towards them. Every original worker in intellectual fields, every man who makes some new thing, is certain to arouse hostility where he does not meet with indifference. He sets out in his chosen path, ignorant of men, but moved by high ideals, content to work in laborious solitude and to wait, and when at last he turns to his fellows, saying, 'See what I have done for you!' he often finds that he has to meet only the sneering prejudices of the few who might have comprehended, and the absolute indifference of the many who are too absorbed in the daily struggle for bread to comprehend any intellectual achievement. The wise worker knows this and arms himself with benevolent contempt, alike against the few and the many. Thus of one of the great men of science on our list, Stephen Hales, it was said that he could look 'even upon those who did him unkind offices without any emotion of particular indignation, not from want of discernment or sensibility; but he used to consider them only like those experiments which, upon trial, he found could never be applied to any useful purpose, and which he therefore calmly and dispassionately laid aside.' But it has to be remembered that the prevailing temperament of men of genius is one of great nervous sensitiveness

and irritability — so that, as Reveillé-Parise puts it, they are apt to 'roar at a pin-prick,' — and even when they are well aware what the opinion of the world is worth, they still cannot help being profoundly affected by that opinion. Hence a fruitful source of melancholy.

The attitude of the world toward the man of original intellect, being not merely one of disdain or indifference, but constantly tending to become aggressive, has certainly reinforced the tendency to melancholy. It is practically impossible to estimate the amount of persecution to which this group of pre-eminent British persons has been subjected, for it has shown itself in innumerable forms, and varies between a mere passive refusal to have anything whatever to do with them or their work and the active infliction of physical torture and death. There is, however, at least one form of persecution, very definite in character, which it is easy to estimate, since the national biographers have probably in few cases passed it over. I refer to imprisonment. I find that at least 160, or over 16 per cent, of our 975 eminent men were imprisoned, once or oftener, for periods of varying length, while many others only escaped imprisonment by voluntary exile. It is true that the causes of imprisonment were various, but even imprisonment for such a cause as debt may usually be taken to indicate an anomalous lack of adjustment to the social environment. The man of genius is an abnormal being, thus

arousing the instinctive hostility of society, which by every means seeks to put him out of the way.

It will be seen that the various personal traits noted in this section, while completing our picture of British persons of genius, may be linked on at numerous points to other traits we have previously noted. It only remains to gather together the threads we have traced and to ascertain how far they may be harmoniously woven into a complete whole.

XII

CONCLUSIONS

The characteristics of men of genius probably to a large extent independent of the particular field their ability is shown in — What is the temperament of genius? — In what sense genius is healthy — The probable basis of inaptitude for ordinary life — In what sense genius is a neurosis.

It may be reasonable to ask, in estimating the significance of those characteristics of British persons of genius we have here ascertained, to what degree an investigation of persons of eminent intellectual aptitude belonging to other countries would bring out different results. It is not possible to answer this question quite decisively. The fact, however, that at many points our investigation simply gives precision to characteristics which have been noted as marking genius in various countries seems to indicate that in all probability the characters that constitute genius are fundamentally alike in all countries, though it may well be that minor modifications are associated with national differences. The point is one that can only be decisively settled when similar investigations are carried out concerning similar groups of persons of superior intellectual ability belonging to various countries.

A further question may be asked: How far has confusion been introduced by lumping together

persons whose intellectual aptitudes have been shown in very different fields? May not the average biological characteristics of the man of science be the reverse of those of the actor, and those of the divine at the other extreme from those of the lawyer? I believe that Galton was inclined to think that the investigation of groups of men with different intellectual aptitudes would yield different results. As, however, we have seen, the investigation of eminent British persons, when carried out without reference to the particular fields in which their activities have been exercised, yields results which, when comparable with those of Galton, do not usually show any striking discrepancies. Nor, so far as I have at present looked into the matter, does it appear that on the whole, when we consider separately the various groups of British eminent persons we are here concerned with, such groups show any widely varying biological characters. Certain variations there certainly are; we have seen that the geographical distribution of the various kinds of intellectual activity to some extent varies, and also that in pigmentation there are in some cases marked variations. On the whole, however, it would appear that, whatever the field in which it displays itself, the elements that constitute the temperament of genius show a tendency to resemble each other.

I shall probably be asked to define precisely what the 'temperament' is that underlies genius.

That, however, is a question which the material before us only enables us to approach very cautiously. There are two distinct tendencies among writers on genius. On the one hand are those who seem to assume that genius is a strictly normal variation. This is the standpoint of Galton.* On the other hand are those, chiefly alienists, who assume that genius is fundamentally a pathological condition and closely allied to insanity. This is the position of Lombroso, who compares genius to a pearl — so regarding it as a pathological condition, the result of morbid irritation, which by chance has produced a beautiful result — and who seeks to find the germs of genius among the literary and artistic productions of the inmates of lunatic asylums.

It can scarcely be said that the course of our investigation, uncertain as it may sometimes appear, has led to either of these conclusions. On the one hand, we have found along various lines the marked prevalence of conditions which can hardly be said to be consonant with a normal degree of health or the normal conditions of vitality; on the other hand, it cannot be said that we have seen any ground to infer that there is any general connection between genius and insanity, or that genius tends to proceed from families in which insanity is prevalent; for while it is certainly true

* In the preface to the second edition of *Hereditary Genius* Galton somewhat modified this view.

that insanity occurs with unusual frequency among men of genius, it is very rare to find that periods of intellectual ability are combined with periods of insanity, and it is, moreover, notable that (putting aside senile forms of insanity) the intellectual achievements of those eminent men in whom unquestionable insanity has occurred have rarely been of a very high order. We cannot, therefore, regard genius either as a purely healthy variation occurring within normal limits, nor yet as a radically pathological condition, not even as an alternation — a sort of allotropic form — of insanity. We may rather regard it as a highly sensitive and complexly developed adjustment of the nervous system along special lines, with concomitant tendency to defect along other lines. Its elaborate organisation along special lines is often built up on a basis even less highly organised than that of the ordinary average man. It is no paradox to say that the real affinity of genius is with congenital imbecility rather than with insanity. If indeed we consider the matter well we see that it must be so. The organisation that is well adapted for adjustment to the ordinary activities of the life it is born into is not prompted to find new adjustments to suit itself. The organic inhibition of ordinary activities is, necessarily, a highly favourable condition for the development of extraordinary abilities, when these are present in a latent condition. Hence it is that so many men of the highest intellectual aptitudes

have so often shown the tendency to muscular inco-ordination and clumsiness which marks idiots, and that even within the intellectual sphere, when straying outside their own province, they have frequently shown a lack of perception which placed them on scarcely so high a level as the man of average intelligence. It is not surprising that by means of the *idiots savants*, the wonderful calculators, the mattoids and 'men of one idea,' and the men whose intellectual originality is strictly confined to one field, we may bridge the gulf that divides idiocy from genius.

Since a basis of organic inaptitude — a condition which in a more marked and unmitigated form we call imbecility — may thus often be traced at the foundation of genius, we must regard it as a more fundamental fact in the constitution of genius than the undue prevalence of insanity, which is merely a state of mental dissolution, in nearly every case temporarily or permanently abolishing the aptitude for intellectual achievement. It must not, however, be hastily concluded that the prevalence of insanity among men of genius is an accidental fact, meaningless or unaccountable. In reality it is a very significant fact. The intense cerebral energy of intellectual reaction involves an expenditure of tissue which is not the dissolution of insanity, for waste and repair must here be balanced, but it reveals an instability which may sink into the mere dissolution of in-

sanity, if the balance of waste and repair is lost and the high pressure tension falls out of gear. Insanity is rather a Nemesis of the peculiar intellectual energy of genius exerted at a prolonged high tension than an essential element in the foundation of genius. But a germinal nervous instability, such as to the ordinary mind simulates some form of insanity, is certainly present from the first in many cases of genius and is certainly of immense value in creating the visions or stimulating the productiveness of men of genius. We have seen how significant a gouty inheritance seems to be. A typical example of this was presented by William Morris, a man of very original genius, of great physical vigour and strength, of immense capacity for work, who was at the same time abnormally restless, very irritable, and liable to random explosions of nervous energy. Morris inherited from his mother's side a peculiarly strong and solid constitution; on his father's side he inherited a neurotic and gouty strain. It is evident that, given the robust constitution, the germinal instability furnished by such a morbid element as this — falling far short of insanity — acts as a precious fermentative element, an essential constituent in the man's genius. The mistake usually made is to exaggerate the insane character of such a fermentative element, and at the same time to ignore the element of sane and robust vigour which is equally essential to any high degree of genius. We may perhaps accept the

ancient dictum of Aristotle as reported by Seneca: 'No great genius without some mixture of insanity.' But we have to remember that the 'insanity' is not more than a mixture, and it must be a finely tempered mixture.

This conclusion, suggested by our survey of British persons of pre-eminent intellectual aptitude, is thus by no means either novel or modern. It is that of most cautious and sagacious inquirers. The same position was, rather vaguely, adopted by Moreau (de Tours) in his *Psychologie morbide dans ses rapports*, etc., published in 1859, though, as his book was prolix and badly written, his proposition has often been misunderstood. He regarded genius as a 'neurosis,' but he looked upon such 'névrose' as simply 'the synonym of exaltation (I do not say trouble or perturbation) of the intellectual faculties. . . . The word "neurosis" would indicate a particular disposition of the faculties, a disposition still in part physiological, but overflowing those physiological limits'; and he presents a genealogical tree with genius, insanity, crime, etc., among its branches; the common root being 'the hereditary idiosyncratic nervous state.' Professor Grasset, again, more recently (*La supériorité intellectuelle et la névrose*, 1900), while not regarding genius as a neurosis, considers that it is united to the neuroses by a common trunk, this trunk being a temperament and not a disease. The slight admixture of morbidity penetrating an otherwise healthy con-

stitution, such as the present investigation suggests as of frequent occurrence in genius, results in an organisation marked by what Moreau calls a 'neurosis' and Grasset a 'temperament.'

It has been necessary to state, as clearly as may be possible, the conclusions suggested by the present study as regards the pathological relationships of genius, because, although those conclusions are not essentially novel, the question is one that is apt to call out extravagant answers in one direction or another. The most fruitful part of our investigation seems, however, to lie not in the aid it may give towards the exact definition of genius — for which our knowledge is not sufficient — but in the promising fields it seems to open out for the analysis of genius along definite and precise lines. The time has gone by for the vague and general discussion of genius. We are likely to learn much more about its causation and nature by following out a number of detailed lines of inquiry on a carefully objective basis. Such an inquiry, as we have seen, is difficult on account of the defective nature of the material and the lack of adequate normal standards of comparison. Yet even with these limitations it has not been wholly unprofitable. It has enabled us to trace a number of conditions which, even if they cannot always be described as factors of the genius constitution, clearly appear among the influences highly favourable to its development. Such a condition seems to be the

great reproductive activity of the parents, the child destined to attain intellectual eminence in many cases alone surviving. The fact of being either the youngest or the eldest child is a condition favourable for subsequent intellectual eminence; and I may add that I could refer to numerous recent instances of large families, in which the eldest and the youngest, but no other members, have attained intellectual distinction. We have further seen that there is a tendency for children who develop genius to be of feeble health, or otherwise disabled, during the period of physical development. It is easy to see the significance of this influence, which by its unfavourable effects on the development of the limbs — an effect not exerted on the head, which may thus remain relatively large — leaves an unusual surplus of energy to be used in other directions; at the same time the child, who is thus deprived of the ordinary occupations of childhood, is thrown back on to more solitary and more intellectual pursuits. The clumsiness and other muscular inco-ordinations which we have found to be prevalent — while there is good reason to believe that they are of congenital origin — co-operate to the same end. Again, it is easy to see how the shock of contact with a strange and novel environment, which we have proved to be so frequent, acts as a most powerful stimulant to the nascent intellectual aptitudes. It is possible to take a number of other common peculiarities in the

course of the development of genius and to show how they either serve to inhibit the growth of genius along unfruitful lines or to further it along fruitful lines.

Such an investigation as the present is far from enabling us to state definitely all the determining factors of genius, or even all the conditions required for its development. It suggests that they are really very numerous and that genius is the happy result of a combination of many concomitant circumstances, though some of the prenatal group of circumstances must remain largely outside our ken. We are entitled to believe that the factors of genius include the nature of the various stocks meeting together in the individual and the manner of their combination, the avocations of the parents, the circumstances attending conception, pregnancy and birth, the early environment and all the manifold influences to which the child is subjected from infancy to youth. The precise weight and value of these manifold circumstances in the production of genius it must be left to later investigation to determine.

XIII

THE CELTIC SPIRIT IN LITERATURE

Definition of the Celtic spirit — Its feeling for the remote — Its decorative sense — Irish and Welsh literature — The Nordic spirit — The *Chanson de Roland* — The blending of Celtic and Nordic spirits in English literature.

Of recent years we have heard much about the Celts, about Celtic aspirations, about the Celtic movement. Yet the people who talk with confident familiarity about these things would be puzzled if they were asked to define a Celt. Even among those who talk most confidently concerning him, there is no agreement at all as to who the 'Celt' is, where he comes from, or even where he is to be found.

I do not propose to discuss these questions here because they are extremely complicated, and involve the consideration of a mass of technical details which even at the end still leave us in some doubt as to the exact solution we are justified in accepting.* There is, however, a related question which we may approach with some reasonable prospect of solving it: I mean the precise nature of

* It is undesirable, and usually misleading, to employ the word 'Celt' in any precise racial sense. It is most correctly used, as I have throughout used it, in a purely conventional sense, to indicate the general population (really of very mixed race) in certain specific regions which were once of Celtic language and culture.

that generally admitted quality which is commonly called by such vague and unsatisfactory names as 'Celtic glamour.' If we seek to escape from the mists with which this question is usually enveloped, what, precisely and specifically, is this 'Celtic glamour'?

At the outset it may be necessary to say that, for the purposes of the question before us, there are two bodies of literature to investigate. There are, indeed, five regions in which more or less allied 'Celtic' traditions may be traced: Ireland, the Highlands of Scotland, Wales, Brittany, and Cornwall. We eliminate three of these, for the Highland traditions coalesce largely with the Irish, the Breton are oral, and the Cornish can scarcely be said any longer to exist at all. There remains Ireland, with a large body of literature which is for a large part primitive in character, and Wales, with a smaller body of literature which is later and sometimes wrought with high artistic skill.*

It may be well, before proceeding, to quote two passages which exhibit in a characteristic manner the special qualities of Celtic literature. I choose two passages in honour of women, always a favourite and felicitous theme to Celtic poets. In the

* The general reader who wishes to gain an idea of ancient Irish literature may do so in Miss Eleanor Hull's collection of the chief Irish stories or in Lady Gregory's *Cuchulain of Muirthemne* (in which, however, there is a considerable amount of manipulation). For the Welsh literature there is Lady Charlotte Guest's admirable translation of the *Mabinogion* (preferably in Mr. Alfred Nutt's edition).

typical and unexcelled description of Olwen, in the *Mabinogion*, we are told: 'She was clothed in a robe of flame-coloured silk, and around her neck was a collar of red gold set with precious stones and rubies. Fairer was her hair than the flower of the broom, whiter her skin than the foam of the waves; brighter her hands and fingers than the blossom of the anemone of the waters emerging with its trefoil flower from the little basin formed by its jetting fountain. Neither the eye of the moulted falcon nor that of the tiercel hawk was clearer than hers. Her bosom was whiter than the swan's, her cheek redder than the reddest roses. It was impossible to see her without loving her. Four white trefoils arose beneath her feet wherever she trod. That was why she was called Olwen, White Footprint.'

The Ossianic bard thus describes Credhe and her household: 'A journey I have in hand to Credhe's mansion against the mountain's breast; it is appointed for me to go thither, to Credhe, at the Paps of Annan. Pleasant is the house where she is, with men and boys and women, magicians and minstrels, cup-bearer and doorkeeper and horsekeeper. The command over all belongs to fair Credhe, the yellow-haired. With coverlet and with down pleasant will my lot be in her *dun*. A bowl she has whence juice of berries flows, and therein she makes her eyebrows black, crystal vats of fermenting grain, cups and goblets. The colour of her *dun* is of lime; coverlets and rushes abound there for the

beds; silk is among them, and many a blue mantle, red gold and the polished drinking horn. Her bower is of silver and yellow gold, its ridgy thatch laid without defect, of the crimson wings of ruddy birds. The door posts are green and the lintel of silver taken as spoil from the slain. Credhe's chair on thy left, overlaid with gold, stands at the foot of her delicate bed, a glittering bed, made in the East, of yellow gold and precious stones. Yet another bed, on thy right, of gold and silver, unerringly wrought, with tent-like curtains, like the foxglove's flower, running upon slender copper rods. Pleasant is the lot of her household; their mantles are neither faded nor worn; their full locks are curly and fair. Wounded men with the blood jetting out from them would fall asleep to the fairy birds' warbling in the eaves of her bower. A hundred men there are in Credhe's house from one angle to the other, and thirty fully measured feet is the width of her noble door. Credhe that owns all these things at low water or flood, hath by a spear cast's length excelled all Ireland's women.' * No one

* It will be seen that I have not gone to the Ulster Cuchulain cycle of legends for typical examples of the Celtic temper in literature. The Welsh *Mabinogion*, Renan long since said, is the true expression of Celtic genius, that is, it should be added, in its most self-consciously artistic forms. The Cuchulain stories, while from some points of view the most interesting of all, are more penetrated by mythic conceptions, and are wilder and harsher; they are genuinely Celtic in tone, but have not attained the finest colour and aroma of that temper. Moreover, it must perhaps be added, Ulster has always stood half outside the Celtic world, and that energetic and ferocious spirit that differentiates Ulster and

could doubt that these two passages possess those peculiar qualities which we term 'Celtic.' The Welsh fragment renders these in a more deliberately artistic fashion, the Scoto-Munster Ossianic fragment in a more wayward, a more decadent manner, but they both appeal to us as having those qualities which we are pleased to term 'Celtic glamour.'

If we attempt to analyse the special characteristics of such passages, certain very constant elements are slowly revealed. In the first place, we have what I believe to be the very fundamental and significant fact that in Celtic literature always there is presented to us *the remote as remote*. This sense of remoteness is deliberately sought in the finest Celtic romances. 'The Dream of Maxen Wledig' leads us over mountains as high as the sky, and down rivers, and across seas, before we reach the far island which holds the enchanted castle of the tale, and its vanished splendour is brought before us with an unparalleled combination of remoteness and precision. 'The Dream of Maxen Wledig' is indeed an unsurpassable example of the remote as remote, of the sense of mystery, of the atmosphere of 'glamour,' not attained by the use of any cheap devices of mistiness or vagueness, but clearly and firmly by the hand of a great artist. It

her legends may well have been infused into the Cuchulain cycle by the stream of Scandinavian invasion pouring into northern Ireland, an invasion which, by way of Scotland and England, has continued during historical times.

is instructive, too, because it enables us to see how the effect was produced. The Celtic mind demands a great and invisible past of impossible magnificence; all Celtic literature is the search for the satisfaction of that demand. The memory of the splendour of Rome which had once been theirs long haunted the Celtic and especially the Cymric mind; the Emperor Maxen Wledig, as Loth points out, is founded on traits of Maxentius, the adversary of Constantine the Great, and when we realise this the whole character of the dream at once becomes intelligible. Sometimes, again, the land of Celtic legend lies on the farther side of a terrifying mist. Geraint once reached such a mist from out of which no man had ever returned. 'Fearlessly and unhesitatingly Geraint dashed forward into the mist. And on leaving the mist he came to a large orchard; and in the orchard he saw an open space, wherein was a tent of red satin; and the door of the tent was open, and an apple-tree stood in front of the door of the tent; and on a branch of the apple-tree hung a large hunting-horn; and no one was in the tent save one maiden sitting on a golden chair.' Such visions only come in Celtic romance to him who fearlessly and unhesitatingly dashes forward into the mist, it may even be but the mist of intoxication, if, as Renan remarked, the Celt's tendency to drunkenness is to be regarded, not as weakness for gross enjoyment which is altogether absent in him, but to the need for illusion, the search for

the vision of the invisible world.* In nearly all poetry, it must be remembered, the element of remoteness is introduced. This element is essential not only for the attainment of any atmospheric effect, but also for all elaborate architectonic construction. In the *Arabian Nights* — the only great work which shows that special romantic quality which we find in the Celtic legends — not only is the ancient and highly idealised age of Haroun-al-Raschid used as a remote mist in which every story may be plunged to become iridescently beautiful, but the element of distance, of long journeys, of great mountains to be overpassed, and great deserts and seas to be traversed, is constantly used with elaborate skill; and when we are taken on board a bark of red sandalwood, with mast of fine amber and ropes of silk, we feel that we are bound for a land of romance exactly identical with the land that Maxen Wledig reached at the end of his long journey, or that Rhonabwy saw in his dream when he fell asleep on the yellow calf-skin. But while the romantic poet, as we universally know him, makes much use of the element of remoteness, it is usually his endeavour to attain — what to the Celtic mind is utterly abhorrent — *the remote as*

* Fiona Macleod, admitting that the Celt makes a remarkably good emigrant, well says: 'Our people have truly loved their land. . . . But it is also true that in that love we love vaguely another land, a rainbow-land, and that our most desired country is not the real Ireland, the real Scotland, the real Brittany, but the vague Land of Youth, the shadowy Land of Heart's Desire.'

present. The remote as remote is alien to him, and antipathetic to the passionate sense of life which stirs him; he is not satisfied unless he has vivified it into the present, however various the devices he may adopt. The Homeric poems are so realistic that they never suggested, what we now know to be the fact, that a vast age of heroic civilization lay behind Homer. Dante placed his comedy in the supernatural world, but he is absolutely in the present and only concerned to sit in judgment on the people he had himself known, quite unlike those Celtic travellers to the underworld in whose visions the prototype of the Divine Comedy has been found. Milton sang the origin of the world, but with an incongruity that often startles us to-day he instinctively occupied himself with the ideals, the discoveries, even the mechanical appliances, of his own time.

This feeling for the remote as remote is a fundamental trait of the Celtic poet's conception of his subject. There is another allied and not less fundamental trait in his technical method of dealing with it. His method is always *decorative.* That is to say, he is always concerned to find the beautiful and harmonious detail. The pages of Celtic romance are like a woven tapestry, with bold outline and strong colour as in the Irish stories, or in the Welsh with softly harmonised colours and delicately flowing lines; in either case they produce more nearly than anything in literature the exact effect of an old tapestry.

It has to be said, one must note, that these qualities of Celtic literature rest on certain psychic qualities of the makers of Celtic literature, of which we may here especially set down inventiveness and quick sensibility, two qualities that are allied, or indeed identical. Swift mental response is shown in the delightful wit of the Celt, in his aptness to embroider statements of fact or (as some will have it) to lie, in his faculty for combining incongruous ideas.* Quick sensibility, again, or rapid feminine response in harmony with, or in reaction against, external stimuli, is of all qualities that which we most readily attribute to the Celt. It is a quality of nervous texture, even to some extent a mental quality, and by no means a pure quality of feeling. It thus becomes very misleading to speak, as Matthew Arnold repeatedly spoke in his Celtic lectures, of the *emotional* qualities of Celtic peoples and Celtic literature. If we wish to speak precisely, and to avoid any misleading confusions, it is best to reserve the term 'emotion' for the deep and inarticulate manifestations of feeling, and to use the term 'sensibility' for the more nervous and intelligent quality of quick sensation and response.†

* I may illustrate what is here meant by the example of an acquaintance of mine, a genial Irish priest, who, after gazing at an exceedingly mediocre seascape in a boarding-house dining-room — he prided himself that he was a connoisseur in painting — turned to me with charmingly blended surprise and modest confidence, and declared that he believed it was a Rossetti. The Irish 'bull' is an example of the same wilful or involuntary tendency.

† Mrs. Sophia Bryant, in an interesting study of 'The Celtic

This quick sensibility is, for instance, well illustrated by the Celtic eye for nature imagery, so often used for decorative purposes in the Welsh and especially in the Ossianic literature.

When we have clearly defined to ourselves these precise qualities of the Celtic mind as it displays itself in literature * — that in vision it regards the remote as remote and in method is decorative — we begin to realise the truth that underlies many of the rhapsodical utterances of the writers on 'Celtic glamour.' For instance, we hear much of fairyland of twilight, in this connection. Mr. Yeats has called one of his books 'The Celtic Twilight.' The atmosphere into which all genuinely Celtic things — the Ulster cycle of legends least of all — brings us is quite accurately and precisely described as one of twilight. Twilight has the curious property of making the scenes it envelops appear at once both near and remote. The glowing high lights and dark shadows of full sunlight have disappeared, as also have the commonplace reflections from the clouds of dull daylight; we are left

Mind' (*Contemporary Review*, October, 1897), has sought to express this in the statement that the main characteristic of the Celtic mind is a *high potential*, or tendency for the potential to pass swiftly into the actual.

* I here confine myself to literature, or it would be easy to show that exactly the same qualities are shown in painting by men belonging to Celtic peoples. Thus the pictures of Burne-Jones, although he was not born in a Celtic land, or bred among Celtic traditions, show conspicuously the two qualities here emphasised: the sense for the remote as remote, and the fundamentally decorative method.

with a vision that is at once both delicate and precise. For a moment a kind of musical silence seems to fill the air; we are conscious of the presence of mystery; we feel as if we had caught a glimpse of a landscape in another world. This impression — fantastic as it may seem, and yet explicable by the conditions of the atmosphere during this brief period of diffused light — very exactly corresponds to the special impression which Celtic romance makes upon us.

II

So far I have tried to define the characteristics of the Celtic spirit in literature without detailed comparison with any other kind of literary temper. Our usual attempts to define the Celtic spirit tend to evaporate in mist because we make no serious effort to put the products of the Celtic imagination beside the products of any other kind of imagination.

It is idle to assert, it may be said in passing, that the characteristics of Celtic literature are simply the characteristics of primitive literature. This is altogether incorrect. In so far as Celtic literature is itself primitive it necessarily shows many features — and more especially the presence of supernatural elements — which have a certain resemblance to primitive literature generally. But it will be found that the literature of savage peoples, however charming or im-

pressive it may be to us at moments, is nearly always essentially a bald statement of what the narrator regards as facts which have their main interest in being facts; its wildest romances are brief, naked, and business-like. Celtic literature, when it is really characteristic, is no longer merely primitive, it has become self-conscious, deliberate, artistic. It can therefore be profitably compared only with literature which has reached a like stage of development.

In Great Britain, and in the northwestern district of Europe, there is one, and only one, literary spirit which can be compared with the Celtic in magnitude, intrinsic force, and permanent influence.* I propose to call it the Nordic spirit, for it is as closely associated with the fair long-headed peoples of Northern Europe (by Deniker termed Nordic) as the Celtic spirit is with the peoples of Central and Southern Europe now or formerly speaking languages of the Celtic family. The Nordic spirit in literature is manifested at first in the Scandinavian lands, then in Northwestern France and Germany, as well as Eastern England and Scotland. The chief of its more primitive embodiments are the Icelandic Eddas, its highest artistic achievement, unmixed

* It would be interesting to compare Celtic literature with the Finnish *Kalevala*. But the curious similarities and dissimilarities which such a comparison would show may be due to both arising, in part, from the same sources.

with other influences, is probably the *Chanson de Roland.*

One's first feeling in turning from Celtic literature to Nordic literature is one of dulness and monotony. It deals with the same main themes, battle and love, but the two elements which are almost omnipresent in the products of the Celtic mind — supernatural invention and vivid detail — and add so much charm to the Celtic narration have almost entirely fallen out of the Nordic stories. When, however, we have become really acclimatised to the Nordic atmosphere we perceive that the undoubted absence of these elements involves a distinction, but not necessarily a loss; we are simply in another world. There is atmosphere here also, as there always is in fine literary art, not indeed the atmosphere of twilight, but of starlit nights and of storm-swept days. Celtic literature takes us into a world where bright sensations, a restless invention, dominate from first to last; profound human passion, with all its painful and stupid limitations, is not there, is not even conceivable there, for we are in a world where all things are possible. The Celtic story of Tristan and Yseult, it may be noted, only assumed tragic vitality and significance when it had been moulded by realistic Nordic hands. Nordic literature is dominated from first to last by emotion, and where emotion is there is limitation, tension, pressure; if the fountain leaps high in the

air it is because of the oppression at its subterranean heart.

To illustrate the spirit of this literature we may turn to the speech of the dying Brynhild in the Volsunga Saga, the greatest primitive achievement of the Nordic mind: '"And now I beg of thee, Gunnar, one last boon. Let make a great pyre on the plain for all of us, for me and for Sigurd, and for those who were slain with him, and let it be covered over with cloth dyed red by the folk of Gaul, and burn me thereon on one side of the King of the Huns, and on the other those men of mine, two at the head and two at the feet, and two hawks withal; so all is shared equally. And lay there betwixt us a drawn sword, as in the other days when we twain stepped into one bed together; and then may we have the name of man and wife, nor shall the door swing to at the heel of him as I go behind him. Nor shall that be a niggard company if there follow him those five bondwomen and eight bondmen, whom my father gave me, and those burn there also who were slain with Sigurd. More yet would I say, but my life-breath flits; the wounds open." . . . And then died Brynhild and was buried there by the side of Sigurd, and thus their life-days ended.'

The highly charged emotional intensity of Nordic narrative — simple, realistic, heart-felt, without reliance on fantastic prodigies — inevitably involves not merely inaptitude, but dis-

dain for deliberately minute picturesque details. It equally involves the denial of supernatural aid. This is so because emotion is a specifically human quality and can only be adequately manifested under the conditions of human personality. The Hebrew Jehovah, with his jealousy, indignation, and pity, the dwellers in Greek Olympus, with their restless lusts and rivalries, were alike anthropomorphic; a god, as Lucretius and the Epicureans rightly felt, must be serene. All Nordic literature impresses us as the expression of a people who are in the highest degree emotional, practical, serious, in a word intensely human. They do not feel, as the Celtic man so easily feels, that after all the boundary between the real and the unreal is very vague, that the nimble invention can easily create a world for itself, that there is no misfortune so great that it may not be straightened out by a twist of the hand of the juggler who has learnt to control it, and no feat so stupendous but that somewhere the charm to perform it may not be found. All Nordic literature is the record of some human passion to be humanly suffered, some human right to be humanly achieved, some human wrong to be humanly wreaked. But Nordic literature reaps the fruits of its abstention from the picturesque and the supernatural in the heroic magnificence which it is thus able to impart to its human figures, a magnificence which the Celtic hero who

finds extra-human aid on every hand can never attain. There the Nordic poet at once reaches the springs of great art. It would be idle to search all Celtic literature for anything so poignant as the speech of the dying Brynhild.

The Nordic poet is, however, an artist in his methods as well as in his conceptions. Those realistic and emotional qualities which in the sagas grow somewhat monotonous, in the more developed manifestations of Nordic art become self-conscious and deliberate. The realism remains, but the emotion is more artfully wrought to a climax, and the monotony, instead of being a helpless accident, becomes a method of heightening the total effect, so that on the basis of the primitive realism, human emotion and monotony, it becomes possible to erect a great architectonic poem far beyond the reach of pure Celtic art.* The supreme Nordic poem of mediæval times — for the Volsunga Saga belongs to a more primitive stage of culture — is without doubt the *Chanson de Roland*. That is indeed the final manifestation of the pure Nordic spirit on a great scale. After the eleventh century literary traditions began to be widely diffused in Europe, and it was no longer

* Mrs. Sophia Bryant, admitting the artistic imperfection of the Irish, traces it, ingeniously and perhaps truly, in part at least, to their positive activity in creativeness, annulling self-criticism, and allowing imperfect work to stand, 'the vividness of the ideal making up for the inadequacy of its realisation.' The deliberation and hesitancy of the Nordic mind, on the other hand, involve perpetual self-criticism and progress.

possible for any great work of genius to grow up in isolation. The *Chanson de Roland* existed in a germinal form before the coming of the Northmen to Western Neustria — to Roland's home in the march of Brittany, where, however, as Gaston Paris suggested, the Nordic spirit probably already existed — but the work of genius in which it has come down to us was, in the opinion of good authorities, probably written by a Norman and it may be in the neighbourhood of Mont Saint Michel. The story of Charlemagne's disastrous expedition into Spain against the infidels and the defeat and death of his faithful paladins in the pass of Roncesvalles is not only the finest manifestation of the special qualities of the Nordic spirit, it is one of the great summits of literature. Rough, firm, precise, realistic, monotonous, with no charming decorative detail, with scarcely a single simile in the whole length of it, the *Chanson de Roland* might have merely been what in one aspect it really is, a record of feats of arms. But it is far more than this. The element of combat sinks into the background, and the epic poem becomes a tragic drama appealing to the universal emotion of mankind. This poet is a supreme artist, and even the baldness and monotony of his narrative, the plain hard roughness of his verse, become elements in the great effects he attains. Charlemagne in his retreat from Saragossa to his palace at Aix-la-Chapelle, unwitting

of danger or treachery yet oppressed by a vague dread, places Roland and the chief of his peers at the head of the little rear-guard, innocent of the fate that is slowly winding its coils around them. In every subtle way the poet makes us realise the tragedy that is approaching as the four hundred thousand infidels slowly close round the undaunted little band of heroes cheerfully affronting their doom, and the fascination of the narrative is not in its record of feats of arms, but its massive and poignant appeal to the most fundamental human emotions, to the pity and terror of the fate of brave men who succumb beneath the stroke of fate, to the depth and the beauty of the bands of affection which bind those who have long faced together the good and the bad chances of life. To the Celtic mind bloodshed and slaughter are as empty of emotional human content as for the child who knows not what they mean; he remains light-hearted throughout, and when the hosts of Queen Meave are flung against the might of Cuchulain and thousands fall in a moment it is all sheer gaiety and not one pulse of the blood is stirred. To the Nordic mind every stroke is felt to vibrate through the fibres of human flesh, and becomes an appeal not to the decorative imagination but to all the emotions that make us men and bind together the world with links of sympathy. It is impossible to claim that the great unknown poet who wrought the *Chanson de Roland* was

ever conscious of this fact, but it is the very stuff of his art; it is the woof in which he worked with such splendid energy and force. When at length the Moslems close on the band of paladins with their men who nearly all lie dead in the pass, and Roland consents to blow his horn, his famous *olifant*, and the aged emperor thirty leagues away hears the long and melancholy blast that the dying paladin sends afar till the blood starts from his eyes, the emotional tension of the *Song of Roland* reaches its highest point. In his own more primitive way and with the limited resources of a single art this poet attains the same kind of massive power in the art of playing on the throbbing pulse of human emotion, which in more recent times and in a more complex manner was achieved by Wagner. We realise how it is that that remote idyllic spot in the land of the Basques, the green plain amid wooded heights and browsing goats, Roncesvalles, is one of the sacred places of our race.

III

The *Chanson de Roland* represents the last great achievement of the pure Nordic spirit on the European mainland. In the isolation of lands cut off by the sea, like Iceland and Ireland, it was possible for the unmixed Nordic spirit, the unmixed Celtic spirit, to develop more or less unhampered by alien traditions during one or two

succeeding centuries — though it must be remembered that the traditions were never quite pure, for even the *Mabinogion* was faintly touched by Norman influence, and even the Icelandic Eddas, it may be, were touched by Irish influence — but on the Continent the growth of civilisation, the spread of written literature, the cosmopolitan authority of the Church, the growing international social intercourse, soon familiarised all the makers of literature with each other's work, and the special themes of Celtic poet and Nordic poet — so far as they were not too subtle for transmission — became common property. In England this fusion was even more complete than in Continental Europe, for here the two spirits, each in its finest form, were brought together. The Danish or Anglian element in Eastern England was thus mightily reinforced when the Normans came, and the *Chanson de Roland* has come down to us in an English manuscript. On the other side of England, in Wales, was the home of the Arthurian legend, the finest manifestation of the Celtic spirit, soon to be revealed to England and the world in the epoch-making work of Geoffrey of Monmouth. The supremacy of England in poetry is due to the accident which brought about the union in our island of the Celtic spirit and the Nordic spirit in their finest forms.

These two elements have now long been exquisitely and inextricably intertwined in our

literature; there has been a mingling of traditions and a mingling of blood. Celtic poet and Nordic poet have seemed to rival each other in aptitude to absorb the spirit and the methods of the other until sometimes in seeming, though in seeming only, each has lost the individuality of his own tribe. A curious illustration is furnished by Malory in his *Morte d'Arthur*. That, we are inclined to say offhand, is essentially a manifestation of the Celtic spirit. Yet it is nothing of the kind. Sir Thomas Malory, it is probable, belonged to the Leicestershire family of that name which settled in Cambridgeshire in the early part of the fourteenth century, a characteristically Danish and Anglian part of England,* and Malory was a man of mainly Nordic spirit. However diligently he may have absorbed the stories and the machinery of Celtic legend, he retains the baldness, the monotony, the avoidance of the supernatural, the instinctive insistence on human interest, which mark the Nordic man. In his hands the Story of King Arthur and his Knights becomes almost as Nordic in its tone as the story of Charlemagne and his paladins is in the *Chanson de Roland*. Again and again we feel in his pages the pulsing throb, the rhythmic swell of the wave of emotion, that we can nowhere hear in pure Celtic literature,

* At the same time, it is of interest to remark, there is a strong element of dark population in Leicestershire, indicating a residuum of primitive British blood.

that we feel below the surface of all Nordic literature.

It is, however, by no means only in the later course of Celtic tradition that we may observe how curiously the two spirits blended or sought to replace each other; we may trace the same phenomenon throughout English literature. Every great English poet, however much he may have leaned to the one side or the other, has combined the Celtic spirit and the Nordic spirit, whether he has absorbed the traditions or inherited the blood. Chaucer, while he certainly belongs in the main to the Nordic side — as we might expect from one so strongly touched by Norman influence and so intimately associated with Eastern England — has yet absorbed the vivacity and imaginative delicacy of the Celtic spirit. Spenser shows the same blending in a more marked and definite form all the more conspicuously since he took up a theme that was more or less Celtic in form. His county, Lancashire, is an old Celtic region greatly overrun by Scandinavian settlers, and we may well believe that he had in his blood an inherited aptitude for both these kinds of literary spirit. We may certainly find it in his work, and the Celtic tapestry of the *Faërie Queene* — happily compared by Landor to an ancient tapestried chamber — is worked with a sober, heartfelt, realistic earnestness altogether Nordic. The intimate way, indeed, in which in Spenser's great poem the web of serious human

emotion is, to use his own favourite phrase, 'subtly wrought' into the woof of a legend of 'faery land' — too sweetly and sincerely conceived to be merely conventional and borrowed — is unique in our literature.

Shakespeare, however, is the supreme example of all that has been gained for our literature by the juxtaposition of the men of Nordic and Celtic spirit. Here indeed there is no intimate fusion of the two spirits, but rather, as it were, a constant dramatic opposition and contrast, a duologue which is sometimes manifested in technical minutiæ and sometimes comprehends the whole scope of a play. Fundamentally Shakespeare would appear to belong to the Celtic side, and as the district he sprang from is known to be an ancient Celtic infolding in the otherwise mainly Anglian midlands, this is not surprising. To realise the special qualities of Shakespeare's work we should bear in mind the qualities of the most conspicuous playwright among his contemporaries, Ben Jonson, a Scandinavian Lowlander with all the Nordic qualities, scarcely indeed in quite their finest form, hardly tinctured at all by any Celtic elements. What we feel by comparison in Shakespeare's work is the happy extravagance of its imagery, its extreme swiftness of thought, the light and delicate touch.* As a poet

* Chapman, a very pronounced representative of the Nordic spirit in its qualities and their defects, furnishes an equally instructive comparison.

Shakespeare is marked by his excessive freedom from bondage to literal fact, by the audacity and profusion of his metaphors, impressionistic rather than precise, qualities which were habitual in old Celtic literature, but are nowhere found in the best English poetry to an extent which even approaches Shakespeare.* As a dramatist, also, Shakespeare rarely presents the typical Englishman; Hamlet, and Falstaff, and Mercutio — all characteristically Shakespearean creations — are emphatically all men of Celtic rather than of Nordic temper, for they all have in highest degree the qualities of mental vivacity and quick sensibility. Except to some extent in the chronicle plays, where the dramatist was somewhat fettered, it is the same throughout, and it is noteworthy that as Shakespeare developed and became more truly himself the more strongly marked is the Celtic spirit in his work. It begins as a play of elves, besides the serious and stolid Nordic realism of *Venus and Adonis*, and it ends by becoming a philosophy of life. Prospero, the exiled duke who dwells in a bare island cell and yet has control over nature, over the world of spirits and the world of man, is the supreme embodiment of the Celtic artist in

* I have elsewhere shown ('The Colour Sense in Literature,' *Contemporary Review*, May, 1896) that Shakespeare's use of colour words tends to be purely imaginative; they are seldom (as in Tennyson, for instance, they usually are) an attempt to render the precise shades of things seen; they are felicitous appeals to the imaginative vision, not to the bodily eye, and are untranslatable into actual fact.

literature. Shakespeare here seems to reveal a deliberate sense of the essential unreality of the visible world; imaginative vision, as in all Celtic work, becomes supreme; in the philosophy of Prospero the actual world has ceased to exist in any serious sense, for all Celtic art is the evocation of a mirage. Yet the Nordic spirit, however it may have become attenuated at the end, is very strong in Shakespeare. The unfailing humanity and concentrated emotion, as well as the architectonic qualities, are alike Nordic. The driving energy is Nordic, and one is inclined to say that while as a pure artist Shakespeare more and more definitely developed the Celtic spirit within him, as a man he remained, as revealed in his early poems and in the Sonnets, the human emotional realistic child of the North.

It is unnecessary to follow the perpetual play of the Celtic spirit and the Nordic spirit as they interweave throughout our poetic literature. Every reader may trace it for himself. It is by no means difficult to extend the inquiry to prose literature. Thus Sir Thomas Browne is the almost pure type of the Celt in literature; he has in full measure both the atmospheric remoteness and the decorative detail which we have found to mark the Celtic spirit, together with the freedom from the bondage of law and order, the pervading sense of the unreality of the world, that so usually flow from those Celtic qualities. Everywhere he sees nothing but

perpetual miracle; he is an experienced physician familiar with hysteria, and a philosophic thinker as well, yet he cannot help finding the capricious movements of the Devil in human affairs, and uses his influence to burn witches when the day of witch-burning was almost over. He has spent his life in professional work among the positive and progressive East Anglians of prosperous Norwich, yet he remains always what the wild and wayward dreams of his Celtic ancestors in Cheshire have made him, the brother of Traherne and Vaughan. His books are mainly philosophic, a would-be scientific discussion of the phenomena of the universe, yet by no possibility could we suppose him to be of the same race with the genuinely Nordic East Anglian philosopher who preceded him by half a century. Bacon delighted to contemplate the natural world; it was the very instinct of his being to reduce it to law and order, to arrange and to classify; the atmosphere of perpetual miracle which Browne loved to breathe — 'Methinks there be not impossibilities enough in Religion' — would have been altogether abhorrent to him. Superficially it might seem that the jewelled speech of the two men was somewhat alike; yet in reality their styles are wholly unlike, and the soaring iridescent fountain of Browne's eloquence has nothing in common with the sombre splendour that glows through the massive prose of Bacon.

To a careless observer it may seem that the

differences between the Celtic and the Nordic spirits are so subtle as to be almost arbitrary, and that in defining their respective spheres much must be left to the play of fancy. In the psychology of literature, however, we have to learn that it is often the subtle things that are the most fundamental and the most pervasive. Moreover, there is one criterion which, when we can apply it, will always furnish an objective test of the soundness of the conclusions reached in this field by processes of psychological analysis. If the poet of mainly Celtic spirit is found to drive his ancestral roots into a Celtic district of our land, the mainly Nordic poet into a Nordic district, or if the poet who conspicuously combines the two spirits is found to belong ancestrally to districts of both characters, then we may reasonably conclude that our psychological analysis is justified. And this is what we constantly find when the facts are within reach. It is certainly no accident that the two poets of the early nineteenth century who have most definitely rendered the Celtic spirit, Keats and Coleridge, come from the southwestern peninsula of England, a region which we know to be still largely occupied by a people once of Celtic speech. Neither poet would have regarded himself as a Celt, and neither had any adequate opportunity of realising what Celtic speech and literature are. Yet, with whatever other demand the genius of Keats held, some of his longer poems take on the dreamy though

decorative character which we have found to characterise all genuine Celtic literature in its finest manifestations and are full of delight in detail which has never been realised; while of his shorter poems 'La Belle Dame sans Merci' is the typical expression of the Celtic imaginative mood, and the 'magic casements' have rightly become the classical example of the kind of vision which characterises the Celt in literature. Coleridge, similarly, in the 'Ancient Mariner,' 'Kubla Khan,' and a few other pieces, has in his own peculiar and personal way attained the expression of like qualities although his genius was less purely confined within poetic limits. How truly the spirit of a poet's work is an inborn grace and not an entirely acquired accomplishment we realise when we turn to Tennyson, who was fascinated by the Celtic Arthurian legend, as Milton had once been, but less wise than Milton determined to adapt himself to the task of a new presentation of it, only to achieve a work of feminine elegance in which the fine qualities of his own art almost altogether disappeared. Tennyson was rooted in the most purely Nordic district of England, his art was Nordic, and all his skill could not enable him to weave a poem in the tapestried manner which to William Morris, for instance, who united the Celtic and Nordic elements, was an effortless task.

It is in Ireland that we should expect to find a typical modern Celtic poet, and it is interesting

to observe how intimately Thomas Moore, who throughout the nineteenth century was the most popular and typical of Irish poets, exactly reproduces the qualities which we find in the old literature of Ireland. This is the more notable since — unlike the more recent poets — Moore certainly knew and cared very little indeed about the ancient literature of Ireland, however happily he sometimes adapted old folk melodies. He had, he once said, 'that kind of imagination which is chilled by the real scene and can but describe what it has not seen.' The attitude of the Celtic poet could not be better defined. The Nordic poet is a realist; he can describe nothing that he has not realised and felt pulsing in his own blood; he cares nothing for the remote as remote; 'I saw it, I was there,' is his perpetual implicit affirmation. The Celtic poet's imagination is 'chilled by the real scene and can but describe what it has not seen.' It is noteworthy that in Mr. Stephen Gwynn's volume on Moore the qualities attributed to Moore's work in verse are precisely those which we have found to mark the Celtic spirit from the first: remoteness, the lack of reality, the taste for decorativeness and ornamentation, a certain diffuseness and lack of concentration and structure, together with an absence of the personal weight which the sense of reality brings. It is true that the author of the 'Loves of the Angels' was a small man in the world of imagination, while the author of, let

us say, 'Hyperion,' was a great poet and imaginative artist, but differences in quality must not blind us to identity of kind.

In another writer of the early nineteenth century we find the Celtic spirit in a finer form than Moore can give it to us, and the example is instructive because it shows how independent spirit is of environmental circumstances. There is no purer example of the Celtic spirit in literature than is furnished by Hawthorne, and even if we never knew that his family sprang from the Welsh Border we could read it in any page of his romances. The early Welsh bards had found their effects in looking back to a remote past when the shadow of the splendour of old Rome had been thrown across their land; their New England child was for ever haunted by a vanished past that was peopled by the sombre heroes driven oversea as exiles from their old English homes. Yet in *The House of the Seven Gables* and the rest, after the lapse of a thousand years we find the exact qualities that we found in the *Mabinogion:* the remote as remote, the minutely realised and decorative detail, the atmosphere of twilight, of a life that is lived in a strange and delicate dream.

I have said nothing of the 'Celtic Movement.' The reason may perhaps be clear. From the point of view of great literature there is no 'Celtic movement' in the petty sense in which it is generally

understood, nor are great poets the outcome of such movements. If at the present time we possess one poet at all events who adequately represents the Celtic spirit, it is equally true that the same poetic qualities may be traced throughout the whole of our literature. This is clear even to one who has, personally, no part or lot in the Celtic world. It may indeed be said that until we realise clearly what the Celtic spirit means and what the Nordic spirit means we are without the clue to guide us through our literature. Sagacious observers in the past have from time to time vaguely seen the significance, now of this element, now of that, perhaps occasionally even of both. But the literary historian of the past has failed to grasp that significance in any broad or definite manner. The clue can only be found when we place ourselves at a standpoint at once psychological and ethnological. As we follow it, our rich and varied literature, for the first time, falls into harmonious order.

XIV

THE EVOLUTION OF PAINTING IN ENGLAND

The two European centres of painting — Main characteristics of these centres — The position of Great Britain in relation to them — The Traditional School of the West Coast — The Naturalistic School of the East Coast.

We cannot understand the course which the art of painting has followed in England, and the influences which have affected that course, unless we understand the main lines along which the art has proceeded in Europe generally. Broadly speaking, there are two primary centres of painting in Europe, differing widely as regards both the races that have constituted them and the conditions that have affected their development. The first of these centres is that of the Mediterranean, that which arose in Greece and Etruria. The other centre is that of the Rhine, more especially the Lower Rhine and the regions extending from its estuary, now known as Holland and Belgium. It is from these two centres that the European art of painting has spread. There are no other primary centres of painting in Europe, and, unless we go back to palæolithic times, it cannot be said that there are any other primary centres of the arts of design generally. There are, however, two secondary centres, of very considerable importance — that of

Venice, which, geographically speaking, merges into that of Etruria, and that of Spain, which is mainly significant through the supreme achievement of a single artist, Velasquez, at his finest point of inspiration in half a dozen pictures. These two secondary centres owe their great interest and charm to the fact that they represent a successful combination of the methods of the North and of the South. Otherwise the two primary centres remain distinct, even although it may be that, if we could go far enough back into the neolithic age, we should find a link of connection between them, for in pre-historic times, as Montelius and others have shown, there were very important commercial routes between the Mediterranean and north-western Europe.

The course of each of the art currents arising in these two centres has been long, in the case of the older of them demonstrably extending over thousands of years, though this southern art-impulse has now been exhausted for several centuries, leaving the northern centre still vigorous and widely diffused. Both continue to exert the influence of their traditions wherever the methods of European painting are practised.

The general characters of the southern and the northern centres are, however, widely different. The southern way of painting expressed the instincts of a people who had not always a close and vivid perception of reality, but who were

artists to the finger-tips. The northern way of painting expressed the instincts of a people who were not apt to create beauty of form or line, but who were infinitely patient in detecting and representing the details of beauty, in colour and light, of the world that was familiar to them. These differences were fostered, if they were not even to some extent caused, by the varying conditions under which the people of these two races lived. In the dry and bright air of the South it was possible to paint external wall spaces. Thus arose a decorative method in which details were subordinated or suppressed for the creation of flowing harmonies; this method found its full expression in fresco painting. In the cold and damp and dark air of the North such a method was impossible; here arose oil painting, and by this method were produced small cabinet works in which were sought the highly elaborated brilliance and colour of great jewels wherewith to decorate the interior of houses. The varying climate of the North and the South influeneed the characteristics of these two art-centres in another way. In the South, where the light is nearly always equally brilliant, the problem of light less easily presents itself to the painter. It is merely a datum which, until his art reaches a high degree of development, he accepts and ignores. Light, indeed, in the South, is a blessing so bountifully bestowed on man that he is constantly seeking to minimise it; so it is that while we find

the architects of northern France always striving to make their church windows larger and larger, in the South of France and in Spain they were always striving either to reduce their windows or so to dispose them that they let in as little light as possible. In the North, light is not only comparatively rare and precious, its manifestations are more varied, and therefore more conspicuous than in the South. The painter is thus irresistibly attracted to the manifold and difficult problems of light, and as his work is small and meant to be seen indoors, instead of seeking the flat and broadly flowing harmonies of the southern artist, he strives to elaborate into one jewel, deeply glowing with light and colour, some single aspect of the visible world floating in its own atmosphere. Thus the southern painter is predominantly a decorative artist who attenuates, traditionalises, or, as we conventionally term it, 'idealises' the actual world; the northern artist is predominantly what we are accustomed to call a 'realist' who seeks to concentrate some corner of the actual world in a dazzling and highly elaborated focus of light and colour. The southern artist has always tended to restrain nature within forms demanded by his own traditional conceptions; the northern artist has always worshipped nature, and has always found it easy to modify his traditions, and to model his own conceptions, to the forms of the natural world. It is dangerous to attempt to set up any all-embrac-

ing formula, but it remains true that we cannot understand the fundamental characteristics of the southern and the northern centres of painting unless we remember that the most typical and significant artists of the one have always set up the canon of tradition, whatever personal modification their own temperaments may have brought to tradition, while the others have at the decisive moment always set up the canon of nature.

I

Great Britain, separated from the Continent, has in painting, as in other matters, been exposed to different influences. It has been affected by the influx alike of races and of traditions from the South and from the North. As regards painting, however, racial impulses remained latent, and traditions non-existent, for very many centuries after the composition of the population had been definitely determined. Mural paintings were no doubt common in English churches, but they are usually of a primitive, crude, and conventional character, and a few fine portraits, a field in which later the English excelled, were produced at an early period. There appears to have been no interest in foreign painting, and no desire to imitate or rival it. At last, towards the middle of the sixteenth century, Holbein was induced by Erasmus to visit England. In all respects an admirable and significant representative of the northern school of paint-

ing, he was the greatest painter who had up to that time visited this country. He painted much in England, drew many portrait sketches, left some of his finest work behind him. But it remains doubtful whether he found here more than a very limited appreciation of his work, and of influence he had absolutely none. So far as the development of painting in England is concerned, Holbein might never have visited our shores at all. He seems to have been forgotten, and some of the most important pictures he left behind, like the portrait group of More's family, have disappeared, while to other pictures his name was affixed at random, as a synonym for 'unknown early master.' A few years later, when Shakespeare tries to think of some great artist, it is not the Rhine master nor indeed any Northerner whose name occurs to his mind, but Julio Romano, Raphael's weak follower of ambiguous reputation, is the name that comes to him in a halo of remote Italian romance.

The decisively initiative moment in the evolution of English painting came indeed from the North, but it was the North at a time when the final southern Renaissance wave was now about to spend itself, last of all, on England.

In 1625 there came to the throne a monarch who, whatever his defects as a constitutional ruler, certainly showed a finer taste in painting and a greater enthusiasm in collecting works of art than any English monarch before or since. In this,

indeed, he was but representing a spirit widely spread in the courts he had visited in youth, but he represented that spirit with great judgment and energy. His collections were dispersed to form the nuclei of some of the most famous foreign galleries; had they been preserved, England would now possess the most magnificent collection of pictures in Europe. Charles I was not content merely to collect pictures; he desired to have great artists around him, and though he was not successful in securing the not very eminent masters whose presence he sought, chance favoured him by bringing to London the most princely and magnificent figure that has perhaps ever reached the highest eminence in painting, the man who still shares with Velasquez the pinnacle of art in that age. Rubens came to London as an ambassador, but at Charles's invitation he stayed to paint. He was thus the second great painter who worked in England. But although Rubens doubtless found among the few cultured English nobles a far more appreciative public than Holbein could find, he was not destined to initiate English painting; his own art was too original and audacious to be understood in a country where the only paintings at all well known were the stiff and angular portraits of the early Flemish and French schools. It was the influence of a pupil of Rubens who shortly followed him to England, as a promising place to achieve fortune, that the taste for painting and the aptitude

to paint in accordance with recognised European methods first appeared in England. Vandyke arrived in London in 1632 at the age of thirty-two, and remained in England many years. He speedily became the fashion; he not only painted the King and the Queen and their family repeatedly, but a great number of persons of quality. He was the first of the long series of fashionable portrait-painters, and unlike his successors he practically had the whole field to himself.

There was good reason why Vandyke rather than either of the two greater painters who preceded him should have exercised this decisive influence on the development and direction of English taste in painting. His unquestionably great and facile talents, his quick impressionability, his accomplished eclecticism, even his monotonous mannerisms, won admiration and applause when more profound and original artists would only have met with indifference and contempt. A public just beginning to awake to æsthetic perception found here exactly what it needed and could understand. To an aristocracy painfully conscious of its unpolished roughness and the barbarism from which it had only just emerged, the particular mannerism of Vandyke and the air of elegant and refined distinction which he shed over his sitters, without too absurdly disguising these robust models, must indeed have been enchanting.* So it is that Van-

* Very significant indeed of Vandyke and of Vandyke's art is

dyke has had the good fortune to leave his mark for ever on the English men and women of that age; and the people who were shortly after found vigorous enough to cut each other's throats in the name of king or country will always appear to us with the idle attenuated hands and the lackadaisical affectations which Vandyke has endowed them with.

Vandyke not only exercised a decisive influence on moulding English taste in painting; it was under his influence that the first genuinely English portrait-painters, Dobson and Walker, arose. Dobson, both in date and importance, came first; although he owed much to Vandyke he was an artist of virile temperament and slow deliberate perceptions, very honest and solid in his methods, with a horror of trickery. So at least he appears in the excellent pictures by which he is represented in our National and National Portrait Galleries. He worthily occupies the place of the first genuinely English painter. Dobson attached himself to the King's party; Walker belonged to the Parliamentary party; it was a seemingly paradoxical division, for

the contrast between his own portrait as painted by himself and as painted by a careful but undistinguished fellow artist — I forget his name — whose picture now hangs in the great gallery at Vienna, which contains so many of the most beautiful and interesting pictures in the world. On himself Vandyke bestowed the same careless air of distinction that he found it so easy to bestow on his sitters, together with an even greater degree of refinement. For his fellow artist the glamour is non-existent, and Vandyke appears before us with an unforgettably veracious face, small-mouthed, sensual, assertive, the face of a clever and ambitious *parvenu*.

whereas Dobson was something of a Puritan in his methods, Walker had the instincts of the Cavalier; he was a follower of Vandyke and nothing more, an artist of feminine sensitive temperament, whose portraits remain pleasing and as portraits interesting, though they can never command the respect and admiration which Dobson still wins from us.

We thus see that the English native school of painting arose under a stimulus that came from the north European centre, though in a form profoundly modified by influences from the secondary centre of Venice. This mixed character has marked most of the art influences that have reached England; they have been predominantly northern, but to some extent southern. When the Civil Wars cut short for the time the native development in painting, the England of Restoration days, like the England of Elizabethan days, fell back on artists more or less of the northern school. For nearly a century after the death of Dobson the art of painting was almost extinct; there were no English artists of merit or of reputation, and the foreign artists who took the place of Vandyke — Lely and Kneller — possessed more reputation than merit.

When English painting arose again it was along new lines. Hogarth, indeed, stands apart; he showed how an artist, while distinctly of the northern school, could yet be genuinely English; but though our first absolutely English artist, he

was somewhat out of the main line of evolution. The painters who carried on this main line of development were still under the inspiration of the northern school as affected by southern influences. Richard Wilson had seen the pictures of the French landscape artists and had lived in Rome; those two facts chiefly moulded his work. While, however, he remained convinced throughout that the typical landscape is a classical landscape with Roman architecture as an essential item, and while he generally assumed that it should be seen as the French landscape painters saw it, he yet went somewhat beyond these canons. He began to perceive the beauty of English landscape and he was fascinated by the problems of atmosphere. His very powerful personality is clearly revealed in his work, which has the sobriety, calm, and thoroughness of an artist who had clearly realised what it was he wanted to do and knew how to do it. Wilson is the Dobson of English landscape, and these two figures are the chief initiators in English painting.

Wilson's work was almost unnoticed in his time, it was eclipsed by the much more brilliant work of a much more brilliant man. Reynolds, indeed, knew and cared very little about landscape; he claimed for himself supremacy in portrait-painting, and compounded for that position by declaring that in landscape Gainsborough was supreme. It is impossible to overrate the in-

fluence of Reynolds on the evolution of English painting. Every English artist before him, even Hogarth with all his originality and aggressive independence, had been but as it were a patient and laborious craftsman. Reynolds took both himself and his art proudly; he desired to show that an English artist can assume something of the princely stateliness of a Titian or a Rubens. The same feeling went into his work; he dealt in traditions, but freely, almost recklessly, and with an accomplished command of his methods which enabled him to infuse his work easily with the sentiment of his own personality. He thus became a sort of English Vandyke, that is to say, a less severely trained Vandyke.

It is no doubt because of the immense services to painting which were directly and indirectly rendered by Reynolds's brilliant and accomplished personality, that his work has always been very indulgently treated in England. The seductive qualities which it must have possessed in the highest degree when fresh from his hand intoxicated his contemporaries, and in more recent times there has never been any inclination to judge harshly a figure in our art history at once so imposing and so amiable. It must, however, be said that the part played by Reynolds in the development of English painting — with which we are alone here concerned — was indirect rather than direct. His seductive brilliancy was not, and

could not be, accompanied by any penetrating and earnest vision of the world, or any desire to see things truly. The judgments on painting contained in his discourses and other writings, and — notwithstanding his professed worship of Michelangelo, Raphael and the 'grand style' — his real admiration for the late Bolognese school reveal a taste which was that of his age, and confirm the impression produced by his paintings. He was fascinated by the epidermis of things, and his desire was to render the fascination of that epidermis, the sheen and bloom of the world. His preoccupation with these aspects rendered it easy for him to adopt the incongruous affectations of a pseudo-classicality which led him into very vapid absurdities, as well as much restless experimentalism in the use of pigments which has brought its own revenge. Delightful and admirable as much of his work still remains, there could scarcely be any progress along those lines.

The line of progress was more truly represented by a less showy if not less accomplished artist. Although Gainsborough doubtless owed much to a sympathetic personality, he lacked the commanding and somewhat superficial personal qualities which contributed so greatly both to the work and the position of Reynolds. A man of sensitively acute æsthetic perceptions and, like so many of the other great painters, a passionate lover of music, he was saved from committing the

pseudo-classicalities and specious superficialities which commended themselves so often and so easily to Reynolds.* He was neither so indiscriminate an admirer of tradition as Reynolds, nor so bold an innovator in technical methods; his penetrating and sensitive love of nature seems indeed usually to have been under a certain restraint due partly to the limitations of a temperament which was not marked by its daring impulses or its ability to withstand the tendencies of the day, but showed a very sound and sober judgment in following the most genuinely English or at all events northern traditions (including that of Vandyke) and in making real progress possible along these lines. Gainsborough was much more English than Reynolds, and even apart from his actual achievements he is a very important figure in the development of English art. In his hands portrait-painting reached a sensitive delicacy combined with intellectual distinction which no Englishman had achieved before, if, indeed, it ever has since; while in land-

* A comparison of Reynolds's 'Mrs. Siddons as the Tragic Muse' (in the Dulwich Gallery and the Duke of Westminster's Collection) with Gainsborough's portrait of Mrs. Siddons (in the National Gallery) may alone serve to indicate this profound difference of personal temperament, and — as may be clearer in the sequel — something even deeper than personal temperament. Reynolds instinctively sought to convey the genius of the actress by the external aid of clouds, a throne, allegorical figures, and a theatrical attitude. It was equally natural to Gainsborough to seek the same end, with no external aids but colour and light, by simply concentrating his vision on the woman herself.

scape he leads directly to the delightful art of Morland, the first English landscape painter who had a kind of international reputation, and, indeed, one cannot help thinking, directly influenced the development of French landscape art.

It may be doubted, however, whether the truly original note was reached in the development of English landscape art until we come to the water-colour painters of the end of the eighteenth century. Here we find an art of very simple and humble origin still unencumbered by traditions. This freedom from traditions, the nature of the media employed, the small and unpretentious scale on which the art was carried out, made it easy for water-colour work to obtain a freshness and naturalness, a swift and delicate reproduction of natural effects, which were to become a little later the characteristics of English painting at its highest point of culmination.

Turner, who is one of these culminating points of English painting, is a very interesting figure from the present point of view, because he represents the fusion of the aboriginal English water-colour manner with the more traditional oil-colour manner. On the one hand, he was a more or less successful disciple of the school of Poussin and Claude, painting the old-fashioned classical scenes, and seeing them in the old-fashioned way, introducing at the same time impossible human figures which were all his own; on the other hand,

taking up the art of water-colour at its highest point of development, he made it the happiest of mediums for expressing his own highly individual vision of the world. He continually tended to leave behind the traditional method and to weld oil-painting more and more into a medium for expressing what he had first learnt to express in water-colour. It may seem an illegitimate impulse, but in Turner's hands it was fully justified by its success, and it certainly achieved the immense service of finally emancipating English painting, rendering it at once the most personal and the most realistic representation of the natural world. Turner is thus the most significant figure in the development of English art.

It may well have been the emancipating influences of Turner which rendered Constable possible, though we have to remember that Constable really represents the climax of a great and fruitful though local movement in landscape art, and is most intimately linked on to Crome, and thereby to the great Dutchmen. In Constable we have the most absolutely and purely English manifestation of the art of landscape painting at its highest point. The exotic and traditional elements that are still clearly traceable in Turner have in Constable disappeared; he painted distinctively English things under truly English aspects, in a characteristically English spirit. And, as ever happens, by force of being national

he became international. He was not only the first great English landscape painter who was completely national, but the first to have really international significance. Whatever pioneering part may be assigned to Huet, it was largely under Constable's influence that the French school of romantic landscape arose.*

After Constable the current of English evolution in painting was transferred to France, and proceeded there on more or less English lines, some of which have flowed back and are still with us. One of the chief purely British initiators in English painting since Constable has been Ford Madox Brown. A singularly forceful temperament, with a very personal vision of the world, Madox Brown possessed a genius that was essentially simple and homogeneous, though very versatile in its manifestations. Whether he turned his hand to landscape, or to dreams of past life, or to scenes of present-day life, his touch remained hard, firm, brilliant, personal, a little fantastic, but essentially realistic. It was once the fashion to belittle Madox Brown's influence, and to question his initiatory impulse on the so-called Pre-Raphaelite movement. The fashion had its excuse in the somewhat unsympathetic character

* Constable's international significance is shared by his contemporary, Bonington, a painter of versatile and accomplished genius who began to do many things which have often been repeated since. Bonington's early association with Delacroix makes it a little difficult to define his originality.

of Brown's genius. Although Rossetti brought an eager receptivity, the sensitive temperament of the poet, the sensuous attitude of the lover of physical beauty (which in turn influenced Brown), much of the force and fibre of his work exists already in Brown before 1848. The term 'Pre-Raphaelite' may have been happily chosen in so far as its inventors sought to fling a slight at the popular ideals of their day, but otherwise it was a misnomer; the movement was indeed not so much Pre-Raphaelite as Flemish. Madox Brown's training was Flemish, his traditions were fundamentally northern, though transformed in his perfervid Scottish temperament; Holbein was the artist who most decisively influenced him and sent him to nature, and though he studied in Rome the visit left no permanent impress on his art. Rossetti, again, remained true to the same northern tradition; he visited no foreign centre of art except Belgium, which ever after left its mark on his work, and though on this basis it is true that his Italian temperament led him to developments which seem sometimes to recall the work of the North Italian masters (those most closely in touch with the Flemish masters), the Italian by blood was still a Northerner by artistic training and tradition. Millais and Holman Hunt also remained essentially Northerners; the one true Pre-Raphaelite was Burne-Jones, and the profound fascination which the Tuscan or Etrus-

can spirit exerted on him swiftly drew him away from those northern influences under which his genius had begun to develop.*

II

It has seemed necessary to trace this rapid sketch of the development of painting in England and the chief traditions and forces that have influenced it, even although it may have recalled many facts that are familiar. When, however, we proceed to study the geographical distribution of the great painters who have played the chief part in this evolution, we reach ground that is comparatively untrodden, and we attain results that are so precise and definite that they furnish pecul-

* The reader will not need to be told that this was written over twenty years ago. To-day the Pre-Raphaelite movement is seldom mentioned save with contempt, and the painters of that group are scarcely considered painters at all. (See, for example, Mr. Clive Bell in the London *Nation* for 19th December, 1925.) But this is a rather shallow view, which will pass, and I see no need to change what I have written. Forty years ago English art was in a sadly moralistic and story-telling way, with a completely dull and slipshod technique. A reaction to a more genuinely æsthetic outlook was necessary, and the Pre-Raphaelites in initiating that reaction were performing a valuable function. For those who were then young Burne-Jones came as the inspiring revelation of a new beauty, by no means as the mere imitator of an old beauty. Some thirty years ago, I remember, a French critic, as he passed an engraving of Burne-Jones's 'Merlin' on my walls, remarked: 'In future ages when men think of English art they will say — "Burne-Jones!"' The French art historian of to-day, like Elie Faure, would not agree. He would be more inclined to say: 'Gainsborough!' and, for my own part, I hope he would be right. The Pre-Raphaelite movement had no significance for European art, but for English art it had an importance we must not belittle though it has now passed away.

iarly brilliant evidence of the intimate connection between race and even the subtlest manifestations of the human spirit.

In the study of British genius we have found that the British painters and designers (I here leave out of account sculptors and architects) of sufficiently high rank to come within the limits of eminence I had set, and concerning whose place of origin adequate information was forthcoming, are forty-five in number. If now, bearing in mind the characteristics of the great English artists, and remembering that they may be roughly divided into the two classes of those who have been mainly influenced by nature, and those who have been mainly influenced by tradition, we proceed to inquire into their origins, we find that the geographical distribution runs as nearly as possible parallel with the distribution by characteristics. In other words, while the painters who have chiefly followed nature came from one part of the British Islands, the painters who have chiefly followed tradition came from another part. Speaking roughly, it may be said that of the two great foci of genius which may be found in England, the East Anglian focus is the headquarters of the painters of nature and the south-western focus, more especially Devonshire, the headquarters of the painters of tradition. The East Anglian district is the centre of an influence which extends along the whole east coast of England

and Scotland and to some distance inland, while Devonshire is, so far as painting is concerned, the centre of a district which may be said to include the whole of the rest of the country including Ireland.

There may be some query as to the propriety of dividing painters into two classes accordingly as they are mainly affected by nature or by tradition. It may be said that no painter is cut off from tradition, and that the worship of nature may itself become a tradition. Although this is true, the distinction between the painter who is mainly influenced by what other painters have done, or by his own imagination, and the painter who is mainly influenced by what his eye actually sees, is fairly clear, both to those who are and those who are not painters, and it may well be retained. A few examples may illustrate both the distinction itself and the accuracy with which it coincides with geographical distribution. Reynolds belonged so far as is known almost entirely to Devonshire, the centre of the south-western focus of British genius; he is likewise the king of the English painters of tradition; his ideals of art were Italian; in theory he was an ardent admirer of Michelangelo, in practice he was a strayed disciple of the later Venetians. A painter, he was accustomed to say, should form his rules not from books or precepts, but (from nature? oh, no!) 'from pictures.' 'Rules,' he would add, 'were first made from pictures.' Very different, indeed,

were the maxims and the practice of Constable. Like Gainsborough, Constable belonged to Suffolk; he was absolutely untouched by Italian tradition, and certainly never formed his rules by the study of pictures. 'Truth only will count,' he said, and he loathed every attempt at *bravura*, the striving to go beyond nature. As a more complex illustration, we may take Turner. It may seem a little difficult to say whether Turner belongs pre-eminently to the school of tradition or the school of nature. His early work was distinctly in large measure traditional; through the greater part of his life he carefully preserved a predilection for pseudo-classical conventions. Yet at the same time he revealed a passionate devotion to nature which in his latest work has altogether survived the classical traditions. The key to this complexity in Turner's genius is, however, at once apparent when we turn to consider his ancestry. His father, like Reynolds, belonged to Devon, coming in early life to London, where he married; the mother's place of origin does not appear to be definitely known, but as her relations were scattered in the eastern counties, we are probably correct in supposing that her family belonged to the east coast. There are no greater names in English painting than Reynolds, Constable, and Turner, and we thus see that all three furnish evidence — at nearly every point definite evidence — of the intimate connection between

a painter's method of painting and his racial heredity.

It would be somewhat tedious to go through the whole group of the forty-five artists in the same manner to show how they illustrate this distribution, even if my own knowledge of second-rate British artists were sufficiently extensive to enable me to do this with complete assurance. In order that the reader may judge for himself, I print the list here:

Barry	Cork.
Bewick	Northumberland and Cumberland.
Blake	Somerset (?).
Bonington	Nottingham.
H. K. Browne	Norfolk.
Cattermole	Norfolk.
Constable	Suffolk.
Cotman	Norfolk.
Copley	Limerick and Clare, but originating in Yorkshire and Lancashire.
Cox	Birmingham.
Crome	Norfolk.
Cruikshank	Leith.
Danby	Wexford.
Dawson	Nottingham.
Dobson	Hertfordshire.
Doyle	Dublin.
Dyce	Aberdeen.
Eastlake	Devon.
Etty	Yorkshire.
Flaxman	Norfolk.
Gainsborough	Suffolk.
Gillray	Lanark.
Haydon	Devon.
Hogarth	Suffolk.
Keene	Westmoreland.
Landseer	Lincoln.
Lawrence	Worcester.
Leech	Irish.
Maclise	Elgin and Cork.
Morland	Norfolk (?) (mother apparently French).
Mulready	Clare.
Northcote	Devon.
Opie	Cornwall.
Phillip	Aberdeen.
Raeburn	Edinburgh and Annandale.
Reynolds	Devon.
Romney	Westmoreland and Cumberland.
Sandby	Nottingham and Lincoln.
Scott (D.)	Lanark.
Stothard	Yorkshire and Shropshire.
Turner	Devon and Nottingham (?).
Varley	Nottingham.
Wilkie	Midlothian and Fife.
Wilson	Montgomery.
Wright	Derby.

It will, I believe, be found that if a line is drawn from London (for the south-eastern corner of England is singularly bare of painters) to Liverpool, the naturalistic painters will be found mainly to the east of that line and the traditionalistic and idealistic painters to the west. There are of course a few dubious and complex cases. Flaxman, for instance, scarcely appears to show the special characteristics of the east country. The case of Wilson, again, seems to resemble that of Turner; he was at once a conserver of traditions and an ardent lover of nature; on his mother's side he was undoubtedly Welsh; his father was a clergyman, and bears a Teutonic or Scandinavian name, which, though widespread, belongs mainly to the east coast. It may be noted that, while the two divisions are nearly equal in size, the whole of Scotland falls into the eastern division; this is due to the fact that the west of Scotland has produced so few painters; if painters were forthcoming here I should expect them to fall mainly into the western group.

If we turn to more recent painters — not included in the present list because still living when the body of the *Dictionary of National Biography* was issued — we shall scarcely find any marked exceptions to the tendency already found to prevail. The chief movement in British painting during the latter half of the nineteenth century was that associated with the 'Pre-Raphaelites.'

Leaving Rossetti, as mainly of Italian race, out of account,* we find that the leaders and precursors of the movement, like Ford Madox Brown and Millais, belonged in character mainly to the followers of nature, and in race mainly to the east country group. But Burne-Jones, notwithstanding all the influences around him, is strictly distinguished from the others by his love of tradition and his affection for early Italian art. In the light of our present knowledge concerning race it is impossible not to connect this fact with his Welsh ancestry.

It is probably unnecessary to elaborate a point which when once indicated is seen to be very clear and simple. The British Islands, roughly speaking, may be said to be divided between two races; one, more ancient, predominantly dark in complexion and commonly called 'Celtic,' but in reality, while containing what may fairly be called Celtic elements, doubtless more correctly denominated Mediterranean. The other element, fairer than the first, lying in its most concentrated form along the east coast of England and Scotland, is Teutonic in its affinities, closely related to the Flemish, Dutch and Scandinavians, as well as to the people of northern France. It is clear that the instincts of one of these two great sections of our popula-

* It is not known (W. M. Rossetti told me) where the Peirces, to whom the Rossettis belong on the English side, came from, and the name itself is not very distinctive.

tion urge them to adopt a traditional or idealistic vision of the world in painting, while the people of the other section are impelled to the direct study of nature, their tradition, when they have one, being the naturalistic tradition of the North European centre of painting to which the other men are insensitive. The first are concerned with what, as it seems to them, ought to be; the others with what is. The first are moved by great ideals or follow lofty traditions; the second are, however, more closely in sympathy with the impulses of the important art-centre, that of North Europe, with which Great Britain is in such close contact; they have produced twice as many notable artists as the men of the western district.* And it is from them, rather than from the others, that the decisively progressive movements in the evolution of British painting have come.† As I have previously pointed out, the east country and the fair element in our population have shown a special predilection for the scientific study of nature,

* That it should be so is not surprising when we recall that even in mediæval times this part of the country was the chief English art-centre. I am inclined to think that more remains of mural painting are found here than elsewhere; it is certain that East Anglia is the chief district for brasses; while the same region, as is recognised, almost alone in our country, has produced an original and attractive architectural style.

† The French school of romantic landscape, which received its impetus from the east coast of England, spread almost exclusively among painters of fair race belonging to northern and north-western France, the regions of France most closely allied to eastern England in race.

though they have no such special pre-eminence in the field of poetry. Now we see the same fundamental racial distinction even in so subtle a matter as methods of painting and modes of æsthetic feeling. Nearly all English painters have been subjected to similar environmental and traditional influences, and have been educated in the same large art-centres. Yet the racial factor, while not all-powerful, still persists. A man's æsthetic feelings are the most delicate, seemingly the most capricious, of his mental possessions. Yet they are, we see, among his most radical and unchangeable possessions; and through a long series of ancestors born to till the soil or to consume its fruits, he may yet retain a spiritual kinship, only waiting for circumstances to make it clear, with the greatest artists of his race, even in foreign lands.*

* When 'The Evolution of English Painting' was first published, Mr. D. S. MacColl sought to explode the view therein put forward in the pages of the *Saturday Review* (22d March, 1902). It may not be necessary to take seriously this playful effort. But if one does so, Mr. MacColl's criticisms are found to resolve themselves into two: (1) there is no 'antenatal necessity' for the character of a painter's art; and (2) we must not accept any 'single cause' of what men do in art. Both these propositions may be accepted without the need for changing a single word in my statement. If the men on the west coast of Great Britain tend on the whole to follow traditional methods in art and those on the east coast naturalistic methods — Mr. MacColl made no serious attempt to deny the fact — that implies no fatal necessity; they were following their own natural bent; that indeed was my point. As to the factor which I had invoked, and which Mr. MacColl would himself admit the existence of, not being a 'single cause,' I had myself already clearly stated that it was 'not all-powerful.' I was dissecting out a single cause, and analysis is not synthesis.

XV

GENIUS AND STATURE

Fallacies of the inquiry — The stature of normal persons — Tall, middle-sized, and short persons of genius — Undue infrequency of the middle-sized — The variational tendency of genius — Some of the problems involved.

THE anthropometry of 'genius' — using the word here and throughout merely to indicate the most highly valued variations of intellectual faculty — is in a much more elementary condition than our knowledge of the physical characters of criminals. There are sufficient reasons why this should be so. The man of genius less obviously belongs to the 'dangerous classes' than the criminal, the idiot, and other varieties of abnormal man; so that we seldom obtain him under favourable conditions for precise measurement. Moreover, persons of artistic genius, at all events, usually possess to an even greater extent than criminals a kind of vanity distinctly opposed to all such proceedings; and few have been found to imitate Zola, who complacently lent himself to the minute scientific investigations of Dr. Toulouse. If, however, there is one anthropological character of genius which ought to be fairly well ascertained, it is stature; for that is the coarsest of all anthropometric characters, and in its roughest degrees can be judged by the unaided eye. This is so obvious

that from time to time the subject has been discussed; but, so far from any agreement having been reached, the conclusions of those who have dealt with the matter are absolutely opposed. And the reflection is inevitable that, if so simple a question as this will not admit of solution, it is impossible to determine any character of genius; and any attempt to consider the study of genius a scientific study is merely an affectation of pseudo-scientific journalists.

When, however, we come to look into the attempts made to settle this question, the cause of their failure is sufficiently obvious. The apparent simplicity of the problem has put the inquirer off his guard. In such a matter it has seemed enough to collect anecdotes concerning little or big 'great men,' to look into a few histories and biographies, or to fall back on one's own reminiscences. No one has attempted to treat the matter in a really serious and methodical manner. So far as I am aware, not a single writer who has undertaken to inquire whether men of genius are 'tall' or 'short' has taken the trouble to explain what he means by 'tall' or 'short.' It is easy to understand the contempt which anyone with the faintest tincture of scientific training must feel for such inquiries. The study of the stature of famous men threatens to resolve itself largely into a psychological analysis of the fallacies of human perception. Men are wont to belittle the physical height of the man of

fluence on the results when it is not exercised in favour of a prejudice; and I must admit that, though the result I have reached seems to me the most simple and the most probable result, it had not occurred to me beforehand as probable. So far as I had any expectation, it was that the small men of genius would predominate; for I remembered Balzac's saying that 'nearly all great men are little,' and the emphasis with which Lombroso and others have followed on this side — which has, indeed, certain biological considerations in its favour. I have included no names which are not really eminent in some field or another. Except in a few unquestionable cases, the names of the living were excluded.

It will be seen that the names are grouped alphabetically into two classes differing in value. The first class contains only those whose height is definitely known, so that we are here free from the influence of mere impressions. It is undoubtedly true that such a list is abnormally deficient in persons of medium height, for it more rarely occurs to the biographers of such to mention the precise height; this is a source of error to be borne in mind, and we may put against it a compensatory error in the second class, for here many of the persons alleged to be of middle height were probably tall, *i.e.*, over five feet nine.

The second class contains those who seemed tall, of medium height, or short to their contemporaries,

whose judgments we are not able to control by precise measurements. Notwithstanding the fallacies I have already mentioned, such judgments have a certain value.*

TALL

George Borrow (6 ft. 2)
J. Bruce (6 ft. 4)
Burke (5 ft. 10)
Burns (nearly 5 ft. 10)
Sir R. Burton (nearly 6 ft.)
Carlyle (5 ft. 11)
Cobbett (over 6 ft.)
Coleridge (5 ft. 9½)
O. Cromwell (5 ft. 10)
Darwin (about 6 ft.)
Dumas *fils* (5 ft. 10)
Fielding (over 6 ft.)
Hawthorne (5 ft. 10½)
J. Hogg (5 ft. 10½)
A. Lincoln (6 ft. 1)
Marryat (5 ft. 10)
Peter the Great (6 ft. 8½)
Sir William Petty (over 6 ft.)
Sir W. Raleigh (about 6 ft.)
C. Reade (over 6 ft.)
Sir W. Scott (about 6 ft.)
Shelley (5 ft. 11)
Southey (5 ft. 11)
Thackeray (6 ft. 4)
Trevithick (6 ft. 2)
A. Trollope (5 ft. 10)
G. Washington (6 ft. 3)
Whitman (6 ft.)
John Wilson (5 ft. 11½)

Hans Andersen ('the Long Poet')
Arago
T. Arnold
Audubon
D'Azeglio
Beaumarchais
Bismarck
Joseph Black
Bolingbroke
Bonington
Boyle
Lord Brougham
Bunyan
Bishop Burnet
Julius Cæsar
Champollion
Charlemagne
Clive
Columbus

* In the case of men belonging to the past we have to reckon with the possibility that the average height of the population may have somewhat changed. In the present century F. D. Maurice was described by his son as 'distinctly below the middle height, not above five feet seven.' In 1745 Otway was described as 'of the middle height, about five feet seven inches'; while Swift at five feet eight was considered tall. But from the present point of view the mainly interesting point is not the absolute height, but the relative height of a certain group of men in comparison with their contemporaries.

Condorcet
Corot
Crabbe
Dalton
Delacroix
Denham
Sir Kenelm Digby ('gigantic')
Dumas *père*
J. Edwards
Emerson
Flaubert
Foscolo
Froude
Gilbert
Goethe
E. de Goncourt
Gounod
Helmholtz
A. von Humboldt
Leigh Hunt
Huxley
Edward Irving
Sir Henry Irving
Dr. Johnson
Ben Jonson
Lamartine
Lavoisier
Lessing
Li Hung Chang ('a giant among Chinamen')
Longfellow
Mazarin
Millet
Mirabeau
Molière
Moltke
Monti
Henry More
A. de Musset
Nietzsche
Petrarch
Poussin
Puvis de Chavannes
Richelieu
J. P. Richter
Romilly
Ruskin
Schiller
Schopenhauer
Adam Sedgwick
Sheridan
Sir Philip Sidney
Smollett
Sterne
Taine
Tasso
Tennyson
St. Thomas Aquinas
J. Thomson
Torrigiano
Tourgueneff
Volta
Waller
D. Webster
William the Silent
Wordsworth

MEDIUM

Lord Beaconsfield (5 ft. 9)
Byron (5 ft. 8½)
Sir A. Cockburn (5 ft. 6)
Dickens (5 ft. 9)
Gladstone (about 5 ft. 9) *
Jeffrey (5 ft. 6)
Bulwer Lytton (about 5 ft. 9)
F. D. Maurice (5 ft. 7)
J. S. Mill (5 ft. 8)
Otway (5 ft. 7)

* It appears, however, that this was Gladstone's height in old age, but that earlier in life he was 5 ft. 11 in., and should therefore be in the tall group.

S. Richardson (about 5 ft. 5)
D. G. Rossetti (barely 5 ft. 8)
Swift (5 ft. 8)
Voltaire (5 ft. 7)
Wellington (5 ft. 7)
Wesley (5 ft. 6)
Zola (5 ft. 7)

Alexander the Great (or short)
Lord Bacon
Baudelaire
St. Bernard
Sir Thomas Browne
Browning
Lord Burleigh
S. Butler
Camoëns
Lord Chesterfield
Chopin
William Collins
Confucius
Cowper
Dante
Defoe
St. Francis of Assisi (rather below)
Hazlitt
Heine
Hood
Keble
Lagrange
Linnæus
J. R. Lowell
Luther
Marvell
Guy de Maupassant
Clerk Maxwell
Michelangelo
J. Mill
Newton (or short)
Poe (or short)
Renan
J. Sansovino
Sydney Smith
Spinoza
Steele
Suckling
Verlaine
Watteau

SHORT

Balzac (nearly 5 ft. 4)
Beethoven (5 ft. 4)
W. Blake (barely 5 ft.)
Hartley Coleridge (about 5 ft.)
St. Francis Xavier (4 ft. 6)
J. Hunter (5 ft. 2)
Kant (about 5 ft.)
Keats (5 ft.)
Meissonier (about 5 ft.)
T. Moore (5 ft.)
Napoleon (5 ft. 1¾)
Nelson (5 ft. 4)
De Quincey (5 ft. 3 or 4)
Thiers (5 ft. 3)
Bishop Wilberforce (5 ft. 3)

Aetius
Albertus Magnus
Aristotle
Augustus Cæsar
Barrow
Baskerville
Beccaria
Beddoes
Bentham
Admiral Blake
Louis Blanc
Bocchoris
Brunelleschi
Burbage
Calvin
Lord Camden
T. Campbell
Chamfort

Chillingworth
Chrysippus
Comte
Condé
Crome
Cruikshank
Curran
David of Angers
Descartes
Sir Francis Drake
Dryden
H. Milne Edwards
Erasmus
Faraday
M. Ficinus
Fromentin
Fuseli
Garrick
Gibbon
Giotto
Godwin
Goldsmith
Gray
Hales
W. Harvey
Warren Hastings
Haüy
Herzen
E. T. A. Hoffmann
Hogarth
O. W. Holmes
Horace
D. Jerrold
Gottfried Keller
Kepler
Admiral Keppel
Lalande
C. Lamb
Lamennais
Larrey
Laud
Lipsius
Locke
Lulli
Marshal Luxembourg
Macaulay
Charles Martel
Melancthon
Mendelssohn
Menzel
Mézeray
Mezzofanti
Milton (or medium)
Montaigne
Sir T. More
Montesquieu
Mozart
Narses ('the body of a child')
Philopœmen
Pomponazzi
Lord John Russell
A. del Monte Sansovino
Shaftesbury (first Lord)
C. Smart (called himself a dwarf)
Socinus
Lord Somers
Spencer
Dean Stanley
Timour
Turner
Voiture
Wagner
H. Walpole
Lord Westbury
Wilberforce
Woolner
Wren

By uniting the two classes, and doubling the number of those in the first class, so as to give due weight to their superior accuracy, we reach a result

which may, I think, be regarded as a fair approximation to the actual state of things. It will be found that we thus obtain 142 tall men of genius, 74 of middle height, while 125 are short.*

We may safely conclude from these figures that the faith cherished by many, that nearly all great men are little — a very venerable faith, as indicated by the ancient sayings collected in Burton's *Anatomy of Melancholy* concerning great wits with little bodies — is absolutely incorrect. Some deduction must doubtless be made in view of the fact that our medium is made on the basis of the general population, while the majority of men of genius belong to the educated classes. This deduction would tend to equalise the two extremes; but that it would not destroy the slight pre-eminence of the tall men of ability is perhaps indicated by the fact, shown by the Anthropometric Committee, that the stature of 98 Fellows of the Royal Society (who from the present point of view may be counted as men of genius) was nearly half an inch above that of the professional class to which they usually belong. At the same time it is clear that the belief in the small size of great men was not absolutely groundless. There is an abnormally large propor-

* This result finds confirmation in the examination of a volume entitled *Word Portraits of Famous Writers* (by their contemporaries), which shows out of 116 famous writers 24 short persons, 20 of middle height, and 40 who are tall — *i.e.*, the same general result in a more irregular form. Even if we assume that the remaining 32 were all of middle height, we still have an undue excess of the tall and short.

tion of small 'great men.' It is mediocrity alone that genius seems to abhor. While among the ordinary population the vast majority of 68 per cent was of middle height, among men of genius, so far as the present investigation goes, they are only 22 per cent, the tall being 41 per cent, instead of 16, and the short 37 instead of 16. The approximate equivalence of the two extremes is probably in favour of the results so far as those extremes are concerned; and although, on grounds already mentioned, the figures I have given probably do not represent the exact state of affairs so far as middle height is concerned, there is considerable ground for believing that, while its precise amount may be doubtful, there is really a considerable deficiency of the middle-sized among men of genius.* The curve of height for genius is thus the opposite of that for the ordinary population; and both extremes are present to an abnormal extent.

The final result is, therefore, not that persons of extraordinary mental ability tend either to be taller or shorter than the average population, but rather that they tend to exhibit an unusual tendency to *variation*. Even in physical structure, men of genius present a characteristic which on other grounds we may take to be fundamental in them: they are manifestations of the variational

* This is confirmed by a later inquiry, which I have not seen (*Grand Magazine*, June, 1906), showing that of 250 men and women of intellect, 89 were tall, 83 short, and only 78 of middle size.

tendency, of a physical and psychic variational diathesis. In a slight and elusive shape, a shape so elusive that it is rarely hereditary, the man of genius represents the same kind of phenomenon which, in organic nature generally, appears to have slowly built up the animated world we know. Just as the visible world is the outcome of the accumulated gross variations of plants and animals, so the world of tradition and culture is the outcome of the accumulated delicate variations of men of genius. The product is different, but it has been obtained by the same method.

It would be interesting if we could trace in a more detailed and precise manner the factor of physical stature in the constitution of the genius variation, and ascertain its precise significance. This is still difficult. One or two points may be noted.

It must be remembered that genius, however it may be defined, is certainly only an excessive development of characteristics which may be traced in much more rudimentary forms. It is thus not impossible to throw light on the subject of genius by investigating the peculiarities of physical stature generally, and the common intellectual accompaniments of under-development and over-development. The conclusion we have reached, that both tall and short individuals tend to predominate unduly among persons of genius, is confirmed and to some extent explained by observa-

tion of the general population. The observations so far made, indeed, are few, but so far as they go perfectly definite. Thus Bohannon — who, under the inspiration of Professor Stanley Hall, collected data concerning over one thousand abnormal children in the United States, dividing them into various groups according to the predominant abnormal character — found that both tall children and short children are intellectually superior to children of medium height. The tall (except in cases of very excessive tallness, which may be regarded as pathological) showed their superiority both in general health and mental ability; at the same time they were notable for their sensitiveness, good nature, even temper, and popularity with others. The small were less often healthy, and consequently were apt to be delicate, ugly, or vicious; but when fairly healthy they tended to show very great activity both of body and mind.

These observations, which will no doubt be confirmed, are in harmony with the results of daily experience with children, and they serve not only to support the conclusion we have reached with regard to men of genius, but they also indicate that genius itself is merely the highest form of a common tendency which puts forth its tender buds in every schoolroom.

It would still remain to show the causes of this tendency; for it is scarcely possible to hold that the

health and ability of the tall is due (as has apparently been suggested) to forced association with their elders in youth, and quite absurd to hold that the activity and mental quickness of the small is due to the arrested development caused by forced association with their juniors. In both cases it seems probable that the primary cause is a greater vital activity, however we may ultimately have to define 'vital activity.' Among the tall such intensity of vital action has shown itself in unimpeded freedom; in the short it is impeded and forced into new channels by pathological or other causes. The latter case is perhaps the more interesting and complicated. An anthropometric examination of short men of genius would throw much light on this question. There are certainly at least two types of short men of genius: the slight, frail, but fairly symmetrical type (approaching what is called the true dwarf), and the type of the stunted giant (a type also to be found among dwarfs proper). The former are fairly symmetrical, but fragile; generally with little physical vigour or health, all their energy being concentrated in the brain. Kant was of this type. The stunted giants are usually more vigorous, but lacking in symmetry. Far from being delicately diminutive persons, they suggest tall persons who have been cut short below; in such the brain and viscera seem to flourish at the expense of the limbs, and while abnormal they often have the good fortune to be

robust both in mind and body. Lord Chesterfield was a man of this type, short for his size, thick-set, 'with a head big enough for a Polyphemus'; Hartley Coleridge carried the same type to the verge of caricature, possessing a large head, a sturdy and ample form, with ridiculously small arms and legs, so that he was said to be 'indescribably elfish and grotesque.' Dryden — 'Poet Squab' — was again of this type, as was William Godwin; in Keats the abnormally short legs co-existed with a small head. The typical stunted giant has a large head; and such stunting of the body has, indeed, a special tendency to produce large heads, and therefore doubtless those large brains which are usually associated with extraordinary intellectual power. It is a curious fact — as a distinguished anatomist, the late Sir George Humphrey, remarked many years ago — that when from any cause the growth of the rest of the body is stunted, the head not only remains disproportionately large, but often becomes actually larger than in ordinary persons. 'Thus short persons and persons with imperfectly developed lower extremities are not uncommonly remarkable for the size of their heads, as though the expenditure of growing force being too great in one direction, other parts are ill-cared for.'* It may be added that the commonest type of dwarf

* Humphrey, *The Human Skeleton*, p. 96. We may perhaps regard these people as highly developed on a basis of infantilism. They need to be studied along the lines laid down by Kretschmer.

possesses a proportionally large head and short legs.

It would doubtless be an attractive task to attempt to trace the causes which lead genius to be associated at once with both abnormal extremes of stature. It must probably be found at an early period of embryonic development, when, as we know from the researches of Dareste and others, the causes of dwarfism may also be found, sometimes in arrest of growth resulting from precocious development. Here, however, it is enough to have ascertained the facts in a roughly approximate fashion. It need only be pointed out, in conclusion, that the result we have reached, although apparently new, is such a result as should have been expected. Geoffroy Saint-Hilaire long since, and Ranke more recently, have pointed out that both giants and dwarfs — the abnormally tall and the abnormally short — are usually abnormal in other respects also. From the biological point of view we know nothing of 'genius,' what is so termed being simply an abnormal aptitude of brain function; so that among those variations and abnormalities which, as is already generally agreed, we find with unusual frequency among the very tall and the very short, extraordinary mental aptitude ought sometimes to occur.

XVI

THE COMPARATIVE ABILITIES OF THE FAIR AND THE DARK

The hair-colour and eye-colour of the British population — The National Portrait Gallery — Eye-colour the chief criterion — The index of pigmentation — The royal family — The aristocracy — The pigmentary character of different groups — Characteristics of the fair and the dark.

We know something concerning the hair-colour and eye-colour of the general population. Many observations have been made on this point during recent years, not only among continental nations but in all parts of the British Islands. It may indeed be said that it was an Englishman, Dr. John Beddoe, who first realised the interest of such observations, and carried them out on a wide scale. To him chiefly we owe the map which shows the relative fairness and darkness of the population of our islands.* When we look at this map we see that there is a certain order in the distribution of the fair population and the dark population, that the fair people are, on the whole, arranged along the eastern sides of the two islands and the dark people along the western sides, so that in each island as we go from east to west the population tends to become darker.

* Much more thorough surveys of special regions have since been made, such as Tocher's 'Pigmentation Survey of School-Children in Scotland,' *Biometrika*, vol. VI, 1908.

At this point, however, it may be said that our knowledge ends. We know which districts of the country are mainly fair and which mainly dark; we even know where particular types of fairness and darkness are chiefly to be found, but we do not know how different classes of the population differ from each other in this respect. It is true that certain results have been reached here too, and for these also we are indebted to Dr. Beddoe, though they were not obtained by the method of direct observation. Dr. Beddoe found, by examining a very large number of the descriptions of 'Persons Wanted' in the *Police Gazette*, that there is a great difference in average degrees of fairness between people of different occupations, more especially that while men connected with horses and cattle, such as grooms and butchers, are notably fair, shoemakers and tailors tend to be notably dark. No doubt such observations will in time be made directly on the general population, and we shall know the relative proportions of the fair and the dark among people following every occupation.

I have not attempted any inquiry of this kind. But I have endeavoured to carry out a somewhat allied inquiry by examining the portraits of eminent persons, and comparing the fairness or darkness of different groups of such persons. The National Portrait Gallery contains portraits of several thousand persons who in some way or other have acquired eminence during the past six hundred

years, and I therefore selected this Gallery for study as furnishing a specially favourable field for the investigation of the question.

This inquiry was by no means so easy as it might appear at the first glance. I have spent many hours in the Gallery, during a period extending over nearly two years, in making the necessary observations. I cannot regret the hours spent in the company of so many wise and noble and gracious personages. But I have acquired a certain scepticism as to the fidelity both of those who paint and those who write portraits. In many cases the painted statements concerning the same person are absolutely unlike; in many cases the painted statements are absolutely unlike the written statements of those who knew the originals. In other cases the discrepancies, though less marked, are still sufficiently considerable to be painful to a careful investigator. I soon realised that the artist was on the whole much more reliable than the literary observer, but, on the other hand, if the artist happens to be dominated by the desire to obtain his own effects at all costs to truth, he may lead us hopelessly astray. An amusing instance of the confusion thus produced many be seen in the neighbouring National Gallery, where Millais in his portrait of Gladstone has represented one eye blue, the other brown. Nor are these the only difficulties with which the anthropologist must contend in the National Portrait Gallery. The age

of a picture may dim or discolour what was once clear and definite, and the same result is attained when a picture is hung high up on the walls in the murky London air. Again, the age of the sitter often enables us to do no more than guess at the probable colour of his hair, or the fashion of his time may have covered it with a wig. Yet when all allowance is made for these causes of error, and a certain amount of care and discretion has been exercised, dubious cases severely disregarded, differing portraits of the same person duly compared, it is still possible to obtain fairly reliable results in the majority of instances.

I decided to take eye-colour as the chief criterion of pigmentation, in preference to hair-colour, mainly on the ground that the eyes were visible in a larger number of cases than the hair. At the same time, hair was also taken into consideration as a secondary criterion, and the judgment as to fairness or darkness obtained from the eyes was modified, if necessary, by that obtained from the hair; thus a person of the so-called 'Celtic' type, with light eyes and dark hair, would be classed as medium. It was scarcely practicable to take into account the actual complexion, and as the depth of colouring of the skin on the whole follows that of the hair and the eyes, it was unnecessary. I found that the degree of precision attainable with my material enabled me to classify my subjects into three classes: light, medium, dark.

The ordinary words used to describe the colour of the eyes, it may not be unnecessary to remark, are very vague and inaccurate. In reality the iris varies from blue (in which case there is a total lack of pigment), through blue-yellow, blue-orange, blue-orange-brown in various combinations, to brown (in which case there is full pigmentation). I find that descriptive writers speak of 'blue' eyes with considerable licence, even when the eye is only very partially blue, while they use the unsatisfactory word 'grey' to describe what is really a blue-yellow eye; 'black' is also liberally applied, usually to brown eyes. There are in reality no black eyes; in examining portraits, however, one sometimes meets with apparently black eyes, which may either be brown or blue, a serious source of confusion, for we thus run the risk of making a totally wrong classification. Thus the eyes of Charles I sometimes seem to be black; in reality they were dark blue.* I have of course omitted the cases in which this important distinction cannot be made with fair probability. Of the three classes — light, medium, dark — into which I have classified all those individuals in the National Portrait Gallery whose portraits enable us to classify them, the first class contains those with completely or almost completely blue eyes and fair

* The same may be said of his daughter Henriette d'Angleterre, whose eyes were greatly admired in France, but while by most of those who knew her they were called blue, by some they were called black.

or brown hair; the last class includes those with completely or almost completely brown eyes and brown or black hair; the medium class includes those whose eyes are of intermediate colour and who usually have brown hair. As already mentioned, any striking contrast between hair-colour and eye-colour involved some shifting of class.

In this way it was possible to ascertain that so many among the distinguished persons represented in the Gallery were fair, so many dark, and so many of intermediate colouring. This result, however, was obviously of no very extraordinary interest. To realise its significance we should have to obtain for comparison a corresponding series of undistinguished persons, and even then we should have to recognise that the personages represented in the Gallery are an extremely miscellaneous collection. In order to obtain results that are really of interest we must break up our data into groups. I have therefore divided the individuals whose colouring I have been able to ascertain into sixteen different groups, according to social rank, occupation, etc., these groups in some cases overlapping, so that one individual sometimes appears in more than one group. It was then possible to ascertain the number of fair, medium, and dark persons in each of the sixteen groups. But it was still necessary to find a convenient method of comparison by reducing the three figures in each group to one figure. To attain this I divided the medium persons

in each group equally between the fair and dark persons, thus reducing the three figures to two, and then I multiplied the fair persons in each group by 100 and divided by the number of dark persons. Thus — in accordance with a method well recognised in anthropology and by which, for instance, the cephalic index is ascertained by measuring the breadth and length of the head — I obtained what may be called the index of pigmentation.*

With these preliminary explanations I can present the results of my investigation. In the following enumeration the groups are arranged in the order of decreasing fairness:

Group with Number of Individuals	Index of Pigmentation
Political Reformers and Agitators (20)	233
Sailors (45)	150
Men of Science (53)	121
Soldiers (42)	113
Artists (74)	111
Poets (56)	107
Royal Family (66)	107
Lawyers (56)	107
Created Peers and their Sons (89)	102
Statesmen (53)	89
Men and Women of Letters (87)	85
Hereditary Aristocracy (149)	82
Divines (57)	58
Men of Low Birth (12)	50
Explorers (8)	33
Actors and Actresses (16)	33

An index of more than 100 means that the fair

* It was not possible for me to adopt Beddoe's index of nigrescence, used for tabulating the results of direct observation of hair-colour on living persons, since I had not found it feasible to make hair-colour the primary basis of classification.

element predominates over the dark in that group, an index of less than 100 means that the dark element predominates. I may add that the lists include persons of both sexes.

The results presented in this simple table — results which in part give precision to recognised tendencies and in part are entirely novel — might well be expounded at considerable length. It will, however, be enough to comment on a few of the conclusions which most clearly emerge.

In the first place, as regards the royal family and the aristocracy, it may seem that the prevalent belief which credits the upper classes with a pronounced tendency to blondness — and which finds expression in the ancient belief, of Spanish origin, in the 'blueness' of noble blood, *sangre azul*, because the veins of fair people are blue — is here shown to be fallacious. That, however, is not the case. It must be remembered that the ordinary population of the middle and lower classes is only slenderly represented in the National Portrait Gallery. It is, however, noteworthy that the small group of persons springing from the working classes is among the darkest of the groups, decidedly darker than any of the aristocratic groups. As regards the royal family, it has also to be remembered that the results have been affected by perpetual infusions of foreign blood from nearly every European country, and as most European populations are darker complexioned than the

English, it is not surprising that the tendency of the royal family to fairness has thus been somewhat reduced. The study of the physical characteristics of the royal family through many centuries is of considerable interest. The early tendency was towards fairness, but by late Tudor times there was a tendency towards darkness, for Henry VIII seems to have inherited his mother's dark eyes, and though Mary I possessed the blue-grey eyes of her Spanish mother and Edward VI's light eyes were presumably inherited from Jane Seymour, Queen Elizabeth inherited brown eyes, probably from both parents. James I brought in a muddy blue Scotch eye, which was probably derived from his father, but Charles I's dark blue eyes were apparently identical with those of his Danish mother. Charles married Henrietta Maria, whose eyes were a clear brown, and two of the children followed the father, two the mother, while two others, in early life at all events, apparently possessed eyes of intermediate colour. The last representatives of the Stuart family were brown-eyed, for though James II (unlike his brother Charles II) inherited his father's eyes, he married a dark Italian wife, whose influence was impressed on all the descendants. William III (like most of the Dutch Orange family) was very dark, and so was Mary II. George I, with his mixed German, Stuart, and Orange blood, brought in a type of mixed eye which had hitherto been apparently

rare in the royal family; in his case it was a dark greenish-brown eye; he married a French wife who appears to have been dark, but while his daughter inherited his eyes, his son, George II, though still showing a mixed eye, is unaccountably fair. This is one of the few slight anomalies we meet with in studying the royal family, and perhaps indicates a return to the fair German grandfather. This light mixed type of eye, usually blue-yellow, has remained persistent, accentuated or increased by German intermarriages, and still prevails at the present day.

The study of the royal family in the National Portrait Gallery is of considerable interest, for, except during the early periods, few links are missing, and it is easy to see how strictly eye-colour is inherited, the rule being — as was noted by Galton and is familiar, indeed, to every observant person — that the eye-colour of the child follows that of one or other of the parents and is very seldom a blend of both parents.

The review of these facts clearly shows also that the average blondness of the English royal family has been modified mainly by intermixture with darker foreign royal stocks, though it may well be that these stocks were fairer than the average population of the countries they belonged to. Our evidence, therefore, indicates that the blondness of the English royal family has been maintained at a considerable height in spite of opposing foreign influences.

If we turn to the hereditary aristocracy, we again find a lower index of pigmentation than we should have been inclined to expect. Foreign intermixture here also may have had some influence. I think it probable, however, that another cause has come into operation; peers have been in a position to select as wives, and have tended to select, the most beautiful women, and there can be little doubt that the most beautiful women, at all events in Great Britain, have tended more to be dark than to be fair. This is proved by the low index of pigmentation of the famous beauties in the Gallery, the selection being made solely on the basis of reputation, independently of any personal judgment of the portraits; while women of letters (fifteen in number) are inclined to be fair and have an index of 100, the index of thirteen famous beauties is as dark as 44. The same tendency is, indeed, illustrated by any series of famous beauties by Reynolds or Romney, and has probably been an important factor, though not the only one, in darkening the old aristocracy.

Our index of pigmentation shows, however, that the new aristocracy is fairer than the old. This seems to be one of the most novel and interesting facts revealed in the whole of this investigation. It answers the question: Why are the aristocracy fair? We see that the aristocracy tend to be fairer than the ordinary population because it is from the fair elements in the ordinary population that the

aristocracy is chiefly recruited. In other words, the fair tend to attain greater success than the dark in those careers which most frequently lead to the peerage. Thus it is that both created peers and their sons (whether taken together or in two separate groups) are decidedly fairer than the old aristocracy. For the same reason lawyers, soldiers and sailors, who all tend towards the peerage, more especially lawyers, also markedly tend to be fair; statesmen, it is true, are not much fairer than the old aristocracy, but that is because they are largely taken from that very class.

A very significant fact, it seems to me, is the extremely high index of pigmentation of the group of political reformers and agitators. These are not persons who reach the House of Lords; their opinions are too radical, they are too violently opposed to the powers that be. But they possess in an extreme degree the sanguine irrepressible energy, the great temporal ambitions, the personal persuasive force, the oratorical aptitudes that in a minor degree tend to mark the class that rises to the aristocracy; it is therefore a notable and curious fact that their index of pigmentation should be as extreme as their mental attitudes and convictions.

If we turn away from the groups which are or tend to become aristocratic, we find that men of science (among whom are here included philosophers and inventors) present a strikingly high index. This seems to be due to the fact that scien-

tific aptitude occurs with especial frequency in the north of England and in Scotland, the most peculiarly fair region of Great Britain, the region, it may be noted also, which has contained the most progressive and successful populations. The fairness of the group of artists, again, must be associated with the fact that artists tend largely to come from among the fair populations along the east coast of England and Scotland. I have noted a similar fairness in an even more marked degree among modern artists in France, who also tend to come from the fairest parts of their country. The fairness of the group of poets can scarcely be put down to a similar cause, for poets are produced by every part of the country.

The large and important group of men of letters, on the other hand, cannot be called predominantly fair; the divines are still darker, and this is so even as regards those among them (like Knox) who were reformers and agitators. The class of men of low birth (including numerous persons of intellectual distinction) is very dark. The actors and the explorers are the darkest of all.

If for the present we neglect the consideration of separate groups and seek to look more broadly at the matter, it seems to me that we may find one or two tendencies fairly well marked. It is clear that a high index of pigmentation, or an excess of fairness, prevails among the men of restless and ambitious temperament, the sanguine energetic

men, the men who easily dominate their fellows and who get on in life, the men who recruit the aristocracy and who doubtless largely form the plutocracy. It is significant that the group of low-class men — artisans and peasants — and the men of religion, whose mission in life it is to practise and preach resignation to a Higher Will, are both notably of dark complexion.

While the men of action thus tend to be fair, the men of thought, it seems to me, show some tendency to be dark. This latter tendency is by no means so clear from the data before us as the other tendency. Still it is indicated, and it would be still clearer if we were to subdivide our groups according to the intellectual eminence of the individuals comprised within them; it would then generally be found, I believe, that in each group the more intellectual showed a somewhat lower index of pigmentation. It is noteworthy that the men of letters, whose intellectual achievements are on the whole decidedly greater, if less brilliant, than those of the poets, show a lower index of pigmentation. It may be said, also, regarding the men of low social class, that though their darkness is partly explainable, as we have seen, on other grounds, they are mostly men of marked intellectual force. If this is so, the dark people may be said to have their consolations; they are by no means lacking in intellectual force, and probably possess such power in a higher average degree than the fair men. The

latter, by virtue of their greater executive energy, are often able to achieve success in the world with the possession of a comparatively minor, though often very considerable, inheritance of intelligence. But the dark men are better able to learn the wisdom that teaches the vanity of worldly success.*

I have hitherto said nothing concerning two groups which may seem somewhat anomalous. I refer to the two darkest groups of all, the explorers and the actors. It may be thought that the darkness of the explorers contradicts the conclusion we have just reached that the people of restless energy tend to be fair. But here a totally new consideration enters into the question. Pigmentation, it is well recognised, is a protection. The veil of dark pigment which the organism weaves for itself against the sun in summer bears evidence to this fact, and there is some reason to believe also that dark persons resist disease better than the fair. The pioneering exploits of sailors, being aided by the climatically modifying influence of the sea and being mostly in cold climates, involve no selection of dark persons. Our group of explorers, however, mostly travellers in the extremely trying climates of tropical lands, especially Africa, have needed all the assistance that constitutional

* As a reader is apt to suspect that any writer on such points as this is moved by personal bias, it may, perhaps, be well to state that the present writer belongs to the medium group, and is therefore able to view this series of phenomena with, as Huxley expressed it, the serene impartiality of the mongrel.

peculiarities furnish; and the life has proved too arduous for the fair, who have mostly succumbed or been discouraged. Thus it is that our most eminent and experienced explorers in hot climates are mostly men of dark eyes and hair.

I cannot furnish so unquestionable an explanation of the darkness of actors, though the phenomena are here at least equally well marked. There have been a few moderately fair actors and actresses of eminence, but scarcely any of them have been of the highest eminence. The Kemble family, to which Mrs. Siddons belonged, was dark, and Garrick was extremely dark. So far as I am aware, no really fair person has ever risen to the highest dramatic eminence in England, and so far as I have been able to observe, it is equally rare for fairness to be associated with histrionic ability in Europe generally. It may certainly be said that in Great Britain the darkest populations are those most fertile in ability of this kind, and also that actors tend, to a considerable extent, to spring from the lower, and darker, social classes. Whether these facts suffice to account for this phenomenon, or whether we must go deeper and assume that the special metabolic processes associated with the organic manufacture of pigment are also associated with dramatic faculty is not clear. I am not at present disposed to accept it, though it is scarcely beyond the bounds of possibility that, other things being equal, a certain kind

of nervous texture, involving a predisposition to certain intellectual aptitudes, may be directly connected with the greater or less tendency to manufacture pigment. It is necessary to introduce the proviso, 'other things being equal,' for we certainly could not assert generally that the unpigmented person or albino shows a native tendency to enter the aristocracy (notwithstanding the case of Lord Sherbrooke), while the existence of highly pigmented lower races suffices to show that pigment alone will not confer intellectual aptitude.

The more reasonable supposition at present seems to be that the relation between pigmentation and mental aptitude is chiefly indirect, and due to race. In other words, the fair man tends to be bold, energetic, restless and domineering, not because he is fair, but because he belongs to an aboriginal fair stock of people who possess those qualities; while the dark man tends to be resigned and religious and imitative, yet highly intelligent, not because he is dark, but because he belongs to a dark stock possessing those characteristics.

An interesting sidelight is thrown on this question by considering the phenomena as they exist in a country having a racial composition in some respects comparable to Great Britain, and, without doubt, closely related to its peoples. In Norway there are, as in Great Britain, fair and dark stocks, the former usually long-headed, the latter broad-headed, and there also the darker stock is, on the

whole, placed more to the south and west of the country. It so happens that a very interesting and acute psychological study of the fair and dark populations of Norway has been made by Dr. A. M. Hansen. This investigation has revealed differences even more marked between the fair and the dark than may easily be discovered in our own islands, and this is not surprising since our racial elements have been more thoroughly mixed. The fair population, he tells us, is made up of born aristocrats, active, outspoken, progressive, with a passion for freedom and independence, caring nothing for equality; the dark population is reserved and suspicious, very conservative, and lacking in initiative, caring little for freedom, but with a passion for equality. The fair people are warlike, quarrelsome when drunk, and furnish, in proportion to numbers, three times as many men for the volunteer force as the dark people; the latter, though brave sailors, abhor war, and are very religious, subscribing to foreign missions nearly three times as much per head as is furnished by the fair people, who are inclined to be irreligious. The fair people value money and all that money can buy, while the dark people are indifferent to money. The reality of the mental distinction is shown by the fact that a map of the proportion of Conservative voters in elections to the Storthing exactly corresponds to an anthropological map of the country, the Conservative majority being found

in the dark and broad-headed districts. While, however, the fair population is the most irreligious and progressive, the dark population is by no means behind in the production of intellect, and the region it inhabits has produced many eminent men.

I have referred to Hansen's remarkable study of Norwegian psychology because it shows that, in a country somewhat allied to England in racial composition, much the same tendency for definite intellectual aptitude to be associated with definite physical types may be traced. There are some discrepancies, it is true; England's dark population is not attracted to seafaring and is by no means specially apt to take the Conservative side in politics. It is probable, indeed, that while the fair population of Norway is without doubt closely allied to our own fair population, the dark population may only be remotely related to ours, which is not broad-headed. Thus, this parallel by no means proves conclusively that the association between special mental aptitudes and pigmentary tendencies can be resolved entirely into a question of race. It may also be remarked that the characteristics of the fair population are especially masculine qualities, while the characteristics of the dark population are more peculiarly feminine qualities; it so happens also that women, as is now beginning to be generally recognised by anthropologists, tend to be somewhat darker than men. Even this fact, however, may possibly receive a racial explanation.

It would, in any case, be rash to state any broad and far-reaching conclusions concerning an inquiry which is still so novel. It is enough for the present that, when we carefully study so large a collection of the representations of eminent British persons as that constituting the National Portrait Gallery, it is possible to show that in the different classes of mental aptitude the proportion of fair and dark persons varies widely, and in some cases to indicate why this is so.

THE END

APPENDICES

APPENDIX A

LIST OF EMINENT BRITISH PERSONS OF ABILITY

(*The names of women are italicised.*)

Abbot, G. (1562–1633)
Abercromby, Sir R. (1734–1801)
Abington, F. (1737–1815)
Adam, R. (1728–1792)
Adams, J. C. (1819–1892)
Adamson, P. (1537–1592)
Addison, J. (1672–1719)
Adrian IV. (——1159)
Ainsworth, H. (1571–1622)
Airy, Sir G. (1801–1892)
Alcuin (735–804)
Alesius, A. (1500–1565)
Alexander of Hales (——1245)
Alexander, W., Earl of Stirling (1567–1640)
Allen, W. (1532–1594)
Amherst, J., Baron (1717–1797)
Andrewes, L. (1555–1626)
Anson, G., Baron (1697–1762)
Arblay, F. d' (1752–1840)
Arkwright, Sir R. (1732–1792)
Arne, T. (1710–1778)
Arnold, M. (1822–1888)
Arnold, T. (1795–1842)
Arthur, Sir G. (1784–1854)
Ascham, R. (1515–1568)
Atterbury, F. (1662–1732)
Austen, J. (1775–1817)
Austin, J. (1790–1859)

Babbage, C. (1792–1871)
Bacon, A. (1558–1601)
Bacon, F., Lord Verulam (1561–1626)
Bacon, Sir N. (1509–1579)
Bacon, R. (1214?–1294)
Bagehot, W. (1826–1877)
Baillie, J. (1762–1851)
Baily, F. (1774–1844)
Baker, Sir S. (1821–1893)
Balfe, M. W. (1808–1870)
Balfour, F. (1851–1882)
Bancroft, R. (1544–1610)
Banim, J. (1798–1842)
Banks, Sir J. (1743–1820)
Banks, T. (1735–1805)
Bannister, J. (1760–1836)
Barbauld, A. (1743–1825)
Barbour, J. (1316?–1395)
Barclay, A. (1475?–1552)
Barclay, J. (1582–1621)
Barclay, R. (1648–1690)
Barham, R. (1788–1845)
Barnes, W. (1801–1886)
Barnfield, R. (1574–1627)
Barrow, I. (1630–1677)
Barrow, Sir J. (1764–1848)
Barry, A. (1734–1801)
Barry, Sir C. (1795–1860)
Barry, E. (1658–1713)
Barry, J. (1741–1806)
Baskerville, J. (1706–1775)
Bateman, W. (1298?–1355)
Bates, H. W. (1825–1892)
Baxter, R. (1615–1691)
Beardsley, A. (1872–1898)
Beaton, D. (1494–1546)
Beaumont, F. (1584–1616)
Becher, E., Lady (1791–1872)
Beckford, W. (1759–1844)
Beddoes, T. (1803–1849)
Bede (673–735)
Bedell, W. (1571–1642)
Behn, A. (1640–1689)
Bell, A. (1753–1832)
Bell, Sir C. (1774–1842)
Bennett, Sir W. S. (1816–1875)
Benson, E. (1829–1896)
Bentham, G. (1800–1884)
Bentham, J. (1748–1832)
Bentley, R. (1662–1742)
Berkeley, G. (1685–1753)
Bessemer, Sir H. (1813–1898)
Bethell, R., Lord Westbury (1800–1873)
Betterton, T. (1635–1710)
Bewick, T. (1753–1828)
Bingham, J. (1668–1723)
Birch, S. (1813–1885)

Bishop, Sir H. (1786–1855)
Black, J. (1728–1799)
Blackmore, R. (1825–1900)
Blackstone, Sir W. (1723–1780)
Blake, R. (1599–1657)
Blake, W. (1757–1827)
Blow, J. (1648–1708)
Boece, H. (1465?–1536)
Boniface, St. (680–755)
Bonington, R. P. (1801–1828)
Bonner, E. (1500?–1569)
Booth, B. (1681–1733)
Borrow, G. (1803–1881)
Boscawen, E. (1711–1761)
Boswell, J. (1740–1795)
Bowen, C., Baron (1835–1894)
Bowring, Sir J. (1792–1872)
Boyce, W. (1710–1779)
Boyle, A., Earl of Cork (1566–1643)
Boyle, R. (1627–1691)
Bracegirdle, A. (1663–1748)
Bradford, W. (1590–1657)
Bradlaugh, C. (1833–1891)
Bradley, J. (1693–1762)
Bradshaw, H. (1831–1886)
Bradshaw, W. (1571–1618)
Bradwardine (1290?–1349)
Breton, N. (1545?–1626)
Brewster, Sir D. (1781–1868)
Bright, J. (1811–1889)
Broke, Sir P. (1776–1841)
Brontë, C. (1816–1855)
Brontë, E. (1818–1848)
Brooke, Sir J. (1803–1868)
Brougham, Lord (1778–1868)
Brown, F. M. (1821–1893)
Browne, H. K. (1815–1882)
Browne, R. (1550?–1633?)
Browne, Sir T. (1605–1682)
Browne, W. (1591–1643?)
Browning, E. B. (1806–1861)
Browning, R. (1812–1889)
Bruce, H., Baron Aberdare (1815–1895)
Bruce, J. (1730–1794)
Bruce, M. (1746–1767)
Buchanan, G. (1506–1582)
Buckle, H. T. (1821–1862)
Bull, J. (1563?–1628)
Bunyan J. (1628–1688)
Burbage, R. (1567?–1619)
Burges, C. (1589–1665)
Burke, E. (1729–1787)
Burne-Jones, Sir E. (1833–1898)
Burnet, G. (1643–1715)
Burns, R. (1759–1796)
Burton, Sir R. (1821–1890)
Burton, R. (1577–1640)
Butler, J. (1692–1752)
Butler, S. (1612–1680)
Butterfield, W. (1814–1900)
Byng, G., Viscount Torrington (1663–1733)
Byrd, W. 1538–1623)
Byron, G., Lord (1788–1824)

Cade, J. (——1450)
Cadogan, W., Earl (1675–1726)
Cædmon (*fl.* 670)
Cairns, H., Earl (1819–1885)
Caius, J. (1510–1573)
Calamy, E. (1671–1732)
Camden, W. (1551–1623)
Campbell, Sir C. (1792–1863)
Campbell, Sir G. (1824–1892)
Campbell, J., Baron (1779–1861)
Campbell, T. (1777–1844)
Campion, E. (1540–1581)
Campion, T. (——1619)
Candlish, R. (1806–1873)
Canning, C., Earl (1812–1862)
Canning, G. (1770–1827)
Canning, S., Viscount S. de Redcliffe (1786–1880)
Cantelupe, St. T. de (1218?–1282)
Canton, J. (1718–1772)
Carey, W. (1761–1834)
Carleton, W. (1794–1869)
Carlile, R. (1790–1843)
Carlyle, T. (1795–1881)
Carpenter, M. (1807–1877)
Carpenter, W. B. (1813–1885)
Carrington, R. (1826–1875)
Carstares, W. (1649–1715)
Cartwright, T. (1535–1603)
Case, T. (1598–1682)
Cattermole, G. (1800–1868)
Cavendish, H. (1731–1810)
Cavendish, M., Duchess of Newcastle (1624?–1674)
Cavendish, T. (1555?–1592)
Caxton, W. (1422?–1491)
Cayley, A. (1821–1895)
Cecil, W., Lord Burghley (1520–1598)
Centlivre, S. (1667?–1723)
Challoner, R. (1691–1781)
Chalmers, T. (1780–1847)
Chantry, Sir F. (1781–1842)
Chapman, G. (1559?–1634)
Chatterton, T. (1752–1770)
Chaucer, G. (1340?–1400)
Cheke, Sir J. (1514–1557)
Cheselden, W. (1688–1752)
Chesney, F. (1789–1872)

Chichele, H. (1362–1443)
Chichester, A. Lord (1563–1625)
Childers, H. (1827–1896)
Chillingworth, W. (1602–1644)
Church, R. (1815–1890)
Churchill, C. (1731–1764)
Churchill, J., Duke of Marlborough (1650–1722)
Cibber, C. (1671–1757)
Cibber, S. (1714–1766)
Clapperton, H. (1788–1827)
Clare, J. (1793–1864)
Clarke, S. (1675–1729)
Clifford, W. G. (1845–1879)
Clive, K. (1711–1785)
Clive, R., Lord (1725–1774)
Clough, A. (1819–1861)
Cobbett, W. (1762–1835)
Cobden, R. (1804–1865)
Cockburn, Sir A. (1802–1880)
Cockerell, C. (1788–1863)
Coke, Sir E. (1552–1634)
Colby, T. (1784–1852)
Colebrooke, H. T. (1765–1837)
Colenso, J. (1814–1883)
Coleridge, H. (1796–1849)
Coleridge, S. T. (1772–1834)
Colet, J. (1467–1519)
Collier, J. (1630–1726)
Collins, W. (1721–1759)
Collins, W. W. (1824–1889)
Colman, G., the elder (1732–1794)
Columba, St. (521–597)
Columban, St. (543–615)
Congreve, W. (1670–1729)
Conington, J. (1825–1869)
Constable, J. (1776–1837)
Cook, J. (1728–1779)
Cooke, G. F. (1756–1811)
Cooke, H. (1788–1868)
Cooper, A., First Lord Shaftesbury (1621–1683)
Cooper, A., Third Lord Shaftesbury (1671–1713)
Cooper, Sir A. (1768–1841)
Cooper, S., (1609–1672)
Copley, J. S. (1737–1815)
Copley, J. S., Lord Lyndhurst (1772–1863)
Cosin, J. (1594–1672)
Cotes, R. (1682–1716)
Cotman, J. (1782–1842)
Cotton, Sir A. T. (1803–1899)
Cotton, C. (1630–1687)
Cotton, Sir R. (1571–1631)
Coutances, W. de (——1207)
Coverdale, M. (1488–1568)
Cowley, A. (1618–1667)
Cowley, H. (1743–1809)
Cowper, W. (1731–1800)
Cox, D. (1783–1859)
Cozens, J. R. (1752–1799)
Crabbe, G. (1754–1832)
Cranmer, T. (1489–1556)
Crashaw, R. (1612–1649)
Creighton, M. (1843–1901)
Crichton, J. (1560–1585?)
Croker, J. W. (1780–1857)
Crome, J. (1768–1821)
Cromwell, O. (1599–1658)
Cromwell, T. (1485?–1540)
Cross, M. A. (1819–1880)
Cruikshank, G. (1792–1878)
Cudworth, R. (1617–1688)
Cullen, W. (1710–1790)
Curran, J. P. (1750–1817)
Cuthbert, St. (——687)

Dalrymple, J., Viscount Stair (1619–1695)
Dalton, J. (1766–1844)
Dampier, W. (1652–1715)
Danby, F. (1793–1861)
Daniel, S. (1562–1619)
Darwin, C. (1809–1882)
Darwin, E. (1731–1802)
D'Avenant, Sir W. (1606–1668)
Davies, Sir J. (1569–1626)
Davy, Sir H. (1778–1829)
Dawson, H. (1811–1878)
Day, T. (1748–1789)
Deane, R. (1610–1653)
Dee, J. (1527–1608)
Defoe, D. (1659–1731)
Dekker, T. (1570?–1641?)
De Morgan, A. (1806–1871)
Dempster, T. (1579?–1625)
Denham, Sir J. (1615–1669)
Denman, Lord (1779–1854)
De Quincey, T. (1785–1859)
D'Ewes, Sir S. (1602–1650)
Dibdin, C. (1745–1814)
Dickens, C. (1812–1870)
Digby, Sir K. (1603–1665)
Dobell, S. (1824–1874)
Dobson, W. (1610–1646)
Doddridge, P. (1702–1751)
Dodgson, C. (1832–1898)
Dodwell, H. (1641–1711)
Dolben, J. (1625–1686)
Donne, J. (1573–1631)
Douglas, G. (1474?–1522)
Dowland, J. (1563?–1626)
Doyle, R. (1824–1883)

Drake, Sir F. (1540?–1596)
Drayton, M. (1563–1631)
Drummond, T. (1797–1840)
Drummond, W. (1585–1649)
Dryden, J. (1631–1700)
Dudley, J., Duke of Northumberland (1502–1553)
Duff, A. (1806–1878)
Dugdale, Sir W. (1605–1686)
Du Maurier, G. (1834–1896)
Dunbar, W. (1465?–1530?)
Duncan, A., Viscount (1731–1804)
Dundas, H., Viscount Melville (1742–1811)
Dunning, J., Baron Ashburton (1731–1783)
Duns, J. S. (1265?–1308?)
Dunstan, St. (924–988)
D'Urfey, T. (1653–1723)
Dyce, W. (1806–1864)

Eastlake, Sir C. (1793–1865)
Eastlake, Lady (1809–1893)
Edgeworth, M. (1767–1849)
Edmund, St. (1170?–1240)
Edwardes, Sir H. (1819–1868)
Edwards, A. B. (1831–1892)
Eliot, Sir J. (1592–1632)
Elliston, R. W. (1774–1831)
Elyot, Sir T. (1490–1546)
Emlyn, T. (1663–1741)
Erskine, E. (1680–1754)
Etherege, Sir G. (1634–1691?)
Etty, W. (1787–1849)

Faber, F. (1814–1863)
Falconer, H. (1808–1865)
Fanshawe, Sir R. (1608–1666)
Faraday, M. (1791–1867)
Farquhar, G. (1678–1707)
Faucit, H. (1817–1898)
Fawcett, H. (1833–1884)
Ferguson, J. (1710–1776)
Fergusson, R. (1750–1774)
Ferrar, N. (1592–1637)
Ferrier, S. (1782–1854)
Fielding, H. (1707–1754)
Fitzgerald, E. (1809–1883)
Fitzgibbon, J., Earl of Clare (1749–1802)
Flamsteed, J. (1646–1719)
Flaxman, J. (1755–1826)
Fletcher, A. (1655–1716)
Fletcher, J. (1579–1625)
Flinders, M. (1774–1814)
Flood, H. (1732–1791)
Flower, Sir W. (1831–1899)
Foote, S. (1720–1777)
Forbes, E. (1815–1854)
Forbes, J. D. (1809–1868)
Ford, J. (1586–1639?)
Forster, W. E. (1818–1886)
Fortescue, Sir J. (1394–1476?)
Fox, C. J. (1749–1806)
Fox, G. (1624–1691)
Foxe, J. (1516–1587)
Foxe, R. (1448?–1528)
Francis, Sir P. (1740–1818)
Frankland, Sir E. (1825–1899)
Franklin, Sir J. (1786–1847)
Franks, Sir A. (1826–1897)
Freeman, E. (1823–1892)
Frere, Sir B. (1815–1884)
Frobisher, Sir M. (1535–1594)
Froude, J. A. (1818–1894)
Fry, E. (1780–1845)
Fuller, T. (1608–1661)

Gainsborough, T. (1727–1788)
Galt, J. (1779–1839)
Gardiner, S. (1483?–1555)
Garnett, H. (1555–1606)
Garrick, D. (1717–1779)
Gascoigne, G. (1523?–1579)
Gaskell, E. C. (1810–1865)
Gauntlett, H. (1805–1876)
Gay, J. (1685–1732)
Geoffrey of Monmouth (1100?–1154)
Gibbon, E. (1737–1794)
Gibbons, O. (1583–1625)
Gibson, J. (1790–1866)
Gifford, W. (1756–1826)
Gilbert, Sir H. (1539?–1583)
Gilbert, Sir J. (1817–1897)
Gilbert, W. (1540–1603)
Gillray, J. (1757–1815)
Giraldus Cambrensis (1146?–1220?)
Girtin, T. (1775–1802)
Gladstone, W. E. (1809–1898)
Glisson, F. (1597–1677)
Godwin, M. W. (1759–1797)
Godwin, W. (1756–1836)
Goldsmith, O. (1728–1774)
Gordon, C. G. (1833–1885)
Gower, J. (1325?–1408)
Graham, Sir G. (1831–1899)
Graham, J., Viscount Dundee (1649?–1689)
Grattan, J. (1746–1820)
Gray, T. (1716–1771)
Green, J. R. (1837–1883)
Greene, R. (1560?–1592)
Grenville, G. (1712–1770)
Grenville, W., Baron (1759–1834)

Gresham, Sir T. (1519?–1579)
Grew, N. (1641–1712)
Grey, Sir G. (1812–1898)
Grocyn, W. (1446?–1519)
Grosseteste, R. (1175?–1253)
Grote, G. (1794–1871)

Hale, Sir M. (1609–1676)
Hales, J. (1584–1656)
Hales, S. (1677–1761)
Hall, J. (1574–1656)
Hallam, H. (1777–1859)
Halley, E. (1656–1742)
Halliwell-Phillips, J. (1820–1889)
Hamilton, A. (1646?–1720)
Hamilton, S. W. (1788–1856)
Hamilton, Sir W. R. (1805–1865)
Hamilton, T., Earl of Haddington (1563–1637)
Hamley, Sir E. (1824–1893)
Hampden, J. (1594–1643)
Hardinge, H., Viscount (1785–1856)
Harrington, J. (1611–1677)
Hartley, D. (1705–1757)
Harvey, W. (1578–1657)
Hastings, W. (1732–1818)
Havelock, Sir H. (1795–1857)
Hawke, E., Lord (1705–1781)
Hawkins, Sir J. (1532–1595)
Hawkwood, Sir J. de (——1304)
Haydon, B. W. (1786–1846)
Hazlitt, W. (1778–1830)
Hemans, F. (1793–1835)
Henderson, A. (1583?–1646)
Herbert, A., Earl of Torrington (1647–1716)
Herbert, of Cherbury, E., Lord (1583–1648)
Herbert, G. (1593–1633)
Herrick, R. (1591–1674)
Herschel, Sir J. (1792–1871)
Heylin, P. (1600–1662)
Heywood, J. (1497?–1580)
Heywood, T. (1650)
Hickes, G. (1642–1715)
Hill, Sir R. (1795–1879)
Hinton, J. (1822–1875)
Hoadley, B. (1676–1761)
Hobbes, T. (1588–1679)
Hodgson, B. (1800–1894)
Hogarth, W. (1697–1764)
Hogg, J. (1770–1835)
Holcroft, T. (1745–1809)
Holl, F. (1845–1888)
Hood, S., Viscount (1724–1816)
Hood, T. (1799–1845)
Hook, T. (1788–1841)
Hook, W. (1798–1875)
Hooke, R. (1635–1703)
Hooker, R. (1554–1600)
Horner, F. (1778–1817)
Horrocks, J. (1617?–1641)
Hort, F. (1828–1892)
Howard, J. (1726–1790)
Howell, J. (1594–1666)
Hubert Walter (——1205)
Hughes, T. (1822–1896)
Hume, D. (1711–1776)
Hunt, L. (1784–1859)
Hunter, J. (1728–1893)
Hunter, Sir W. (1840–1900)
Huskisson, W. (1770–1830)
Hutcheson, F. (1694–1746)
Hutton, J. (1726–1797)
Hutton, R. H. (1826–1897)
Huxley, T. H. (1825–1895)
Hyde, E., Earl of Clarendon (1609–1674)

Inchbald, E. (1753–1821)
Ireton, H. (1611–1651)
Irving, E. (1792–1834)

Jameson, A. (1794–1860)
Jeffrey, F., Lord (1773–1850)
Jenner, E. (1749–1823)
Jerrold, D. (1803–1857)
Jervis, J., Earl of St. Vincent (1735–1823)
Jevons, W. S. (1835–1882)
Jewel, J. (1522–1571)
John of Salisbury (——1180)
Johnson, S. (1709–1784)
Johnston, A., Lord Warriston (1610?–1663)
Jones, I. (1573–1652)
Jones, Sir J. T. (1783–1843)
Jones, Sir W. (1746–1794)
Jones, W. B. (1822–1897)
Jonson, B. (1573–1637)
Jordan, D. (1761–1816)
Joule, J. P. (1818–1889)
Jowett, B. (1817–1893)
Juxon, W. (1582–1663)

Kean, E. (1787–1833)
Keats, J. (1795–1821)
Keble, J. (1792–1866)
Keeley, M. A. (1805–1895)
Keene, C. (1823–1891)
Kelly, F. (1790–1882)
Kemble, F. A. (1809–1893)
Kemble, J. M. (1807–1857)
Kemble, J. P. (1757–1823)

Kemp, J. (1380–1447)
Ken, T. (1637–1711)
Kennett, W. (1660–1728)
Kenyon, L., Lord (1732–1802)
Killigrew, T. (1612–1683)
King, T. (1730–1805)
King, W. (1650–1729)
Kingsley, C. (1819–1875)
Kingsley, M. (1862–1900)
Kirkcaldy, Sir W. (1573)
Knight, G. (1713–1772)
Knollys, Sir R. (1407)
Knowles, J. S. (1784–1862)
Knox, J. (1505–1572)

Lake, G., Viscount (1744–1808)
Lamb, C. (1775–1834)
Lambert, J. (1619–1683)
Lancaster, J. (1778–1838)
Lander, R. (1804–1834)
Landon, L. E. (1802–1838)
Landor, W. S. (1775–1864)
Landseer, Sir E. (1802–1873)
Lane, E. (1801–1876)
Langland, W. (1330?–1400?)
Langton, S. (1228)
Langton, W. (1321)
Lardner, N. (1684–1768)
Latimer, H. (1485?–1555)
Laud, W. (1573–1645)
Law, E., Baron Ellenborough (1750–1818)
Law, E., Earl of Ellenborough (1790–1871)
Law, J. (1671–1729)
Law, W. (1686–1761)
Lawes, H. (1596–1662)
Lawes, Sir J. B. (1814–1900)
Lawrence, Sir H. (1806–1857)
Lawrence, J., Lord (1811–1879)
Lawrence, S. (1698–1775)
Lawrence, Sir T. (1769–1830)
Layard, Sir A. H. (1817–1894)
Leake, Sir J. (1656–1720)
Lee, N. (1653?–1692)
Leech, J. (1817–1864)
Lefroy, Sir J. (1817–1890)
Leighton, F., Baron (1830–1896)
Leighton, R. (1611–1684)
Leland, J. (1506?–1552)
Leslie, A., Earl of Leven (1582–1661)
Leslie, C. (1650–1722)
Leslie, J. (1527–1596)
L'Estrange, Sir R. (1616–1704)
Lever, C. J. (1806–1872)
Lewes, G. H. (1817–1878)
Lewis, Sir G. C. (1806–1863)
Lewis, J. F. (1805–1876)
Lewis, W. T. (1748?–1811)
Liddon, H. P. (1829–1890)
Lightfoot, J. B. (1828–1889)
Lilburne, J. (1614?–1657)
Lillo, G. (1693–1739)
Linacre, T. (1460?–1524)
Lindsay, Sir D. (1490–1555)
Linguard, J. (1771–1851)
Linnell, J. (1792–1882)
Linton, E. L. (1822–1898)
Linton, W. J. (1812–1898)
Lister, J. (1786–1869)
Liston, J. (1776–1846)
Littleton, Sir T. (1422–1481)
Livingstone, D. (1813–1873)
Lloyd, J. (1627–1717)
Locke, J. (1632–1704)
Lockhart, J. (1794–1854)
Lodge, T. (1558–1625)
Loftus, A. (1533–1605)
Lovelace, R. (1618–1658)
Lover, S. (1797–1868)
Lowe, R., Viscount Sherbrooke (1811–1892)
Lowth, R. (1710–1787)
Lucus, C. (1713–1771)
Ludlow, E. (1617–1692)
Lydgate, J. (1370?–1451)
Lyell, Sir C. (1797–1875)
Lyly, J. (1554?–1606)
Lytton, E. B., Earl of (1831–1891)
Lytton, E. B., Lord (1803–1873)

Macaulay, T., Lord (1800–1859)
Macdonald, Sir J. A. (1815–1891)
Macfarren, Sir G. (1813–1887)
Mackay, H. (1640?–1692)
Mackintosh, Sir J. (1765–1832)
Mackenzie, H. (1745–1831)
Macklin, C. (1697?–1797)
Maclaurin, C. (1698–1746)
Maclise, D. (1806–1870)
Macnaghten, Sir W. (1793–1841)
Macready, W. C. (1793–1873)
Maginn, W. (1793–1842)
Maine, Sir H. S. (1822–1888)
Malcolm, Sir J. (1769–1833)
Malone, E. (1741–1812)
Malthus, T. (1766–1834)
Manning, H. E. (1807–1892)
Map, W. (*fl.* 1200)
Marlowe, C. (1564–1593)
Marryat, F. (1792–1848)
Marsh, H. (1757–1839)
Marshall, S. (1594?–1655)
Marston, J. (1575–1634)

Marten, H. (1602–1680)
Martineau, H. (1802–1876)
Martineau, J. (1805–1900)
Marvell, A. (1621–1678)
Massinger, P. (1583–1640)
Mathews, C. (1776–1835)
Mathews, C. J. (1803–1878)
Maurice, F. D. (1805–1872)
Maxwell, J. C. (1831–1879)
Mayow, J. (1643–1679)
Mead, R. (1673–1754)
Melville, A. (1545–1622)
Merivale, C. (1808–1893)
Middleton, C. (1683–1750)
Middleton, T. (1570?–1627)
Mill, J. (1773–1836)
Mill, J. S. (1806–1873)
Millais, Sir J. (1829–1896)
Miller, H. (1802–1856)
Milman, H. (1791–1868)
Milner, I. (1750–1820)
Milner, J. (1752–1826)
Milton, J. (1608–1674)
Mitchell, Sir T. (1792–1855)
Mitford, M. (1787–1855)
Moffat, R. (1795–1883)
Monck, G., Duke of Albemarle (1608–1670)
Monson, Sir W. (1569–1643)
Montagu, C., Earl of Halifax (1661–1715)
Montagu, E. (1720–1800)
Montagu, R. (1577–1641)
Moore, Sir J. (1761–1809)
Moore, T. (1779–1852)
More, H. (1745–1833)
More, Sir T. (1478–1535)
Morgan, Sir G. O. (1826–1897)
Morgan, Sir H. (1635?–1688)
Morgan, Lady S. (1783?–1859)
Morland, G. (1763–1804)
Morland, Sir S. (1625–1695)
Morley, G. (1597–1684)
Morris, W. (1834–1896)
Morton, T. (1564–1659)
Mulready, W. (1786–1863)
Mun, T. (1571–1641)
Munday, A. (1553–1633)
Mundella, A. J. (1825–1897)
Munden, J. (1758–1832)
Munro, Sir T. (1761–1827)
Murchison, Sir R. (1792–1871)
Murdock, W. (1754–1839)
Murray, J. (1778–1843)
Myers, F. W. (1843–1901)

Nairne, C., Baroness (1766–1845)
Napier, Sir C. (1786–1860)
Napier, Sir C. J. (1782–1853)
Napier, J. (1550–1617)
Napier, Sir J. (1804–1882)
Napier, R. C., Lord (1810–1890)
Napier, Sir W. J. P. (1785–1860)
Nash, T. (1567–1601)
Nasmyth, J. (1808–1890)
Nasmyth, P. (1787–1831)
Naylor, J. (1617?–1660)
Neale, E. V. (1810–1892)
Neale, J. M. (1818–1866)
Needham, M. (1620–1678)
Neill, J. G. S. (1810–1857)
Neilson, J. (1792–1865)
Neilson, L. A. (1848–1880)
Nelson, H., Lord (1758–1805)
Newcomen, T. (1663–1729)
Newman, F. W. (1805–1897)
Newman, J. H. (1801–1890)
Newton, Sir I. (1642–1727)
Nicholson, J. (1821–1857)
Northcote, J. (1746–1831)
Norton, T. (1532–1584)
Nott, Sir W. (1782–1845)
Nowell, A. (1507?–1602)
Noye, W. (1577–1634)

Ochterlony, Sir D. (1758–1825)
Ockham, W. (——1349?)
Ockley, S. (1678–1720)
O'Connell, D. (1775–1847)
Oglethorpe, J. E. (1696–1785)
Oldcastle, Sir J. (——1417)
Oldfield, A. (1683–1730)
Oldys, W. (1696–1761)
O'Leary, A. (1729–1802)
Oliphant, L. (1829–1888)
Oliphant, M. (1828–1897)
O'Neill, D. (1612–1664)
Opie, A. (1769–1853)
Opie, J. (1761–1807)
Ordericus Vitalis (1075–1143?)
Otway, T. (1652–1685)
Oughtred, W. (1575–1660)
Outram, Sir J. (1803–1863)
Owen, J. (1616–1683)
Owen, Sir R. (1804–1892)
Owen, R. (1771–1858)

Paget, Sir J. (1814–1899)
Paget, W., Baron (1505–1563)
Paine, T. (1737–1809)
Paley, W. (1743–1805)
Palmer, E. H. (1840–1882)
Palmer, J. (1742?–1798)

Palmer, R., Earl Selbourne (1812–1895)
Palmer, S. (1805–1881)
Paris, M. (——1259?)
Park, M. (1771–1806)
Parker, M. (1504–1575)
Parker, T., Earl Macclesfield (1667–1732)
Parkes, E. A. (1819–1876)
Parkes, Sir H. S. (1828–1885)
Parkes, Sir H. (1815–1896)
Parnell, C. S. (1846–1891)
Parr, S. (1747–1825)
Parsons, R. (1546–1610)
Parsons, W. (1736–1795)
Pater, W. H. (1839–1894)
Paterson, W. (1658–1719)
Patmore, C. (1823–1896)
Patrick, St. (373–463)
Pattison, M. (1813–1884)
Payne, P. (1380?–1455)
Pearson, J. (1613–1686)
Pearson, J. L. (1817–1897)
Pecock, R. (1395?–1460?)
Peel, Sir R. (1788–1850)
Peele, G. (1558?–1597?)
Peirce, J. (1674?–1726)
Pellew, E., Viscount Exmouth (1757–1833)
Penn, Sir W. (1621–1670)
Penn, W. (1644–1718)
Penry (1559–1593)
Pepys, S. (1633–1703)
Perkins, W. (1558–1602)
Perry, J. (1756–1821)
Peters, H. (1598–1660)
Petty, Sir W. (1623–1687)
Phelps, S. (1804–1878)
Phillip, J. (1817–1867)
Picton, Sir T. (1758–1815)
Pitman, Sir I. (1813–1897)
Pitt, W., Earl of Chatham (1708–1778)
Pitt, W. (1759–1806)
Pococke, E. (1604–1691)
Pollock, Sir G. (1786–1872)
Pope, A. (1688–1744)
Popham, Sir H. R. (1762–1820)
Porson, R. (1759–1808)
Pott, P. (1714–1788)
Powell, V. (1617–1670)
Pownall, T. (1722–1802)
Pratt, C., Earl Camden (1714–1794)
Preston, J. (1587–1628)
Prestwich, Sir J. (1812–1896)
Price, R. (1723–1791)
Priestley, J. (1733–1804)
Prior, M. (1664–1721)
Prynne, W. (1600–1669)
Pugin, A. W. (1812–1852)
Pulteney, W., Earl of Bath (1684–1764)
Purcell, H. (1658?–1695)
Pusey, E. B. (1800–1882)
Pym, J. (1584–1643)

Quarles, F. (1592–1644)
Quin, J. (1693–1766)

Radcliffe, A. (1764–1823)
Raeburn, Sir H. (1756–1823)
Raffles, Sir T. (1781–1826)
Raleigh, Sir W. (1552?–1618)
Randolph, T. (1605–1635)
Ray, J. (1627–1705)
Reade, S. (1814–1884)
Reid, T. (1710–1796)
Reid, Sir W. (1781–1858)
Reynolds, Sir J. (1723–1792)
Richardson, S. (1689–1761)
Ridley, N. (1500?–1555)
Ritson, J. (1752–1803)
Robertson, W. (1721–1793)
Robinson, H., Baron Rosmead (1824–1897)
Rodney, G., Baron (1719–1792)
Roe, Sir T. (1581?–1644)
Rogers, S. (1763–1855)
Romney, G. (1734–1802)
Roscoe, W. (1753–1831)
Rose, G. (1744–1818)
Ross, Sir H. D. (1779–1868)
Ross, R. (1766–1814)
Rossetti, C. (1830–1894)
Rossetti, D. G. (1828–1882)
Rowe, N. (1674–1718)
Rowlandson, T. (1756–1827)
Ruskin, J. (1819–1900)
Russell, C., Baron (1832–1900)

Sabine, Sir E. (1788–1883)
Sacheverell, W. (1638–1691)
Sadler, M. T. (1780–1835)
St. John, O. (1598?–1673)
St. Leger, Sir A. (1496?–1559)
Sale, Sir R. (1782–1845)
Salesbury, W. (1520?–1600?)
Sancroft, W. (1617–1693)
Sandby, P. (1725–1809)
Savage, R. (——1743)
Savile, Sir H. (1549–1622)
Scarlett, J., Baron Abinger (1769–1844)
Scott, D. (1806–1849)

Scott, Sir G. G. (1811–1878)
Scott, J., Earl of Eldon (1751–1838)
Scott, Sir W. (1771–1832)
Scott, W., Lord Stowell (1745–1836)
Scotus Erigena (*fl.* 850)
Sedgwick, A. (1785–1873)
Seeley, Sir J. (1834–1895)
Selden, J. (1584–1654)
Shakespeare, W. (1564–1616)
Sharp, J. (1645–1714)
Sheil, R. L. (1791–1851)
Sheldon, G. (1598–1677)
Shelley, P. B. (1792–1822)
Sheridan, R. B. (1751–1816)
Shirley, J. (1596–1666)
Siddons, S. (1755–1831)
Sidgwick, H. (1838–1899)
Sidney, Sir P. (1554–1586)
Simpson, Sir J. Y. (1811–1870)
Sinclair, Sir J. (1754–1835)
Skelton, J. (146–?–1529)
Smart, C. (1722–1771)
Smith, A. (1753–1790)
Smith, Sir H. G. (1787–1860)
Smith, H. J. S. (1826–1883)
Smith, R. A. (1817–1884)
Smith, Sydney (1771–1845)
Smith, Sir T. (1513–1577)
Smith, W. (1769–1839)
Smith, W. R. (1846–1894)
Smith, Sir W. S. (1764–1840)
Smollett, T. (1721–1771)
Somers, J., Lord (1651–1716)
Somerville, M. (1780–1872)
South, R. (1634–1716)
Southey, R. (1774–1843)
Southwell, R. (1561?–1595)
Speke, J. (1827–1864)
Spelman, Sir H. (1564?–1641)
Spencer, E. (1552?–1599)
Sprat, T. (1635–1713)
Stanhope, W., Earl of Harrington (1690?–1756)
Stanley, A. P. (1815–1881)
Steele, Sir R. (1672–1729)
Steevens, G. (1736–1800)
Stephen, Sir J. F. (1829–1894)
Stephenson, G. (1781–1848)
Sterne, L. (1713–1768)
Stevens, A. (1818–1875)
Stevenson, R. L. (1850–1894)
Stewart, D. (1753–1828)
Stothard, T. (1755–1834)
Stow, J. (1525–1605)
Street, G. E. (1824–1881)
Stubbs, G. (1724–1806)
Sturgeon, W. (1783–1850)
Suckling, Sir J. (1609–1642)
Sullivan, Sir A. (1842–1900)
Swift, J. (1667–1745)
Sydenham, T. (1624–1689)
Symonds, J. A. (1840–1893)

Tait, A. C. (1811–1882)
Tallis, T. (1510?–1585)
Tarleton, Sir B. (1754–1833)
Taylor, Sir H. (1800–1886)
Taylor, J. (1613–1667)
Taylor, W. (1765–1836)
Telford, T. (1757–1834)
Temple, Sir W. (1628–1699)
Tennyson, A., Baron (1809–1892)
Thackeray, W. M. (1811–1863)
Thirlwall, C. (1797–1875)
Thomas, W. (——1554)
Thompson, W. (1785?–1833)
Thomson, J. (1700–1748)
Thurloe, J. (1616–1668)
Thurlow, E., Baron (1731–1806)
Tillotson, J. (1630–1694)
Toland, J. (1670–1722)
Tone, T. W. (1763–1798)
Tooke, J. H. (1736–1812)
Trelawney, E. J. (1792–1881)
Trevithick, R. (1771–1833)
Trollope, A. (1815–1882)
Trollope, Sir H. (1756–1839)
Tunstall, C. (1474–1559)
Turner, J. M. W. (1775–1851)
Tye, C. (1497?–1572)
Tyndale, W. (1490?–1536)
Tyndall, J. (1820–1893)

Udall, N. (1505–1556)
Urquhart, Sir T. (1611–1660)
Ussher, J. (1581–1656)

Vanbrugh, Sir J. (1663–1726)
Vane, Sir H., the younger (1613–1662)
Varley, J. (1778–1842)
Vaughan, H. (1622–1695)
Vere, Sir F. (1560–1609)
Vere, Sir H. (1565–1635)
Vernon, E. (1684–1757)

Wakley, T. (1795–1862)
Walker, F. (1840–1875)
Wallace, Sir W. (1272?–1305)
Waller, E. (1606–1687)
Waller, Sir W. (1597?–1668)
Wallis, J. (1616–1703)
Walpole, H., Earl of Orford (1717–1797)

Walpole, R., Earl of Orford (1676–1745)
Walsh, P. (1618?–1688)
Walsingham, Sir F. (1530?–1590)
Walter, J. (1739–1812)
Walton, I. (1593–1683)
Warburton, W. (1698–1779)
Ward, M. (1585–1645)
Ward, S. (1617–1689)
Ward, W. G. (1812–1882)
Warham, W. (1450?–1532)
Warton, T. (1728–1790)
Watson, R. (1737–1816)
Watson, T. (1557?–1592)
Watt, J. (1736–1819)
Waynflete, W. of (1395?–1486)
Webster, B. (1797–1882)
Wedgwood, J. (1730–1795)
Wentworth, W. C. (1793–1872)
Wesley, C. (1707–1788)
Wesley, J. (1703–1791)
Westmacott, Sir R. (1775–1856)
Whately, R. (1787–1863)
Wheatstone, Sir C. (1802–1875)
Whewell, W. (1794–1866)
Whiston, W. (1667–1752)
Whitbread, S. (1758–1815)
White, G. (1720–1793)
White, J. B. (1775–1841)
Whitefield, J. (1714–1770)
Whitehead, G. (1636?–1723)
Whitelocke, B. (1605–1675)
Whitgift, J. (1530?–1604)
Whittington, R. (——1423)
Whitworth, Sir J. (1803–1887)
Wilberforce, S. (1805–1873)
Wilberforce, W. (1759–1833)
Wilde, O. (1856–1900)
Wilfrid, St. (634–709)
Wilkes, J. (1727–1797)
Wilkie, Sir D. (1785–1841)
Wilkins, J. (1614–1672)
Wilks, R. (1665?–1732)
Willet, A. (1562–1621)
William of Malmesbury (——1143?)
William of Newburgh (1136–1198?)
Williams, Sir C. H. (1708–1759)
Williams, D. (1643?–1716)
Williams, Sir R. (1540?–1595)
Williams, R. (1604?–1683)
Williams, Sir W. (1634–1700)
Williamson, Sir J. (1633–1701)
Williamson, W. C. (1816–1895)
Willoughby, Sir N. J. (1777–1849)
Wilson, J. (1785–1854)
Wilson, R. (1714–1782)
Wilson, Sir R. (1777–1849)
Wilson, T. (1663–1755)
Windham, W. (1750–1810)
Winthrop, J. (1588–1649)
Winwood, Sir R. (1563?–1617)
Wiseman, N. (1802–1865)
Wishart, G. (1513?–1546)
Wither, G. (1588–1667)
Woffington, M. (1714?–1760)
Wolcot, J. (1738–1819)
Wolfe, J. (1727–1759)
Wollaston, W. H. (1766–1828)
Wolsey, T. (1471?–1530)
Woodward, H. (1714–1777)
Woolner, T. (1825–1892)
Wordsworth, Charles (1806–1892)
Wordsworth, Christopher (1807–1885)
Wordsworth, W. (1770–1850)
Wotton, Sir H. (1568–1639)
Wotton, N. (1497?–1567)
Wren, Sir C. (1632–1723)
Wright, J. (1734–1797)
Wright, T. (1810–1877)
Wulfstan, St. (1012?–1095)
Wyatt, Sir T. (1503?–1542)
Wycherley, W. (1640?–1716)
Wycliffe, J. (1324?–1384)
Wykeham, W. of (1324–1404)
Wyse, Sir T. (1791–1862)

Yates, M. A. (1728–1787)
Yorke, P., Earl of Hardwicke (1690–1764)
Young, A. (1741–1820)
Young, E. (1683–1765)
Young, T. (1773–1829)

At various points it has been necessary to classify our eminent persons into groups, according to the character of their intellectual activities. It may be convenient here to present these groupings. It should be noted that a few individuals (distinguished by an asterisk) appear in more than one list, and that some miscellaneous per-

sons have been omitted altogether. In a large number of cases the question of classification is difficult and remains doubtful, although a considerable amount of care has been exercised in such cases. Difference of opinion must also necessarily exist on the question of duplication and the extent to which it should be carried. The eminent women have been grouped separately.

Actors. — Bannister, Betterton, Booth, Burbage, Cibber, Cooke, Elliston, Foote, Garrick, Kean, Kemble, King, Lewis, Liston, Macklin, Macready, C. Mathews, C. J. Mathews, Munden, Palmer, Parsons, Phelps, Quin, Webster, Wilks, Woodward.

Artists. — Adam, Banks, C. Barry, J. Barry, Beardsley, Bewick, Blake,* Bonington, Brown, Browne, Burne-Jones, Butterfield, Cattermole, Chantrey, Cockerell, Constable, Cooper, Copley, Cotman, Cox, Cozens, Crome, Cruikshank, Danby, Dawson, Dobson, Doyle, Du Maurier, Dyce, Eastlake, Etty, Flaxman, Gainsborough, Gibson, Gilbert, Gillray, Girtin, Haydon, Hogarth, Holl, Inigo Jones, Keene, Landseer, Lawrence, Leech, Leighton, Lewis, Linnell, Linton, Maclise, Millais, Morland, Morris,* Mulready, Nasmyth, Northcote, Opie, Palmer, Pearson, Phillip, Pugin, Raeburn, Reynolds, Romney, Rossetti,* Rowlandson, Sandby, D. Scott, G. Scott, Stevens, Stothard, Street, Stubbs, Turner, Vanbrugh,* Varley, Walker, Westmacott, Wilkie, Wilson, Woolner, Wren, Wright.

Divines. — Abbot, Adrian IV, Ainsworth, Alesius, Allen, Andrewes,* Atterbury, Bancroft, Barclay, Barrow,* Baxter, Bedell, Benson, St. Boniface, Bonner, Bradshaw, Browne, Burges, Burnet,* Butler,* Campion, Candlish, St. Thomas de Cantelupe, Carey, Cartwright, Challoner, Chalmers, Chichele, Chillingworth, Church, Clarke, Colenso, St. Columba, St. Columban, Cooke, Cosin, Coverdale, Cranmer, Cudworth, St. Cuthbert, Dolben, Doddridge, Donne,* Duff, St. Dunstan, St. Edmund, Emlyn, Erskine, Faber, Ferrar, Fox, Foxe,* Fuller, Garnett, Henderson,* Heylin, Hoadley, Hook, Hooker, Irving, Jewel, Jones, Juxon, Keble,* Ken, King, Knox,* Langton,* Lardner, Latimer, Laud, Law, Leighton, Leslie, Liddon, Lightfoot, Lloyd, Loftus, Manning, Marsh, Marshall, Martineau, Maurice, Melville, Middleton, Milner, Moffat, Montagu, Morley, Naylor, Neale, Newman, Nowell, Owen, Paley,* Parker, Parsons, St. Patrick, Payne, Pearson,* Pecock, Peirce, Penry, Perkins, Peters, Powell, Preston, Pusey, Ridley, Sancroft, Sharp, Sheldon, South, Stanley,* Tait, Taylor, Tillotson, Tyndale,* Walsh, Warham, C. Wesley, J. Wesley, Blanco White, Whitefield, Whitehead, Whitgift, Wilberforce, St. Wilfrid, Willett, D. Williams, R. Williams, Wilson, Wiseman, Wishart, Wordsworth, St. Wulfstan, Wycliffe.*

Doctors. — Caius,* Cheselden, Cooper, Cullen, Linacre,* Mead, Paget, Pott, Simpson, Sydenham. (Others are included among *Men of Science.*)

Lawyers. — Abinger, Ashburton, Austin, Blackstone, Bowen, Cairns, Camden, Campbell, Clare, Cockburn, Coke, Curran, Denman, Eldon, Ellenborough, Fortescue, Haddington, Hale, Hardwicke, Kenyon, Littleton, Lyndhurst, Macclesfield, Maine, More,* J. Napier, Noye, Russell, St. John, Selbourne, Selden, Somers, Stair, Stephen, Stowell, Thurlow, Westbury, Williams.

Men of Letters. — Addison, Alcuin, Ascham, Bagehot, Banim, Barclay, Beck-

ford, Bede, Blackmore, Borrow, Boswell, Browne, Buchanan,* Buckle, Bunyan, Burton, Calamy, Camden, Carleton, Carlile, Carlyle, Cibber,* Cobbett,* Collier, Wilkie Collins, Colman, Congreve, Cotton, Cowley, Crocker, D'Avenant, Day, Defoe, Dekker, Dempster, De Quincey, D'Ewes, Dickens, Digby, Dodgson,* Dugdale, Elyot, Etherege, Fanshawe, Farquhar, Fielding, Foxe, Francis, Freeman, Froude, Galt, Geoffrey of Monmouth, Gibbon, Gifford, Giraldus, Goldsmith, Green, Grote, Hall, Hallam, Halliwell-Phillips, Hamilton, Harrington, Hazlitt, Herbert, Holcroft, Hood, Hook, Howell, Hughes, Hume,* Hunt, Hunter, Hutton, Jeffrey, Jerrold, Johnson, Jonson, Kemble, Kennett, Killigrew, Kingsley, Knowles, Lamb, Landor, Lee, Leland, L'Estrange, Lever, Lewes, Lillo, Lingard, Lockhart, Lodge, Lover, Lyly, Lytton, Macaulay, Mackenzie, Maginn, Malone, Map, Marryat, Marston, Miller,* Merivale, Milman, More,* Myers, W. J. P. Napier, Nash, Needham, Newman, Oliphant, Oldys, Ordericus Vitalis, Paine, Paris, Pater, Pepys, Perry, Prynne, Raleigh,* Reade, Richardson, Ritson, Robertson, Roscoe, Ruskin, Scott, Seeley, Sheil, Sheridan,* Smollett, Southey, Sprat, Sidney Smith, Stanley,* Steele, Sterne, Steevens, Stevenson, Stow, Swift, Symonds, H. Taylor, W. Taylor, Temple,* Thackeray, Thirlwall, Trelawney, Trollope, Tyndale, Udall, Urquhart, Vanbrugh,* Wakley,* H. Walpole, Walton, Warburton, Warton, Whately, Wilde, William of Malmesbury, William of Newburgh, Williams, Wilson, Wolcot, Wright, Wycherley.

Men of Science. — Adams, Airy, Arkwright, Armstrong, Babbage, R. Bacon,* Baily, Balfour, Banks, Barrow,* Baskerville, Bates, Bell, Bentham, Bessemer, Birch, Black, Boyle, Bradley, Brewster, Canton, Carpenter, Carrington, Cavendish, Cayley, Caxton, Clifford, Colby, Cotes, Cotton, Dalton, C. Darwin, E. Darwin, Davy, Dee, De Morgan, Dodgson,* Drummond, Falconer, Faraday, Ferguson, Flamsteed, Flinders,* Flower, E. Forbes, J. D. Forbes, Frankland, Franks, Gilbert, Glisson, Grew, Hales, Halley, Hamilton, Harvey, Herschel, Hodgson, Hooke, Horrocks, Hunter, Hutton, Huxley, Jenner, Jevons, Joule, Knight, Lawes, Lefroy, Lister, Lyell, Maclaurin, Malthus, Mayow, Maxwell, Miller,* Milner, Morland, Mun, Murchison, Murdoch, Napier, Nasmyth, Neilson, Newcomen, Newton, Oughtred, Owen, Parkes, Petty, Priestley, Ray, Sabine,* Sadler, Sedgwick, Sidgwick, Sinclair, A. Smith, H. J. Smith, R. A. Smith, W. Smith, Stephenson, Sturgeon, Telford, Thompson, Trevithick, Tyndall, Wallis, Ward, Watson, Watt, Wedgwood, Wheatstone, Whewell, White, Whitworth, Wilkins, Williamson, Wollaston, A. Young, T. Young.

Musical Composers. — Arne, Balfe, Bennett, Blow, Boyce, Byrd, Dowland, Gauntlett, Gibbons, Lawes, Macfarren, Purcell, Sullivan, Tallis, Tye.

Philosophers. — Alexander of Hales, F. Bacon, Roger Bacon,* Bentham, Berkeley, Bradwardine, Butler,* Duns, Erigena, Godwin, Hamilton, Hartley, Hinton, Hobbes, Hume,* Hutcheson, Locke, Mackintosh, J. Mill, J. S. Mill, Ockham, Paley,* Price, Reid, Shaftesbury, Stewart, Toland, Ward, Wycliffe.*

Poets. — Arnold, Barbour, Barclay, Barham, Barnes, Barnfield, Beaumont, Beddoes, Blake,* Breton, Browne, Browning, Bruce, Burns, Butler, Byron, Cædmon, Campbell, Campion, Chapman, Chatterton, Chaucer, Churchill, Clare, Clough, H. Coleridge, S. T. Coleridge, Collins, Cotton, Cowper, Crabbe, Crashaw, Daniel, Davies, Denham, Dibdin, Dobell, Donne,* Douglas, Drayton, Drummond, Dryden, Dunbar, D'Urfey, Fletcher, Ford, Fergusson, Fitzgerald, Gascoigne, Gay, Gower, Gray, Greene, Herbert, Herrick, J. Heywood, T. Heywood, Hogg, Hood, Keats, Keble,* Langland, Lindsay, Lovelace, Lydgate, Marlowe, Marvell, Massinger, Middleton, Milton, Moore, Morris,* Munday, Norton, Otway, Patmore, Peele, Pope, Prior, Quarles, Randolph, Rogers, Rossetti,* Rowe, Savage, Shakespeare, Shelley, Shirley, Sidney,* Skelton, Smart, Southwell, Spenser, Suckling, Tennyson, Thomson, Vaughan, Waller, Watson, Wither, Wordsworth, Wotton, Wyatt, Young.

Politicians, etc. — Arthur, A. Bacon, N. Bacon, Bateman, Beaton, Bradford, Bradlaugh, Bright, Brooke, Brougham, Bruce, Burke, Burghley, Burnet,* Cade, Campbell, Canning, Earl Canning, Carstares, Chatham, Chichester, Childers, Clarendon, Clive, Cobbett,* Cobden, Cork, Coutances, O. Cromwell, T. Cromwell, Eliot, Ellenborough, Fawcett, Fletcher, Forster, Fox, Foxe,* Frere, Gardiner, Gladstone, Grattan, G. Grenville, W. Grenville, Grey,* Hampden, Harrington, Hastings, Henderson,* Horner, Hubert Walter, Huskisson, Ireton, Kemp, Kirkcaldy, Knox,* S. Langton, W. Langton, Law, Lawrence, Leslie, Lewis, Lilburne, Lucas, Ludlow, Lytton, Macdonald, Macnaghten, Malcolm, Marten, Melville, C. Montagu, Morgan, Mundella, Northumberland, O'Connell, Oldcastle, O'Leary, O'Neill, Paget, Sir Harry Parkes, Sir Henry Parkes, Parnell, Peel, Penn, Pitt, Pownall, Pulteney, Pym, Raffles, Reid,* Robinson, Roe, Rose, Sacheverell, St. Leger, Shaftesbury, Sherbrooke, Sheil,* Sheridan,* T. Smith,* Stratford de Redcliffe, Stirling, Temple,* Thurloe, Tone, Tooke, Tunstall, Vane, Wallace,* Walpole, Walsingham, Warriston, Waynflete, Wentworth, Whitbread, Whitelocke, Wilberforce, Wilkes, Williamson, Windham, Winthrop, Winwood, Wolsey, Wotton, Wykeham, Wyse.

Sailors. — Anson, Blake, Boscawen, Broke, Byng, Cavendish, Cook, Dampier, Deane, Drake, Duncan, Exmouth, Flinders,* Franklin, Frobisher, Gilbert, Hawke, Hawkins, Hood, Leake, Monson, C. Napier, Nelson, Penn, Popham, Raleigh,* Rodney, Smith, St. Vincent, Trollope, Vernon, Willoughby.

Scholars. — Andrewes,* Adamson, Barrow,* Bentley, Bingham, Boece, Bradshaw, Buchanan,* Caius,* Cheke, Colebrooke, Colet, Conington, Creighton, Crichton, Dodwell, Grocyn, Grosseteste, Hales, Hickes, Hort, John of Salisbury, Jones, Jowett, Lane, Lightfoot, Linacre,* Lowth, Montagu, Morton, Ockley, Palmer, Pattison, Pearson,* Pococke, Porson, Salesbury, Savile, T. Smith, W. R. Smith, Spelman, Thomas, Ussher, Whiston, Wordsworth.

Soldiers. — Abercromby, Amherst, Cadogan, Campbell, Dundee, Edwards, Gordon, Graham, Hamley, Hardinge, Havelock, Hawkwood, Jones, Knollys, Lake, Lambert, H. Lawrence, S. Lawrence, Leven, Mackay, Marlborough, Monck, Moore, Morgan, Munro, Napier of Magdala, C. J. Napier, Neill, Nicholson, Nott, Ochterlony, Oglethorpe, Outram, Picton, Pollock, Raleigh,* Reid, H. D. Ross, R. Ross, Sabine,* Sale, Sidney,* Smith, Tarleton, F. Vere, H. Vere, Wallace,* Waller, Williams, Wilson, Wolfe.

Travellers. — Baker, Barrow, Bowring, Bruce, Burton, Chesney, Clapperton, Grey,* Lander, Livingstone, Mitchell, Park, Speke.

The women fall into the following groups:

Actresses. — Abington, Anne Barry, Elizabeth Barry, Becher, Bracegirdle, Cibber, Clive, Faucit, Jordan, Keeley, Kelly, Kemble, Neilson, Oldfield, Siddons, Woffington, Yates.

Philanthropists. — Carpenter, Fry.

Poets. — Baillie, Browning, Hemans, Landon, Nairne, Rossetti.

Religious. — Ward.

Traveller. — Kingsley.

Women of Letters. — D'Arblay, Austen, Barbauld, Behn, C. Brontë, E. Brontë, Cavendish, Centlivre, Cowley, Cross, Eastlake, Edgeworth, Edwards, Ferrier, Gaskell, Godwin, Inchbald, Jameson, Linton, Martineau, Mitford, Montagu, More, Morgan, Oliphant, Opie, Radcliffe.

Woman of Science. — Somerville.

APPENDIX B

ORIGINS OF BRITISH PERSONS OF ABILITY

THE significance of the place-names in the following list varies with their position. When the place-name occurs between that of the grandfather and grandmother it refers to the father (or the mother), our knowledge not going back so far as the grandparents. When the place-name comes in the centre of the page our knowledge is still more imperfect, only comprehending the fact that the eminent person's family belonged to the district in question. A query mark (?) means that the statement is fairly probable, and has been accepted in the body of the book, but is not absolutely certain. The place-names in square brackets indicate origins that are either doubtful or further back than the grandparents; no account of such origins has been taken in the summaries given in the body of the book.

	Paternal grandfather.	Paternal grandmother.	Maternal grandfather.	Maternal grandmother.
Abbot			Surrey	
Abercromby		Clackmannan		
Abington			England	
Adam			Scotland	
Adams		Cornwall		Cornwall
Adamson			Perth	
Addison		Westmoreland		
Adrian IV			England [? Herts]	
Ainsworth		Lancashire		Yorks
Airy		Lincs [Westmoreland and Yorks]		Suffolk
Alcuin			Yorks	
Alesius			Midlothian	
Alexander of Hales			Gloucester	
Alexander (W.)		Clackmannan		
Allen		Lancashire		Yorkshire
Amherst		Kent		
Andrewes		Suffolk [Essex]		
Anson		Staffs		Derbyshire
Arblay, D'		Shropshire	France	
Arkwright			Lancashire	
Armstrong		Cumberland		Northumberland (?)
Arne			England	

	Paternal grand-father.	Paternal grand-mother.	Maternal grand-father.	Maternal grand-mother.
Arnold (M.)	Hants and Suffolk [Ireland]			Cornwall
Arnold (T.)	Suffolk and Hants			Ireland [Huguenot]
Arthur			Devon [? Cornwall]	
Ascham	Yorks			Yorks
Atterbury			England	
Austen	Kent			Warwick
Austin	Suffolk			
Babbage			Devon	
Bacon (A.)	Suffolk	Suffolk		Essex
Bacon (F.)	Suffolk	Suffolk		Essex
Bacon (N.)	Suffolk			Suffolk
Bacon (R.)			Somerset	
Bagehot	Somerset			Somerset
Baillie				Ayr and Lanark
Baily			England	
Baker	Gloucester			Middlesex
Balfe			Ireland	
Balfour	Haddington			England
Bancroft	Lancashire			
Banim	Kilkenny			
Banks (J.)	Lincs			
Banks (T.)			England	

	Paternal grand-father.	Paternal grand-mother.	Maternal grand-father.	Maternal grand-mother.
Bannister		Gloucester (?)		
Barbauld	Yorks			
Barbour			Aberdeen	
Barclay (A.)			Scotland	
Barclay (J.)		Scotland		France
Barclay (R.)		Elgin		
Barham		Kent		
Barnes		Dorset		Dorset
Barnfield		Shropshire		
Barrow (I.)		Suffolk		Kent
Barrow (J.)		Lancashire		Lancashire
Barry (A.)			Somerset	
Barry (C.)			England	
Barry (E.)			England (?)	
Barry (J.)			Cork	
Baskerville			Worcester	
Bateman			Norfolk	
Bates		Leicester		
Baxter		Shropshire		Shropshire
Beardsley		Scotland		England
Beaton		Fife		
Beaumont		Leicester		
Becher		Ireland		
Beckford	Glo'ster			
Beddoes		Shropshire		England and Ireland
Bede			Durham	

	Paternal grand-father.	Paternal grand-mother.	Maternal grand-father.	Maternal grand-mother.
Bedell		Essex		Essex
Behn			Kent	
Bell (A.)		Fife		Holland
Bell (C.)		Lanark		
Bennett	Kent			
Benson				Cambs
Bentham (G.)		Hants		
Bentham (J.)				Hants
Bentley		Yorks		
Berkeley		England		Ireland (?)
Bessemer			England [Huguenot]	
Bethell		Wilts		
Betterton			England	
Bewick		Northumberland		Cumberland
Bingham			Yorks	
Birch			England	
Bishop		Shropshire		
Black		Antrim [Scotland]		Aberdeen
Blackmore		Devon		Glamorgan [and Devon & Glo'ster]
Blackstone		Wilts		Wilts
Blake (R.)		Somerset		
Blake (W.)		Somerset (?)		

	Paternal grand-father.	Paternal grand-mother.	Maternal grand-father.	Maternal grand-mother.
Blow			Notts (?)	
Boece			Forfar	
Boniface			Devon	
Bonington	Notts			Notts
Bonner			England	
Booth	Lancashire			
Borrow	Cornwall			Norfolk [Huguenot]
Boscawen	Cornwall			
Boswell	Ayr			
Bowen	Mayo			Ireland and Austria
Boyle (A. Earl of Cork)	Hereford			Kent
Boyle (Robert)	Hereford	Kent		
Bracegirdle	Northants			
Bradford	Yorks			
Bradlaugh	Suffolk			
Bradley	Durham			Wilts
Bradshaw (H.)	Ireland [Cheshire and Derby]			Antrim
Bradshaw (W.)	Lancashire			
Bradwardine	Hereford (?)			
Broke	Suffolk			

	Paternal grand-father.	Paternal grand-mother.	Maternal grand-father.	Maternal grand-mother.
Brooke		England [? Norfolk]		
Breton	Essex			
Brewster		Scotland		
Bright	Warwick [Wilts]			
Brontë (C.)	Down		Cornwall	
Brontë (E.)	Down		Cornwall	
Brougham	Cumberland		Fife	Ayr
Brown	Berwick	Midlothian	Kent	
Browne (H.)	Norfolk			
Browne (R.)	Lincs		Herts	
Browne (T.)	Cheshire		Sussex	
Browne (W.)	Devon			
Browning (E.)		Northumberland		
Browning (R.)	Dorset		Germany	Scotland
Bruce (H.)	Glamorgan [and Scotland]			
Bruce (J.)	Stirling		Stirling	
Bruce (M.)		Kinross		
Buchanan	Stirling		Haddington	
Buckle			Yorks	
Bull		Somerset		

	Paternal grand-father.		Paternal grand-mother.		Maternal grand-father.		Maternal grand-mother.
Bunyan		Bedford				Bedford	
Burbage		Herts					
Burges				Somerset			
Burke		Dublin				Ireland	
Burne-Jones		Wales				England	
Burnet		Aberdeen			Dumfries		Ayr
Burns		Kincardine				Ayr	
Burton (Richard)	West-moreland		Ireland [and Fr. Huguenot]		Herts		Scotland
Burton (Robert)		Leicester					
Butler (J.)				Berks			
Butler (S.)				Worcester			
Butterfield				England			
Byng		Kent					
Byrd				Lincoln (?)			
Byron			Cornwall			Aberdeen	
Cade				Ireland (?)			
Cadogan		Ireland [Somerset]					
Cædmon				Yorks			
Cairns		Down [Scotland]					
Caius				Norfolk			
Calamy	France		Suffolk				
Camden		Staffs			Lancs		Cumberland

	Paternal grandfather.	Paternal grandmother.	Maternal grandfather.	Maternal grandmother.
Campbell (C.)	Lanark			Argyle
Campbell (G.)	Fife			Fife
Campbell (J.)			Scotland	
Campbell (T.)	Argyle			Argyle
Campion (E.)			Essex	
Campion (T.)	Essex			Essex
Candlish	Ayr			Ayr
Canning (C.)	Londonderry [Wilts]			
Canning (G.)	Wilts and Londonderry			
Canning (S.)	Wilts and Londonderry			
Cantelupe	Bucks			France
Canton			Gloucester	
Carey			Northants	
Carleton	Tyrone [Londonderry]			Tyrone
Carlile	Devon			
Carlyle	Dumfries			
Carpenter (M.)	Worcester			Worcester
Carpenter (W.)	Worcester			Worcester
Carrington	Middlesex			
Carstares	Lanark			Ayr
Cartwright			Herts	
Case	Kent			
Cattermole			Norfolk	

	Paternal grand-father.	Paternal grand-mother.	Maternal grand-father.	Maternal grand-mother.
Cavendish (H.)			England	
Cavendish (M.)	Essex			
Cavendish (T.)			Suffolk	
Caxton			Kent	
Cayley	Yorks [Norfolk]			
Cecil	Northants			Lincoln
Centlivre	Lincoln			Norfolk
Challoner			Sussex	
Chalmers	Fife			
Chantrey			Yorks	
Chapman			Herts	
Chatterton	Gloucester			Gloucester
Chaucer	Suffolk [? Essex]			
Cheke	Hants			Cambs
Cheselden			Rutland	
Chesney	Antrim [Scotland]			
Chichele	Northants (?)			
Chichester	Devon			Devon
Childers			England [partly Jewish both sides]	
Chillingworth	Oxford			
Church		Yorks	Germany	England
Churchill (C.)	England			Scotland (?)

	Paternal grand-father.	Paternal grand-mother.	Maternal grand-father.	Maternal grand-mother.
Churchill (J.)	Dorset			Devon
Cibber (C.)	Denmark			Rutland
Cibber (S.)			England	
Clapperton	Dumfries			
Clare	Northants			
Clarke	Norfolk			
Clifford			Devon	
Clive (K.)	Kilkenny			England
Clive (R.)	Shropshire			Lancs
Clough	Denbigh			Yorks
Cobbett			Suffolk (?)	
Cobden			Sussex	
Cockburn	Berwick			France
Cockerell	Somerset			
Coke	Norfolk			
Colby	Wales			
Colebrooke	England			
Colenso	Cornwall			
Coleridge (H.)	Devon			Gloucester
Coleridge (S.)	Devon			
Colet	Bucks			Norfolk
Collier				Cambs
Collins (W.)			Sussex	
Collins (W. Wicklow W.)				Scotland
Colman			England	
Columba	Ireland (Connaught)			Ireland (Leinster)

	Paternal grandfather.	Paternal grandmother.	Maternal grandfather.	Maternal grandmother.
Columban			Ireland (Leinster)	
Congreve	Staffs			
Conington	Lincs			
Constable	Suffolk [Yorks]			Suffolk
Cook	Northumberland (?)			
Cooke (G.)	England (?)			Scotland (?)
Cooke (H.)	Down [England]			[Scotland]
Cooper (First Lord Shaftesbury)	Hants			Dorset
Cooper (Third Lord)			England	
Cooper (Astley)	Norfolk			
Cooper (S.)			England	
Copley (J. S.)	Yorks and Limerick			Lancs and Clare
Copley (Lord Lyndhurst)	Limerick	Clare		England (?)
Cosin	Norfolk			Norfolk
Cotes				Leicester
Cotman			Norfolk	
Cotton (A.)	Cheshire			Essex

	Paternal grandfather.	Paternal grandmother.	Maternal grandfather.	Maternal grandmother.
Cotton (C.)	Staffs		Derby	
Cotton (R.)	[Cheshire]		Leicester	
Coutances				
Coverdale		Cornwall		
Cowley (A.)		Yorks		
Cowley (H.)		England		
Cowper	Devon			
Cox	Herts		Norfolk	
Cozens	Warwick		Warwick	
Crabbe	Russia	Kent		
Cranmer	Suffolk		Suffolk	
Crashaw	Lincs and Notts		Lincs	
Creighton	Yorks			
Crichton	Cumberland		Cumberland	
Croker	Dumfries		Fife	
Crome	Devon		Galway	
Cromwell (O.)		Norfolk		
Cromwell (T.)	Glamorgan and Hunts		Cambs (?)	
Cross	Notts			
Cruikshank	Flint		Derby (?)	
Cudworth	Midlothian			
Cullen		England		
Curran	Lanark			
	Cumberland and Cork			

	Paternal grandfather.	Paternal grandmother.	Maternal grandfather.	Maternal grandmother.
Cuthbert			Scotland (? Lothians)	
Dalrymple		Ayr		
Dalton		Cumberland		Cumberland
Dampier			Somerset [? Huguenot]	
Danby		Wexford		
Daniel			Somerset	
Darwin (C.)	Lincoln			
Darwin (E.)		Lincoln [Norfolk and Notts]	Staffs	Cheshire
D'Avenant			Oxford	
Davies		Wilts		
Davy	Cornwall [Norfolk]			Wilts
Dawson		Notts		
Day			England	
Deane		Gloucester		
Dee		Radnor		Bucks (?)
Defoe		Flanders (?) and Northants		England (?)
Dekker			England	
De Morgan			England	
Dempster		Aberdeen		Scotland
Denham		England		Ireland
Denman	Notts			Scotland

	Paternal grandfather.	Paternal grandmother.	Maternal grandfather.	Maternal grandmother.
De Quincey		Lancashire		
D'Ewes	Holland		Dorset	Kent
Dibden		Cambs		
Dickens		Hants		
Digby		Hants		
Dobell		Rutland		
Dobson		Kent		
Doddridge		Herts		
Dodgson		Devon		
Dodwell				Bucks
Dolben				
Donne				
Douglas				
Dowland				
Doyle		Denbigh		
Drake		England		
Drayton		[and Wales?]		
Drummond (T.)			England	
Drummond (W.)				Germany
Dryden				
Dudley				
Duff				
Dugdale				
Du Maurier				
				Yorks (?)
				Carnarvon

	Paternal grandfather.	Paternal grandmother.	Maternal grandfather.	Maternal grandmother.
Dunbar			Haddington (?)	
Duncan		Perth		
Dundas				Ross
Dunning		Devon		Devon
Duns			Northumberland [or Berwick] Somerset (?)	
Dunstan				
D'Urfey		France		Hunts
Dyce		Aberdeen		Aberdeen
Eastlake (C.)		Devon		Devon
Eastlake (Lady)		Lancashire		Norfolk
Edgeworth		Longford [England]	Germany	Oxford
Edmund			Berks	
Edwardes		Shropshire [Wales]		
Edwards		Suffolk		Ireland and Norfolk
Eliot		Cornwall		
Elliston		Suffolk		
Elyot		Somerset		
Emlyn		Rutland (?)		Kent
Erskine		Berwick		Orkney
Etherege		Oxford		

	Paternal grand-father.		Paternal grand-mother.		Maternal grand-father.		Maternal grand-mother.
Etty		Yorks				Yorks	
Faber		[Huguenot]				Yorks	
Falconer		Elgin					
Fanshawe		Derby				Kent	
Faraday				Yorks	[?Ire-land]		
Farquhar				Ireland			
Faucit		England			France		
Fawcett		Westmore-land				Wilts (?)	
Ferguson				Banff			
Fergusson		Aberdeen				Aberdeen	
Ferrar						Cheshire	
Ferrier		Renfrew				Forfar	
Fielding	Warwick		Somerset			Somerset	
Fitzgerald		Ireland (?)				Ireland	
Fitzgibbon		Limerick					
Flamstead				Derby			
Flaxman		Norfolk					
Fletcher (A.)		Haddington					
Fletcher (J.)		Norfolk					
Flinders		Lincoln					
Flood				Ireland			
Flower		Herts				Warwick	
Foote		Cornwall					
Forbes (C.)		Isle of Man				Isle of Man	
Forbes (J.)		Aberdeen				Perth	

	Paternal grandfather.		Paternal grandmother.		Maternal grandfather.		Maternal grandmother.
Ford		Devon				Devon	
Forster						Norfolk	
Fortescue		Devon (?)					
Fox (C. J.)	Wilts		Lincoln				
Fox (G.)		Leicester					
Foxe (J.)				Lincoln			
Foxe (R.)							
Francis		Ireland		Lincoln			
Frankland				Lancashire			
Franklin		Lincoln [Norfolk]					
Franks					Worcester		Norfolk
Freeman		Warwick				Warwick	
Frere	Norfolk [Suffolk]		Surrey				
Frobisher		Yorks [Wales]					
Froude		Devon				Cumberland	
Fry		Norfolk					
Fuller		[? Berks]			Essex [and Suffolk]		Surrey
Gainsboro'		Suffolk				Suffolk	
Galt				Ayr			
Gardiner				Suffolk			
Garnett				Derby			

	Paternal grand-father.	Paternal grand-mother.	Maternal grand-father.	Maternal grand-mother.
Garrick	France		Ireland	
Gascoigne	Beds		Yorks	
Gaskell	Berwick		Lancashire	
Gauntlett	Wilts		Glamorgan	
Gay	Devon			
Geoffrey			Monmouth	
Gibbon	Kent and Shropshire [Suffolk]			
Gibbons	Cambridge [Norfolk]			
Gibson	Carnarvon		Wales	
Gifford	Devon		Devon	
Gilbert (H.)			Devon	
Gilbert (J.)	Derby			
Gilbert (W.)	Suffolk			
Gillray	Lanark			
Giraldus	England		Wales	
Girtin			England	
Gladstone	Midlothian	Midlothian	Ross	
Glisson	Dorset			
Godwin (M.)	Ireland	England (?)	Ireland	
Godwin (W.)			Cambs (?)	
Goldsmith	Ireland [England]		Ireland	
Gordon	Scotland	England	England	
Gower	Kent			

	Paternal grandfather.	Paternal grandmother.	Maternal grandfather.	Maternal grandmother.
Graham (G.)		Cumberland	Yorks	
Graham (J.)		Kincardine		
Grattan		Dublin		
Gray				Bucks
Green		Oxford		Oxford
Greene			Norfolk	
Grenville (G.)		Bucks		
Grenville (W.)		Bucks		Norfolk (?)
Gresham		Norfolk		Northampton
Grew		Warwick		Notts
Grey			England	
			[Leicester]	
Grocyn			Wilts	
Grosseteste			Suffolk	
Grote	Germany [Flemish Huguenot]			Lincoln [French Huguenot]
Hale			Gloucester	
Hales (J.)		Somerset		
Hales (S.)		Kent		Herts
Hall		Leicester		
Hallam		Lincs		
Halley		Derby		
Halliwell-Phillips		Lancashire		
Hamilton (A.)			Ireland and Scotland	

	Paternal grand-father.		Paternal grand-mother.	Maternal grand-father.		Maternal grand-mother.
Hamilton (W.)		Lanark			Lanark	
Hamilton (W. R.)	Ireland [Scotland]		Wigton		Ireland (?)	
Hamilton (T.)					Berwick	
Hamley		Cornwall			Shetland	
Hampden		Bucks			Hunts	
Hardinge					Kent	
Harrington		Lincs			Northants	
Hartley					Yorks (?)	
Harvey		Kent			Kent	
Hastings		Worcester				
Havelock		Durham [Lincoln]			Durham	
Hawke		Cornwall		Yorks		Yorks
Hawkins	Cornwall		Devon		Cornwall	
Hawkwood		Essex				
Haydon		Devon				
Hazlitt		Antrim			Cambs	
Hemans		Sligo		Italy		Lancashire
Henderson			Fife			
Herbert (A.)		Montgomery			England (?)	
Herbert (E.)		Montgomery [Monmouth]			Shropshire	
Herbert (G.)		Montgomery [Monmouth]			Shropshire	
Herrick		Leicester				
Herschel		Germany			England	

	Paternal grand-father.	Paternal grand-mother.	Maternal grand-father.	Maternal grand-mother.
Heylin		Montgomery		Kent
Heywood (J.)			England	
Heywood (T.)			Lincoln	
Hickes		Yorks		Yorks
Hill		Worcester		
Hinton		Oxford and Bucks [and Essex]		
Hoadley			England	
Hobbes		Wilts (?)		Wilts
Hodgson		Cheshire		Lancashire
Hogarth		Westmore-land		
Hogg			Selkirk	
Holcroft			England	
Holl	Germany			England
Hood (S.)		Somerset		Dorset
Hood (T.)		Scotland		
Hook (T.)		Norfolk		
Hook (W.)		Norfolk		Aberdeen
Hooke			England	
Hooker		Devon		
Horner		Midlothian		
Horrocks		Lancashire		
Hort		Ireland [and Somerset and Hants]		England [? Suffolk]

	Paternal grand-father.	Paternal grand-mother.	Maternal grand-father.	Maternal grand-mother.
Howard			England	
Howell	Wales			Wales
Hubert	Suffolk [or Norfolk]			
Hughes				Yorks
Hume	Berwick			
Hunt				England
Hunter (J.)	Ayr			Lanark
Hunter (R.)	Roxburgh			Roxburgh
Huskisson	Staffs			Staffs
Hutcheson	Ayr	Ireland		Armagh (?)
Hutton (J.)	Midlothian			
Hutton (R.)	Ireland (?)			Notts
Huxley	Warwick [? Staffs]			Wilts
Hyde	Cheshire			Wilts
Inchbald	Suffolk			
Ireton	Derby			
Irving	Dumfries [Fr. Huguenot]			Dumfries
Jameson	Dublin			
Jeffrey	Midlothian			Lanark
Jenner	Glo'ster (?)			Gloucester
Jerrold			England	
Jervis	Staffs			Staffs and Cheshire

	Paternal grandfather.		Paternal grandmother.		Maternal grandfather.		Maternal grandmother.
Jevons		Staffs			Lancashire		Lancashire
Jewel		Devon					
John of Salisbury				Wilts			
Johnson		Staffs				Worcester	
Johnston		Dumfries				Ayr	
Jones (I.)		Denbigh (?)					
Jones (J. T.)		Suffolk and Norfolk					
Jones (W.)		Anglesey				England	
Jones (W. B.)		Cardigan				Essex	
Jonson		Dumfries (?)				England (?)	
Jordan						Ireland	
Joule		Derby				Lancashire	
Jowett	[Yorks]		Yorks			Lancashire	
Juxon				England			
Kean		Ireland					
Keats		Devon [or Cornwall]					
Keble		Gloucester				Scotland [& Hants ?]	
Keeley				Suffolk			
Keene		Suffolk				Suffolk	
Kelly	Dublin		Westmeath			England	
Kemble (F.)	Hereford		Ireland		France		Switzerland

	Paternal grandfather.		Paternal grandmother.		Maternal grandfather.		Maternal grandmother.
Kemble (J.)	Hereford		Ireland		France		Switzerland
Kemble (J. P.)		Hereford [? Wilts]				Ireland	
Kemp		Kent					
Ken		[Somerset ?]				Middlesex	
Kennett		Kent				Kent	
Kenyon		Flint				Cheshire	
Killigrew		Cornwall				Norfolk	
King (T.)				England			
King (W.)		Aberdeen					
Kingsley (C.)		Devon					
Kingsley (M.)		Devon					
Kirkcaldy		Fife				Fife	
Knight				England			
Knollys				Cheshire			
Knowles		Dublin				Cork	
Knox				Haddington			
Lake						Middlesex	
Lamb		Lincoln				Herts	
Lambert		Yorks					
Lancaster				England			
Lander				Cornwall			
Landon		Hereford				Wales	
Landor		Staffs				Warwick	
Landseer		Lincoln					
Lane		Hereford				Suffolk (?)	

	Paternal grand-father.	Paternal grand-mother.	Maternal grand-father.	Maternal grand-mother.
Langland			Shropshire (?)	
Langton (S.)			England	
Langton (W.)			Leicester	
Lardner	Hants			
Latimer	Leicester			
Law (E., Baron Ellenboro')	West-moreland			Cumberland
Law (E., Earl of Ellenboro')	West-moreland	Cumberland		
Law (J.)	Edinburgh			
Law (W.)	Northampton			
Lawes (H.)	Wilts (?)			
Lawes (J. B.)	Herts			Oxford
Lawrence (H.)	Londonderry			Donegal [Scotland]
Lawrence (J.)	Londonderry			Donegal [Scotland]
Lawrence (S.)	Hereford			
Lawrence (T.)				Worcester
Layard	[Huguenot]			Kent
Leake	Suffolk			
Lee			England [Herts or Leicester?]	
Leech	Ireland			

	Paternal grand-father.	Paternal grand-mother.	Maternal grand-father.	Maternal grand-mother.
Lefroy			England [Huguenot]	
Leighton (F.)	Yorks [Shropshire]			Middlesex
Leighton (R.)	Forfar			
Leland	Lancashire			
Leslie (A.)	Aberdeen			Perth
Leslie (C.)	Aberdeen			
Leslie (J.)	Aberdeen			
L'Estrange	Norfolk			Norfolk
Lever	Lancashire			Ireland [England]
Lewes	Wales			
Lewis (J. F.)	Germany			England (?)
Lewis (G. C.)	Radnor			Hereford
Lewis (W. T.)	Wales			
Liddon	Hants (?)			Surrey
Lightfoot	Yorks			Northumberland
Lilburne	Durham			
Lillo	Holland			England
Linacre			Kent (?)	
Lindsay	Haddington			
Lingard	Lincoln			
Linnell	Bucks [? Northants]			
Linton (E.)	Norfolk	Norfolk		

	Paternal grand-father.		Paternal grand-mother.		Maternal grand-father.		Maternal grand-mother.
Linton (W.)	Aberdeen						
Lister		Yorks (?)					
Liston				England (?)			
Littleton		Devon					
Livingstone		Inverness				Lanark	
Lloyd		Anglesey					
Locke		Somerset				Somerset	
Lockhart		Lanark				Midlothian	
Lodge		Shropshire				Northants	
Loftus		Yorks					
Lovelace		Kent					
Lover		Dublin					
Lowe							
Lowth		[Lincs and Hunts]				Worcester Dorset	
Lucas		Clare					
Ludlow		Wilts					
Lydgate				Suffolk		Somerset	
Lyell		Forfar					
Lyly				Kent		Yorks	
Lytton (Earl of)	Norfolk		Herts				
Lytton (Lord)		Norfolk				Ireland Herts	
Macaulay		Argyll					
Macdonald		Sutherland				Gloucester	
Macfarren							
Mackay		Sutherland				Lanark Ross	

	Paternal grandfather.	Paternal grandmother.	Maternal grandfather.	Maternal grandmother.
Mackintosh		Inverness		
Mackenzie		Midlothian		Nairn
Macklin		Down (?)		Westmeath (?)
Maclaurin		Argyll		
Maclise		Elgin		Cork
				[Scotland]
Macnaghten		Antrim		Tyrone
Macready		Dublin		Lincoln and Derby
Maginn		Cork		
Maine		Roxburgh		Berks
Malcolm		Fife and Dumfries		Dumfries
Malone		Westmeath		Essex
Malthus		Surrey		
Manning	Herts			
Map			Hereford and Wales	
Marlowe		Kent		Kent (?)
Marryat		England [Huguenot]		Germany
Marsh			England	
Marshall		Hunts		
Marston		Shropshire		Italy
Marten		Berks		
Martineau (H.)		Norfolk [Huguenot]		Northumberland

	Paternal grand-father.		Paternal grand-mother.		Maternal grand-father.		Maternal grand-mother.
Martineau (J.)		Norfolk [Huguenot]				Northumberland Yorks	
Marvell							
Massinger		Wilts					
Mathews (C.)	Glamorgan	England				England (?)	
Mathews (C. J.)		[Glamorgan]					
Maurice		Wales				Norfolk	
Maxwell		Midlothian				Northumberland	
Mayow				Cornwall			
Mead		Bucks					
Melville		Forfar				Forfar	
Merivale	Devon [Northants, Notts & France]		Germany		Norfolk		Devon
Middleton (C.)				Yorks (?)			
Middleton (T.)				England			
Mill (J.)		Forfar				Forfar	
Mill (J. S.)	Forfar		Forfar			England	
Millais		Jersey [France]				England	
Miller		Cromarty (?)				Ross	
Milman	Devon		Devon			Gloucester	
Milner (I.)		Yorks					
Milner (J.)		Lancashire					
Milton		Oxford					

	Paternal grand-father.	Paternal grand-mother.	Maternal grand-father.	Maternal grand-mother.
Mitchell		Stirling		
Mitford		Northumberland		Hants
Moffat				Haddington
Monck		Devon		Devon
Monson		Lincs		Lincs
Montagu (C.)		Northants		Lincs
Montagu (E.)		Yorks		Cambs and Kent
Montagu (R.)			England	
Moore (J.)		Stirling		Lanark
Moore (T.)		Kerry		Wexford
More (H.)		Norfolk and Suffolk		Gloucester
More (T.)		Herts (?)		[Beds ?]
Morgan (G. O.)		Wales		Sweden (?) [Huguenot & England]
Morgan (H.)		Glamorgan		
Morgan (S.)		Mayo		Shropshire
Morland (G.)		Berks (?)		
Morland (S.)			England	
Morley			England	Ireland
Morris	Worcester [from Welsh Border]	Notts		Worcester

	Paternal grand-father.	Paternal grand-mother.	Maternal grand-father.	Maternal grand-mother.
Morton	Yorks			
Mulready	Clare			
Mun			England	
Munday			Staffs (?)	
Mundella	Italy			Wales
Munden			England	
Munro	Lanark			
Murchison	Ross			Ross
Murdock	Ayr			
Murray	Edinburgh [Perth]			
Myers	Yorks			Cumberland
Nairne	Perth			Perth
Napier (C.)	Stirling			Lanark (?)
Napier (C. J.)	Scotland	Dublin		[France]
Napier (J.)	Midlothian			
Napier (Sir J.)	Antrim			Antrim
Napier (R. C.)	Scotland (?)			
Napier (W. J. P.)	Scotland	Dublin		[France]
Nash	Hereford			[? Suffolk]
Nasmyth (J.)	Midlothian			Midlothian
Nasmyth (P.)	Midlothian			Midlothian
Naylor			Yorks	

	Paternal grand-father.	Paternal grand-mother.	Maternal grand-father	Maternal grand-mother.
Neale (E. V.)	Berks			Warwick
Neale (J. M.)		Staffs		Essex
Needham		Derby		Oxford
Neill		Ayr		
Neilson (J.)		Lanark		England
Neilson (L. A.)		Spain (?)		
Nelson		Norfolk		Suffolk and Norfolk
Newcomen		Devon [Lincs]		
Newman (F.)		Cambs [Holland]		[Huguenot]
Newman (J.)		Cambs [Holland]		[Huguenot]
Newton		Lincoln [English family in Haddington]		Rutland
Nicholson		Down		Antrim
Northcote		Devon		
Norton				Bucks
Nott		Hereford		Norfolk
Nowell		Lancashire		Lancashire
Noye		Cornwall		
Ochterlony		Forfar		
Ockham			Surrey (?)	

	Paternal grandfather.	Paternal grandmother.	Maternal grandfather.	Maternal grandmother.
Ockley	Norfolk			
O'Connell	Kerry			Cork
Oglethorpe	Yorks			Tipperary
Oldcastle	Hereford			
Oldfield	[and Wales]		England	
Oldys	Dorset and Gloucester			
O'Leary			Cork	
Oliphant (L.)	Perth			[Highlands]
Oliphant (M.)	Midlothian			Fife
O'Neill	Tyrone			
Opie (A.)	Suffolk			Norfolk
Opie (J.)	Cornwall			Cornwall
Ordericus	France			England
Otway	[Yorks ?]		England	
Oughtred	Northumberland			
Outram	Derby			Aberdeen
Owen (J.)	Wales			
Owen (Sir R.)	Bucks			Lancashire [Huguenot]
Owen (R.)	Montgomery			Montgomery
Paget (J.)	Norfolk		Cheshire	
Paget (W.)	Staffs			

	Paternal grandfather.	Paternal grandmother.	Maternal grandfather.	Maternal grandmother.
Paine		Norfolk		Norfolk
Paley		Yorks		Yorks
Palmer (E. H.)		Cambs		Norfolk and Scotland [Highlands]
Palmer (J.)			England	
Palmer (R.)		Leicester and Essex		Yorks
Palmer (S.)	Devon [or Wilts]			
Paris			England	
Park		Selkirk		
Parker (M.)		Norfolk		
Parker (T.)		Staffs		Cheshire
Parkes (E.)		Warwick		
Parkes (H. S.)		Staffs		Shropshire
Parkes (H.)		Warwick		
Parnell		Queen's County		[United States]
Parr		Leicester		France
Parsons (R.)		Somerset		
Parsons (W.)				Kent
Pater	Bucks and Norfolk [Flanders]			
Paterson		Dumfries		

	Paternal grandfather.		Paternal grandmother.		Maternal grandfather.		Maternal grandmother.
Patmore		England [& Germany]				Scotland	
Patrick				Dumbarton			
Pattison		Yorks				Yorks	
Payne		France				Lincoln (?)	
Pearson (J.)		Westmoreland				Merioneth [or Carnarvon]	
Pearson (J. L.)		Durham					
Pecock				Wales			
Peel		Lancashire [Yorks]					
Peele		Devon (?)					
Peirce				England			
Pellew		Cornwall					
Penn (Sir W.)		Gloucester [or Wilts]				Yorks	
Penn (W.)	Glo'ster		Yorks			Holland	
Penry		Brecknock					
Pepys		Cambs					
Perkins		Warwick					
Perry		Aberdeen					
Peters		Cornwall				Cornwall	
Petty		Hants					
Phelps		Somerset					
Phillip		Aberdeen					
Picton		Pembroke					

	Paternal grand-father.	Paternal grand-mother.	Maternal grand-father.	Maternal grand-mother.
Pitman		Wilts		
Pitt (Earl of Chatham)	Dorset	Elgin		Waterford
Pitt (W.)	Dorset	Waterford		Bucks
Pococke		Hants		England
Pollock		Berwick		Yorks
Pope		Hants (?)	England	
Popham		[Devon ?]		Norfolk
Porson		Norfolk	England	
Pott				Montgomery
Powell		Radnor	Cheshire [& Lincoln]	
Pownall				Carnarvon
Pratt		Oxford [Devon]	Northants	
Preston				Shropshire
Prestwich		Shropshire [Lancs. & Ireland]		
Price		Glamorgan		Yorks
Priestley		Yorks		Somerset
Prior		Dorset		
Prynne	Glo'ster and Somerset [Shropshire ?]			

	Paternal grand-father.	Paternal grand-mother.	Maternal grand-father.	Maternal grand-mother.
Pugin		France		England
Pulteney		Leicester		
Purcell		Shrop-shire (?)		
Pusey		Norfolk [Walloon Huguenot]		
Pym		Somerset		Kent
Quarles		Essex		
Quin		Dublin		
Radcliffe		Rutland [Holland]		Nottingham [or Essex]
Raeburn				Dumfries
Raffles		Yorks		
Raleigh		Devon [and Cornwall]		Devon
Randolph		Sussex		Northants
Ray		Essex		
Reade		Oxford		
Reid (T.)		Aberdeen		Banff
Reid (W.)		Aberdeen		
Reynolds		Devon [and Holland]		Devon
Richardson		Surrey		
Ridley		Northum-berland		
Ritson		Westmoreland		

	Paternal grand-father.		Paternal grand-mother.	Maternal grand-father.		Maternal grand-mother.
Robertson		Fife			Ayr	
Robinson	West-meath		Kilkenny			
Rodney		Somerset				
Roe		Essex			Norfolk	
Rogers	Wales [& France]				Cheshire	
Romney		Westmore-land			Cumberland	
Roscoe		Lancashire				
Rose		Nairn				
Ross (H. D.)		Wigton			Haddington	
Ross (R.)		Down			Cork	
Rossetti (C.)		Italy		Italy		England
Rossetti (D. G.)		Italy		Italy		England
Rowe		Devon			Beds	
Rowlandson			England			
Ruskin		Midlothian				
Russell		Down			Antrim	
Sabine		Kent			Shropshire	
Sacheverell	Notts & Derby				Leicester	
Sadler	Warwick & Derby				[Huguenot]	
St. John		Beds			Beds	
St. Leger		Kent			Kent	
Sale					Hunts	

	Paternal grandfather.	Paternal grandmother.	Maternal grandfather.	Maternal grandmother.
Salesbury				Denbigh
Sancroft		Suffolk		Suffolk
Sandby		Notts		
Savage			England	
Savile		Yorks		
Scarlett			England	
Scott (D.)		Lanark		
Scott (G. G.)		Lincoln		
Scott (J.)		Northumberland		Northumberland
Scott (Walter)		Midlothian		
Scott (William)		Northumberland		Northumberland
Scotus			Ireland	
Sedgwick			Yorks	
Seeley		Bucks		
Selden		Sussex		Kent
Shakespeare		Warwick		Warwick
Sharp		Yorks		
Sheil		Kilkenny		Tipperary
Sheldon		Staffs		
Shelley		Sussex [? Suffolk]		Surrey
Sheridan	Cavan			England
Shirley			England	
Siddons		Hereford [? Wilts]		Ireland
Sidgwick		Yorks		

	Paternal grand-father.	Paternal grand-mother.	Maternal grand-father.	Maternal grand-mother.
Tait	Aberdeen & Midlothian			
Tallis			England [? Essex]	
Tarleton	Lancs			Lancs
Taylor (H.)	Northumberland			Durham
Taylor (J.)	Gloucester & Cambs			
Taylor (W.)	Norfolk			Norfolk
Telford			Dumfries	
Temple	Warwick & Derby			Lancs (?) & Surrey
Tennyson	Lincoln			Lincoln
Thackeray	Yorks	Wilts		
Thirlwall	Northumberland			Radnor
Thomas			Radnor (?)	
Thompson			Cork	
Thomson	Roxburgh			Berwick
Thurloe			Essex (?)	
Thurlow	Norfolk			Suffolk
Tillotson	Cheshire			Yorks
Toland			Londonderry	
Tone	Kildare			
Tooke			England	

	Paternal grandfather.		Paternal grandmother.		Maternal grandfather.		Maternal grandmother.
Trelawney		Cornwall				Cornwall	
Trevithick		Cornwall				Cornwall	
Trollope (A.)	Lincoln		Holland				
Trollope (H.)		Lincoln					
Tunstall		Lancs				Yorks (?)	
Turner		Devon				Notts (?)	
Tye				England			
Tyndale		Gloucester (?)					
Tyndall	Carlow [Glo'ster]						
Udall				Hants			
Urquhart		Cromarty					
Ussher				Ireland [England]			
Vanbrugh	Flanders [Huguenot]					England	
Vane	Kent		Kent			Essex	
Varley		Lincoln [or Notts]				Yorks	
Vaughan		Brecknock					
Vere (F.)		Essex				Essex	
Vere (H.)		Essex				Essex	
Vernon		Cheshire & Staffs					
Wakley		Devon					

	Paternal grand-father.	Paternal grand-mother.	Maternal grand-father.	Maternal grand-mother.
Walker			England	
Wallace	Renfrew and Ayr [? Shropshire]			Ayr
Waller (E.)		Bucks		
Waller (W.)		Kent		
Wallis		Northants		Kent
Walpole (H.)	Norfolk			Kent
Walpole (R.)		Suffolk		Suffolk
Walsh		Norfolk	Kildare	
Walsingham		Kent [Norfolk]		Herts
Walter			England	
Walton		Staffs		
Warburton		Cheshire		
Ward (M.)		Yorks		Yorks
Ward (S.)		Herts		
Ward (W. G.)			England	
Warham		Hants		
Warton				Surrey
Watson (R.)		Westmoreland		
Watson (T.)			England	
Watt		Aberdeen & Renfrew		Lanark
Waynflete		Lincoln [? & Essex]		

	Paternal grand-father.		Paternal grand-mother.		Maternal grand-father.		Maternal grand-mother.
Webster		Yorks				Yorks	
Wedgwood		Staffs				Shropshire	
Wentworth		Armagh					
Wesley (C.)	Devon [& Ireland]		Staffs			Warwick	
Wesley (J.)	Devon [& Ireland]		Staffs			Warwick	
Westmacott				England			
Whately		Surrey [and Oxford ?]				Herts	
Wheatstone		Gloucester					
Whewell		Lancashire					
Whiston				England			
Whitbread		Beds				Bucks	
White (G.)		Hants				Sussex	
White (J. B.)	Waterford [Dublin]					Spain	
Whitefield		Gloucester					
Whitehead				Westmore-land			
Whitelocke						Bucks	
Whitgift		Lincoln					
Whittington		Glo'ster (?)					
Whitworth		Yorks and Lancashire					
Wilberforce (S.)	Yorks		Oxford			Warwick	

	Paternal grand-father.	Paternal grand-mother.	Maternal grand-father.	Maternal grand-mother.
Wilberforce (W.)	Yorks			Oxford
Wilde	Ireland [Durham]	Galway		
Wilfrid			England	
Wilkes	Beds			
Wilkie	Midlothian			Fife
Wilkins	Oxford			Cheshire
Wilks	Worcester & Dublin			
Willet			England	
William of Malmesbury	France			Somerset (?)
William of Newburgh			Yorks	
Williams (C. H.)	Monmouth [Worcester]			
Williams (D.)	Denbigh			Denbigh
Williams (Sir R.)	Monmouth			
Williams (R.)	Wales (?)			
Williams (W.)	Anglesey			Denbigh

	Paternal grand-father.		Paternal grand-mother.		Maternal grand-father.		Maternal grand-mother.
Williamson (J.)				England			
Williamson (W. C.)	Yorks		Yorks		Had-dington		Yorks
Willoughby		Notts				Perth	
Wilson (J.)				Renfrew			
Wilson (R.)						Flint	
Wilson (Sir R.)		Yorks					
Wilson (T.)						Cheshire	
Windham		Norfolk				Essex	
Winthrop		Suffolk				Suffolk	
Winwood		Northants					
Wiseman	Waterford [settled in Spain]					Kilkenny	
Wishart				Forfar			
Wilton		Hants					
Woffington		[Lanca-shire]		Ireland			
Wolcot				Devon			
Wolfe		Ireland [Wales]				Yorks	
Wollaston		Staffs [? & French Huguenot]					
Wolsey				Suffolk			

	Paternal grand-father.	Paternal grand-mother.	Maternal grand-father.	Maternal grand-mother.
Woodward			England	
Woolner	Suffolk			
Wordsworth (Charles)	Yorks		Warwick [Mont-gomery]	Glo'ster
Wordsworth (Christopher)	Yorks		Warwick [Mont-gomery]	Glo'ster
Wordsworth (W.)	Yorks			
Wotton (H.)	Kent			Kent
Wotton (N.)	Kent			
Wren	Warwick [Durham]			Wilts
Wright (J.)	Derby			
Wright (T.)	Yorks			
Wulfstan			Warwick	
Wyatt	Kent (?)			Surrey
Wycherley	Shropshire			
Wycliffe			Yorks	
Wykeham			Hants	
Wyse	Waterford			Waterford
Yates			England (?)	
Yorke	Wilts			Kent
Young (A.)	Suffolk			Holland
Young (E.)			England	
Young (T.)	Somerset			Somerset

APPENDIX C

OCCUPATION OR SOCIAL POSITION OF FATHERS

Abbot	clothworker
Abercromby	upper class
Abington	soldier
Adam	architect
Adams	farmer
Adamson	baker
Addison	Church
Airy	collector of excise
Alexander	upper class
Allen	upper class
Andrewes	merchant and sea captain
Arblay, D'	musician and author
Arkwright	humble
Arne	upholsterer
Armstrong	corn merchant
Arnold (M.)	schoolmaster
Arnold (T.)	collector of customs
Arthur	official
Ascham	yeoman
Atterbury	Church
Austen	Church
Bacon (A.)	upper class
Bacon (F.)	upper class
Bacon (N.)	sheepreeve
Bacon (R.)	upper class
Bagehot	banker
Baillie	minister *
Baily	banker
Baker	merchant
Balfour	upper class
Bancroft	upper class
Banim	farmer
Banks (T.)	steward
Bannister	actor
Barbauld	Church
Barclay (J.)	lawyer
Barclay (R.)	army
Barnes	farmer
Barnfield	upper class
Barrow (I.)	draper
Barrow (J.)	peasant
Barry (A.)	apothecary
Barry (C.)	stationer
Barry (E.)	lawyer
Barry (J.)	builder
Baskerville	humble
Bates	manufacturer
Baxter	yeoman
Beardsley	brewery manager
Beaumont	upper class lawyer
Beckford	upper class commerce
Beddoes	doctor
Bedell	yeoman
Becher	actor
Behn	barber
Bell (A.)	barber
Bell (C.)	Church
Bennett	musician
Benson	manufacturer
Bentham (G.)	naval architect
Bentham (J.)	lawyer
Bentley	yeoman
Bessemer	engineer
Bethell	doctor
Betterton	cook
Bewick	farmer
Birch	Church
Bishop	merchant
Black	wine merchant
Blackmore	Church
Blackstone	silk mercer
Blake (R.)	merchant
Blake (W.)	hosier
Bonington	governor of gaol
Bonner	priest (?)
Booth	upper class
Borrow	maltster soldier

* 'Minister' is here throughout applied to all religious denominations except the Church of England. 'Priest' has reference to the Roman Catholic Church, whether before or since the Reformation.

Boscawen	upper class
Boswel	upper class lawyer
Bowen	Church
Bowring	woollen trade
Boyce	cabinet maker
Boyle (R.)	upper class
Bracegirdle	innkeeper
Bradford	yeoman
Bradlaugh	clerk
Bradley	upper class
Bradshaw (H.)	banker
Breton	trade
Brewster	minister
Bright	miller
Brontë (C.)	Church
Brontë (E.)	Church
Burke	civil service
Brown	purser
Browne (R.)	upper class
Browne (T.)	mercer
Browning (R.)	clerk
Bruce (H.)	upper class
Bruce (M.)	weaver
Buchanan	farmer
Buckle	merchant
Bunyan	whitesmith
Burke	lawyer
Burne-Jones	carver and gilder
Burnet	upper class lawyer
Burns	farmer
Burton (Sir Richard)	army
Butler (J.)	draper
Butler (S.)	farmer
Byng	upper class
Byron	upper class
Cadogan	lawyer
Cairns	army
Calamy	minister
Camden	painter stainer
Campbell (C.)	carpenter
Campbell (G.)	upper class
Campbell (J.)	minister
Campbell (T.)	trade
Campion (E.)	bookseller
Candlish	doctor
Canning (C.)	upper class
Canning (G.)	upper class
Canning (S.)	banker
Cantelupe	upper class
Canton	business
Carey	schoolmaster
Carleton	peasant farmer
Carlile	shoemaker
Carlyle	mason
Carpenter (M.)	minister
Carpenter (W. B.)	minister
Carrington	brewer
Carstares	minister
Case	Church
Cattermole	upper class
Cavendish (H.)	upper class
Cavendish (M.)	upper class
Cavendish (T.)	upper class
Cayley	merchant
Cecil	upper class
Challoner	wine cooper
Chalmers	merchant
Chantrey	carpenter farmer
Chatterton	shoemaker
Chaucer	vintner
Chesney	army
Chichele	yeoman draper
Chichester	upper class
Childers	upper class Church
Church	merchant
Churchill (C.)	Church
Churchill (J.)	upper class
Cibber (C.)	sculptor
Cibber (S.)	upholsterer
Clapperton	doctor
Clare	labourer
Clive (R.)	upper class
Clough	cotton merchant
Cobbett	peasant
Cobden	yeoman
Cockburn	upper class
Cockerell	architect
Coke	upper class
Colby	army
Colebrooke	banker
Colenso	mineral agent
Coleridge (H.)	author
Coleridge (S.)	Church
Colet	merchant
Collier	Church
Collins (W.)	hatter
Collins (W. W.)	artist
Colman	upper class
Columba	upper class
Congreve	army
Conington	Church
Constable	miller
Cook	agricultural labourer
Cooke (G.)	army
Cooke (H.)	farmer
Cooper (First Lord Shaftesbury)	upper class
Cooper (Third Lord Shaftesbury)	upper class
Cooper (A.)	Church

Copley (Lord Lyndhurst)	artist
Cotes	Church
Cotman	mercer
Cotton (A.)	upper class
Cotton (C.)	upper class
Cowley	trade
Cowper	upper class Church
Cox	blacksmith
Cozens	artist
Crabbe	collector of customs
Crashaw	Church
Crichton	upper class
Croker	surveyor of customs
Crome	journeyman weaver
Cromwell (O.)	upper class
Cromwell (T.)	blacksmith innkeeper
Cross	carpenter
Cruikshank	artist
Cudworth	Church
Cullen	lawyer
Dalrymple	upper class
Dalton	weaver
Dampier	farmer
Danby	farmer
Daniel	music master
Darwin (C.)	doctor
D'Avenant	vintner and innkeeper
Davy	yeoman
Dawson	cheesemonger
Day	collector of customs
Deane	upper class
De Foe	butcher yeoman
De Morgan	army
Dempster	upper class
Denham	upper class
Denman	doctor
De Quincey	merchant
D'Ewes	upper class
Dibdin	merchant
Dickens	clerk
Digby	upper class
Dobell	wine merchant
Doddridge	oilman
Dodgson	Church
Dodwell	army
Dolben	Church
Donne	trade
Douglas	upper class
Doyle	artist
Drake	upper class
Drummond (T.)	lawyer
Drummond (W.)	upper class
Dryden	upper class
Dudley	upper class
Du Maurier	upper class glass mfr.
Dundas	upper class lawyer
Dunning	lawyer
Dunstan	upper class
Dyce	doctor
Eastlake (C.)	admiralty agent
Eastlake (Lady)	doctor
Edgeworth	upper class
Edwardes	Church
Edwards	army
Eliot	upper class
Elyot	lawyer
Emlyn	trade
Erskine	minister
Etherege	army
Etty	miller and baker
Fanshawe	upper class
Faraday	smith
Farquhar	Church
Faucit	actor
Fawcett	draper
Ferguson	day labourer
Fergusson	clerk
Ferrar	merchant
Ferrier	law
Fielding	upper class army
Fitzgerald	upper class
Fitzgibbon	lawyer
Flamsteed	maltster
Fletcher (A.)	upper class
Fletcher (J.)	Church
Flinders	doctor
Flood	lawyer
Foote	trade
Forbes (E.)	banker
Forbes (J.)	upper class
Ford	upper class
Forster	minister
Fox (C. J.)	upper class
Fox (G.)	weaver
Foxe (R.)	yeoman
Francis	Church
Franklin	trade
Franks	navy
Frere	ironmaster
Froude	Church
Fry	banker
Fuller	Church

Gainsborough	woollen manufacturer
Galt	sea captain
Gardiner	clothworker
Garrick	army
Gascoigne	upper class
Gaskell	minister
Gauntlett	Church
Geoffrey	priest
Gibbons	musician
Gibson	market gardener
Gifford	sailor
Gilbert (J.)	estate agent
Gilbert (W.)	recorder
Gillray	soldier
Giraldus	upper class
Girtin	rope-maker
Gladstone	merchant
Godwin (W.)	minister
Goldsmith	Church
Gordon	army
Gower	upper class
Graham (G.)	doctor
Graham (J.)	upper class
Grattan	lawyer
Gray	money scrivener lawyer
Grenville (G.)	upper class
Grenville (W.)	upper class
Gresham	merchant
Grew	minister
Grey	army
Grote	banker
Hale	lawyer
Hallam	Church
Halley	soap-boiler
Hamilton (A.)	upper class
Hamilton (W.)	doctor
Hamley	navy
Hampden	upper class
Hardinge	Church
Harrington	upper class
Hartley	Church
Harvey	yeoman
Havelock	shipbuilder
Hawke	lawyer
Hawkwood	tanner
Haydon	printer
Hazlitt	minister
Hemans	merchant
Henderson	farmer
Herbert (A.)	lawyer
Herbert (E.)	upper class
Herbert (G.)	upper class
Herschel	man of science
Hickes	farmer
Hill	schoolmaster
Hinton	minister
Hoadley	Church schoolmaster
Hobbes	Church
Hodgson	banker
Hogarth	yeoman
Hogg	farmer
Holcroft	shoemaker
Holl	engraver
Hood (S.)	Church
Hood (T.)	publisher
Hook (T.)	composer
Hook (W.)	Church
Hooke	Church
Horner	merchant
Horrocks	farmer
Hort	upper class
Howard	upholsterer
Howell	Church
Hughes	author
Hunter (J.)	farmer
Hutcheson	minister
Hutton (J.)	merchant
Hutton (R.)	minister
Huxley	schoolmaster
Hyde	upper class
Inchbald	farmer
Irving	tanner
Jameson	artist
Jeffrey	lawyer (Clerk in court of sessions)
Jenner	Church
Jerrold	actor
Jervis	upper class lawyer
Jevons	nail maker
Johnson	trade
Johnston	trade
Jones (I.)	clothworker
Jones (W.)	yeoman
Jonson	minister
Jordan	stage underling
Joule	brewer
Jowett	furrier
Keats	livery stableman
Keble	Church
Keene	law
Kemble (F.)	actor
Kemble (J. M.)	actor
Kemble (J. P.)	actor
Kemp	upper class
Ken	lawyer
Kennett	Church

Kenyon	farmer
Killigrew	upper class
King (T.)	trade
King (W.)	miller
Kingsley (C.)	Church
Kingsley (M.)	doctor
Kirkcaldy	upper class
Knight	Church
Knowles	author
Knox	peasant
Lancaster	soldier shopkeeper
Lander	innkeeper
Landor	doctor
Landseer	artist
Lane	Church
Lardner	minister
Latimer	yeoman
Laud	clothier
Law (J.)	goldsmith
Law (E., Baron Ellenborough)	Church
Law (E., Earl of Ellenborough)	upper class
Law (W.)	grocer
Lawes (H.)	musician
Lawes (J.)	upper class
Lawrence (H.)	army
Lawrence (J.)	army
Lawrence (S.)	trade
Lawrence (T.)	innkeeper
Layard	civil service
Leake	naval gunner
Lee	Church
Leech.	coffee house keeper
Lefroy	Church
Leighton (F.)	doctor
Leighton (R.)	doctor
Leslie (A.)	upper class army
Leslie (C.)	Church
Leslie (J.)	upper class Church
L'Estrange	upper class
Lever	builder
Lewis (G. C.)	upper class
Lewis (J. F.)	engraver
Lewis (W. T.)	actor
Liddon	navy
Lightfoot	accountant
Lillo	jeweller
Lingard	carpenter
Linnell	wood carver
Linton (E.)	Church
Lister	wine merchant
Livingstone	small tea dealer
Lloyd	Church
Locke	lawyer
Lockhart	minister
Lodge	grocer
Lovelace	upper class
Lover	stockbroker
Lowe	Church
Lowth	Church
Lucas	upper class
Ludlow	upper class
Lyell	botanist
Lytton (B.)	army
Lytton (Earl)	upper class
Macaulay	author
Macfarren	theatrical manager
Mackenzie	doctor
Mackintosh	army
Maclaurin	minister
Maclise	soldier shoemaker
Macnaghten	lawyer
Macready	actor-manager
Maginn	schoolmaster
Maine	doctor
Malthus	author
Manning	merchant
Marlowe	shoemaker
Marsh	Church
Marshall	poor glover
Marston	lawyer
Marten	lawyer
Martineau (H.)	manufacturer
Martineau (J.)	manufacturer
Marvell	Church
Mathews (C.)	bookseller minister
Mathews (C. J.)	actor
Maurice	minister
Mead	minister
Merivale	lawyer
Middleton (C.)	Church
Mill (J.)	shoemaker
Mill (J. S.)	author
Miller	captain of sloop
Milman	doctor
Milner (I.)	business
Milner (J.)	tailor
Milton	scrivener yeoman (?)
Mitford	upper class
Moffat	custom house
Monck	upper class
Monson	upper class
Montagu (E.)	upper class
Montagu (R.)	Church
Moore (J.)	doctor author
Moore (T.)	provision dealer
More (T.)	lawyer

Morgan (G. O.)	Church
Morgan (H.)	upper class
Morgan (S.)	actor
Morland (G.)	artist
Morland (S.)	Church
Morris	bill broker
Morley	upper class
Morton	mercer
Mulready	leather breeches maker
Mun	merchant
Munday	draper
Munden	poulterer
Munro	merchant
Murchison	doctor
Murdock	millwright
Murray	publisher
Myers	Church
Nairne	upper class
Napier (C.)	upper class
Napier (C. J.)	upper class army
Napier (J.)	upper class
Napier (Sir J.)	merchant
Napier (R.)	army
Napier (W. J. P.)	upper class army
Nash	Church
Nasmyth (J.)	artist
Nasmyth (P.)	artist
Naylor	yeoman
Neale (E.)	Church
Neale (J.)	Church
Neill	army
Neilson (J.)	millwright
Nelson	Church
Newman (F. W.)	banker
Newman (J. H.)	banker
Newton	yeoman farmer
Nicholson	doctor
Northcote	watchmaker
Norton	business
Nott	yeoman farmer
Oglethorpe	army
Oldcastle	upper class
Oldfield	army
Oldys	lawyer
Oliphant (L.)	lawyer
Oliphant (M.)	business
O'Neill	upper class
Opie (A.)	doctor
Opie (J.)	carpenter
Ordericus	priest (married)
Otway	Church
Oughtred	Church
Outram	civil engineer
Owen (J.)	Church
Owen (Sir R.)	merchant
Owen (R.)	saddler
Paget (J.)	brewer shipowner
Paine	farmer
Paley	Church
Palmer (E. H.)	schoolmaster
Palmer (J.)	soldier
Palmer (R.)	Church
Palmer (S.)	bookseller
Park	farmer
Parker (M.)	calenderer of stuffs
Parker (T.)	lawyer
Parkes (H.)	farmer
Parkes (H. S.)	ironmaster
Parnell	upper class
Parr	doctor
Parsons (R.)	yeoman blacksmith
Parsons (W.)	carpenter
Pater	doctor
Patmore	author
Patrick	deacon (married)
Pattison	Church
Pearson (J.)	Church
Pearson (J. L.)	artist
Peel	manufacturer
Peele	business
Pellew	sea captain
Penn (Sir W.)	merchant sea captain
Penn (W.)	navy
Pepys	tailor
Perry	builder
Petty	clothier
Phelps	outfitter
Phillip	soldier
Pitman	factory overseer
Pitt (W., Earl of Chatham)	upper class
Pitt (W.)	upper class
Pollock	saddler
Pope	merchant
Porson	weaver
Pott	lawyer (scrivener)
Powell	ale keeper
Pratt	lawyer
Preston	farmer
Prestwich	wine merchant
Price	minister
Priestley	cloth dresser
Prior	joiner
Pugin	architect
Pulteney	upper class
Purcell	music copyist

Pusey	upper class
Quarles	upper class
Quin	lawyer
Radcliffe	trade
Raeburn	mill owner
Raffles	sea captain
Raleigh	upper class
Randolph	steward
Ray	blacksmith
Reid (T.)	minister
Reid (W.)	minister
Reynolds	Church
Richardson	carpenter
Ritson	yeoman
Robertson	minister
Robinson	navy
Rogers	merchant
Romney	builder and cabinet maker
Roscoe	market gardener tavern keeper
Rose	Church
Ross (H. D.)	army
Ross (R.)	army
Rossetti (C.)	opera librettist, etc.
Rossetti (D. G.)	opera librettist, etc.
Rowe	lawyer
Rowlandson	merchant
Ruskin	wine merchant
Sadler	upper class
St. John	upper class
St. Leger	upper class
Sale	army
Sancroft	yeoman
Scott (D.)	engraver
Scott (G. G.)	Church
Scott (J.)	coal factor
Scott (Walter)	lawyer
Scott (William)	coal factor
Sedgwick	Church
Seeley	publisher
Selden	yeoman
Shakespeare	yeoman trade
Sharp	salter
Sheil	upper class
Sheldon	menial servant
Shelley	upper class
Sheridan	actor
Siddons	actor
Sidgwick	Church
Sidney	upper class
Simpson	baker
Sinclair	upper class
Smart	nobleman's steward
Smith (A.)	lawyer
Smith (H. J. S.)	lawyer
Smith (S.)	business
Smith (T.)	upper class
Smith (W.)	farmer
Smith (W. R.)	minister
Smith (W. S.)	army
Somers	lawyer
Somerville	navy
South	merchant
Southey	farmer
Southwell	upper class
Speke	army
Spelman	upper class
Spenser	cloth maker
Sprat	Church
Stanhope	upper class
Stanley	Church
Steele	lawyer
Stephen	official
Stephenson	fireman
Sterne	army
Steevens	house painter
Stevens	sea captain
Stevenson	engineer
Stewart	minister
Stothard	publican
Street	lawyer
Stubbs	currier
Sturgeon	shoemaker
Suckling	upper class
Sullivan	musician
Sydenham	upper class
Symonds	doctor
Tait	upper class
Tarleton	merchant
Taylor (H.)	upper class
Taylor (J.)	barber surgeon
Taylor (W.)	manufacturer
Telford	shepherd
Temple	upper class
Tennyson	Church
Thirlwall	Church
Thompson	upper class
Thomson	minister
Thurloe	Church
Thurlow	Church
Tillotson	clothworker
Toland	priest
Tone	coach maker
Tooke	poulterer
Trelawney	army

Trevithick	mine manager of humble origin
Trollope (A.)	lawyer
Trollope (H.)	Church
Tunstall	upper class
Turner	barber
Tyndall	upper class
Urquhart	upper class
Ussher	lawyer
Vanburgh	sugar baker
Vane	upper class
Varley	tutor
Vaughan	upper class
Vere (F.)	upper class
Vere (H.)	upper class
Vernon	upper class
Walker	working jeweller
Wallace	upper class
Waller (E.)	upper class
Waller (W.)	upper class
Wallis	Church
Walpole (H.)	upper class
Walpole (R.)	upper class
Walsingham	lawyer
Walter	coal merchant
Walton	yeoman
Warburton	town clerk
Ward (M.)	upper class
Ward (S.)	lawyer
Ward (W. G.)	financier
Warham	upper class
Warton	author
Watson (R.)	Church
Watt	carpenter
Webster	actor and musical composer
Wedgwood	potter
Wentworth	doctor
Wesley (C.)	Church
Wesley (J.)	Church
Westmacott	sculptor
Whately	Church
Wheatstone	music seller
Whewell	carpenter
Whiston	Church
Whitbread	brewer
White (G.)	lawyer
White (J. B.)	merchant
Whitefield	innkeeper
Whitelocke	lawyer
Whitgift	merchant
Whitworth	minister
Wilberforce (W.)	upper class
Wilde	doctor
Wilfrid	upper class
Wilkes	malt distiller
Wilkie	minister
Wilkins	goldsmith
Willett	lawyer
Williams (C. H.)	manufacturer
Williams (Sir R.)	upper class
Williams (R.)	tailor
Williams (W.)	Church
Williamson (J.)	Church
Williamson (W.)	gardener
Wilson (J.)	manufacturer
Wilson (R.)	Church
Wilson (R. T.)	artist
Windham	army
Winthrop	lawyer
Wiseman	merchant
Woffington	bricklayer
Wolcot	doctor
Wolfe	army
Wollaston	Church
Wolsey	grazier
Woodward	tallow chandler
Woolner	post office official
Wordsworth (Chas.)	Church
Wordsworth (Christopher)	Church
Wordsworth (W.)	lawyer
Wotton (H.)	upper class
Wotton (N.)	upper class
Wren	Church
Wright (J.)	lawyer
Wright (T.)	printer
Wulfstan	upper class
Wyatt	upper class
Wycherley	lawyer
Yates	ship's steward
Yorke	lawyer
Young (A.)	Church
Young (E.)	Church

APPENDIX D

STATURE

5 ft. 0 in.	W. Blake T. Moore
5 ft. 1 in.	Caius H. Coleridge Keats
5 ft. 2 in.	Hunter
5 ft. 3 in.	De Quincey G. White S. Wilberforce
5 ft. 4 in.	Nelson
5 ft. 5 in.	Linnell Richardson
5 ft. 6 in.	Cockburn R. Fergusson Jeffrey* B. Lytton J. Wesley
5 ft. 7 in.	Bright Madox Brown Maurice C. J. Napier Otway
5 ft. 8 in.	Byron T. Lawrence Macaulay J. S. Mill Rossetti Swift† Tooke
5 ft. 9 in.	Burns S. Coleridge Dickens Gordon Paine Priestley W. Wordsworth
5 ft. 10 in.	Burke O. Cromwell Grote Hogg Huxley Kenyon Marryat C. Mathews
5 ft. 10 in.	Mulready Prestwich Ruskin Stevenson Street A. Trollope Wakley
5 ft. 11 in.	Sir R. Burton Carleton Carlyle Froude Liston O'Connell Porson Sedgwick Southey J. Wilson.
6 ft. 0 in.	R. Boyle Clapperton C. Darwin Millais W. J. Napier Park W. Scott Selden Tait
6 ft. 1 in.	Cobbett J. Cook Fielding Galt Hobbes Leech Petty Reade Tennyson
6 ft. 2 in.	Trevithick
6 ft. 3 in.	Borrow Fawcett Irving‡ Thackeray
6 ft. 4 in.	J. Bruce Duncan Graham

* According to one description Jeffrey was 'scarcely five feet.'
† It is worth noting that Swift was considered tall by his contemporaries.
‡ The estimates of Irving's height vary between 6 ft. 2 in. and 6 ft. 4 in.

APPENDIX E

PIGMENTATION

THE individuals whose pigmentation I have been able to ascertain are here arranged alphabetically in their groups: Fair, Medium, Dark. To facilitate reference no note is here taken of the three sub-divisions of the medium group.

I. — FAIR

Addison, Amherst, Arkwright, Beaton, Berkeley, Blackmore, Bright, Brown, Buchanan, C. Campbell, J. Campbell, S. Canning, Cantelupe, Clifford, Congreve, Copley (Lord Lyndhurst), Cowper, Cullen, Dee, Denham, Etty, Fergusson, Fitzgerald, A. Fletcher, J. Fletcher, Freeman, Frobisher, Gordon, Gray, Hardinge, Hogarth, Hogg, Hort, Hutcheson, A. Leslie, B. Lytton, Earl Lytton, Munden, Newton, H. S. Parkes, Peel, Pellew, Sir W. Penn, Pusey, Randolph, Richardson, Ruskin, Sabine, Shelley, A. Smith, Smollett, Street, Thackeray, Tooke, Trevithick, Turner, Tyndall, Vane, Wakley, Walker, W. Waller, Wallis, Westmacott, Whitefield, Whitgift, J. Wilson, Wolfe.

II. — MEDIUM

Anson, M. Arnold, Austen, Austin, F. Bacon, N. Bacon, Baillie, Bancroft, J. Banks, Barnes, I. Barrow, J. Barrow, E. Barry, J. Barry,* Becher, C. Brontë, Bennett, J. Bentham, Bentley, Bewick, Blackstone, W. Blake, Bonington, Boscawen, Boswell, Bowring, R. Boyle, Bradley, H. Bradshaw, Brewster, Brougham, E. Browning, R. Browning, Burbage, Burke, Burns, S. Butler, Byng, Byron, Cadogan, T. Campbell, Canton, Carlyle, M. Carpenter, Cayley, Cecil, Chalmers, Chantrey, Chatterton, Chaucer, Chillingworth, C. Churchill, C. Cibber, Clark, R. Clive, Cobbett, Cockburn, Coke, S. Coleridge, William Collins, Colman, Cooper (First Lord Shaftesbury), R. Cotton, A. Cowley, Crabbe, Cranmer, Crichton, Croker, O. Cromwell, Cross, Cruikshank, C. Darwin, E. Darwin, Davy, Defoe, Denman, De Quincey, Dickens, Dobson, Dryden, Flaxman, Flowers, C. J. Fox, Francis, Fry, Gainsborough, Gifford, Girtin, Gladstone, Goldsmith, G. Graham, Grattan, Grote, Harrington, Harvey, Hastings, Haydon, Hazlitt, Hill, Hoadley, Hobbes, Holcroft, T. Hood, Hooke, Horner, J. Hunter, Huxley, Hyde, Inchbald, Jenner, Jerrold, Jervis, Johnson, I. Jones, Jonson, Jowett, Keats, F. Kemble, Kenyon, Knox, Lambert, Lander, Landon, Landor, Landseer, E. Law (Baron Ellenborough), J. Law, W. Law, Latimer, H. Lawrence, J. Lawrence, S. Lawrence, Leech, J. Leslie, Lever, G. H. Lewes, Livingstone, Locke, Macaulay, Mackenzie, Mackintosh, Maclise, Macready, Maginn, Malone, Manning, Marryat, H. Martineau, J. Martineau, Mead, C. Middleton, J. S. Mill, Millais, Miller, Milton, Mitford, C. Montagu, T. More, G. Morland, Morris, Murchison, C. Napier, C. J. Napier, Nelson, J. H. Newman, O'Connell, Oldfield, A. Opie, J. Opie, Sir R. Owen, R. Owen, W. Paget,

---

* I have since noted that in his own portrait of himself Barry's eyes are blue and hair light.

Paine, Park, Patmore, Pepys, Petty, Perkins, Pitt (Lord Chatham), Pitt, Pococke, Pope, Popham, Pratt, Priestley, Prior, Pulteney, Raffles, Reynolds, Rogers, Roscoe, Rose, C. Rossetti, D. G. Rossetti, Sancroft, J. Scott, Walter Scott, William Scott, Selden, Shakespeare, Sidgwick, Sidney, Sinclair, Smart, W. S. Smith, Somers, Somerville, Spelman, Spenser, Stanley, Stephenson, Stewart, Stothard, Suckling, Swift, Sydenham, Tait, H. Taylor, Thomson, Thurloe, H. Vere, E. Waller, R. Walpole, Warburton, Warham, Watt, J. Wesley, Whiston, G. White, S. Wilberforce, W. Wilberforce, Wilde, Wilkie, C. H. Williams, W. Williamson, Wolcot, W. Wordsworth, Wren, Wyatt, Wycherley.

III. — DARK

Abercromby, Babbage, Bagehot, Baxter, Betterton, Bishop, Black, Borrow, Bracegirdle, J. Bruce, Burnet, Burton (Sir R.), Camden, J. Churchill, S. Cibber, Cobden, H. Coleridge, J. Cook, Crome, T. Cromwell, Curran, Dampier, Day, Dempster, Dibdin, Digby, Dolben, W. Drummond, Faraday, Ferrier, Fielding, J. Foxe, Froude, Galt, Garrick, Gay, Gibson, M. Godwin, Grenville (Baron), Gresham, Hale, Henderson, E. Herbert, T. Hook, Hooker, Howard, Hunt, Ireton, Irving, Jeffrey, Jewel, Juxon, Kean, Keble, Keene, J. M. Kemble, J. P. Kemble, Ken, Lamb, Lancaster, Laud, T. Lawrence, A. Leslie, Lovelace, Marvell, Melville, J. Milner, J. Moore, T. Moore, H. More, L. A. Neilson, Nicholson, Northcote, M. Oliphant, Otway, Oughtred, Outram, J. Owen, Paley, Parr, R. Parsons, Phillip, Picton, Prestwich, Quarles, Raleigh, Raeburn, Ray, Reade, R. Reid, Ridley, Romney, Sedgwick, Sheridan, Siddons, S. Smith, Southey, Steele, Steevens, Stevenson, Symonds, J. Taylor, Temple, Tennyson, Thurlow, Tillotson, Ussher, H. Walpole, Whitelocke, J. Williamson, Windham, Winwood, Wishart, Woffington, Wolsey, J. Wright, Yates.

INDEX

Aberdeen, 52, 53.
Actors, great, distribution of, 63, 64; preponderance of Irish element in, 64; frequently of low and obscure birth, 75, 76; why generally dark, 304.
Adams, John Couch, 61.
Ahlfeld, 114.
Airy, Sir George B., 36.
Akenside, Mark, 8.
Albinos, 305.
Alexander the Great, 9.
Alexander of Hales, 41.
Alfred, King, 38.
American Academy, Annals of, 79.
Andrewes, Lancelot, 36.
Angina pectoris, 168, 169.
Anglo-Danish district of England, limits of, 58, 59; eminent scientists in, 42 and *n.*, 43.
Ansell, C., *On the Rate of Mortality*, etc., 94, 97, 98, 99, 110, 113, 116, 139, 140, 143.
Anthropometric Committee of the British Association, tables of stature of, 274, 275.
Anthropometry of genius, knowledge of, in elementary state, 27 *ff.*; lists of eminent men arranged according to height, 278–81.
Apoplexy, 161.
Arabian Nights, The, 219.
Arbuthnot, John, 8.
Architectural Review, quoted, 62, 63.
Aretæus, 167.
Aristocracy, hereditary British, pigmentation of, 299, 300.
Aristotle, 111, 199, 209.
Armstrong, John, 8.
Arnold, Matthew, 36, 39, 221.
Arnold, Thomas, 36.
Arréat, *Psychologie du Peintre*, 74.
Arthurian legend, Wales the home of, 232.
Artistic genius, rarely inherited, 84, 85.
Artists, distribution of, 62, 63; occupational heredity among, 72–74; precocity of, 126.
Asthma, spasmodic, 168.
Austen, Jane, 4.
Awkwardness in use of hands and feet, 181–83.

Bach, Johann S., 84.
Bacon, Francis, Lord Verulam, 44, 60, 115, 238.
Bacon, Nathaniel, 36.
Bacon, Roger, 39, 46.
Bacons, the, a gouty family, 163.
Bagehot, Walter, 46, 177.
Baillie, Joanna, 84, 118.
Balde, Father, *Solatium Podagricorum*, 164.
Balzac, H. de, 277.
Banks, Sir J., 126.
Barbauld, Anna Letitia, 173 *n.*
Barbauld, Rochemont, 173 *n.*
Barrow, Isaac, 36, 126, 127.
Barry, J., 125, 170.
Baxter, Richard, 161.
Beardsley, Aubrey, 161.
Beauties, famous, pigmentation of, 299.
Beauty, physical, 196, 197.
Becket, Thomas, 23.
Beddoe, John, his observations of relative fairness and darkness of British people, 289, 290, 295 *n.*; 30 *n.*, 40 *n.*, 74, 189 *n.*, 190 *n.*, 191, 193 *n.*
Beddoes, Thomas L., 84.
Bell, Clive, 262 *n.*
Bentham, Jeremy, 120.
Biological data, lack of, in *Dic-*

tionary of National Biography, 14–16; how supplied, 16.
Birthplace, and genius, 19, 2[illegible] and *n.*
Black, Joseph, 161.
Blackstone, Sir W., 39, 121.
Blake, Robert, 39, 45.
Blake, William, 45 *n.*, 171.
Boniface, Saint, 39.
Bonington, Richard P., 161.
Booth, J. B., 75.
Borrow, George, 170, 186.
Boswell, James, 171.
Boyle, Robert, 41, 115, 177.
Boys and girls, relative numbers of, in genius-producing families, 98–101; and in families of persons of genius, 151, 152.
Bradlaugh, Charles, 36.
Bradley, James, 39.
Bradshaw, John, 5.
Bright, John, 41.
Brontë, Charlotte, 142.
Brougham, Henry, Lord, 180.
Brown, Ford Madox, 260, 261, 262 and *n.*, 268.
Brown, Thomas, 8.
Browne, R., 171.
Browne, Sir Thomas, 41, 47, 197, 237, 238.
Browning, Elizabeth B., 142, 198.
Browning, Robert, 39.
Bruce, James, 120.
Bryant, Sophia, *The Celtic Mind*, 221 *n.*, 228 *n.*
Brythons, in Ireland, 54.
Brythonic Ordovices, in Wales, 50.
Buchanan, George, 133.
Buchanan, W. J., 276.
Burke, Edmund, 120.
Burne-Jones, Sir E., 222 *n.*, 261, 262 *n.*, 268.
Burney, Fanny, 125, 142.
Burns, Robert, 53, 196, 197.
Burton, Robert, *The Anatomy of Melancholy*, 282.
Butler, Samuel, 41.
Byron, George Gordon, Lord, 39, 115, 125.
Caine, Hall, 273.
Cambridge University, and Oxford, respective influence of, 128, 129, 130.
Campbell, Henry, *Causation of Disease*, 37, 105.
Canning, George, 39.
Canning, Stratford, 39.
Cantlie, *Degeneration amongst Londoners*, 37.
Carman, Miss, 104.
Cassel, *Was lehrt die Untersuchung*, etc., 96; 74, 179.
Cattell, J. McKeen, *A Statistical Study of Eminent Men*, 7–9, 10, 13, 14, 109.
Cavendish, H., 171.
Cavendish, Thomas, 36.
Caxton, William, 29, 133.
Celibacy, comparative tendency to, of men of genius, 144, 145.
Celibates, 136 and *n.*, 137.
Celt, proper use of the term, 213 and *n.*
'Celtic glamour,' defined, 214 *ff.*
'Celtic Movement,' the, 242, 243.
Chalmers, Thomas, 126.
Chamberlain, A. F., *The Child*, 121 *n.*
Chanson de Roland, 225, 228–31, 232.
Chapman, George, 235 *n.*
Charles I, 30, 249, 250, 293, 297.
Charles II, 297.
Chatham, Earl. *See* Pitt, William.
Chatterton, Thomas, 121, 125, 156, 197.
Chaucer, Geoffrey, 36, 56, 70, 115, 234.
Chesterfield, Lord. *See* Stanhope.
Children, first-born and last-born, particulars concerning, 103–05, 188.
Children of eminent persons, comparative numbers of, 148 *ff.* And *see* Families.
Churchill, John, Duke of Marlborough, 44, 61, 169 *n.*

Clare, John, 170.
Clergy, as fathers of eminent men, 68, 69; prevalence of ill-health among, 159, 160.
Clifford, William K., 39, 161.
Clive, Robert, Lord, 41.
Clouston, *Neuroses of Development*, 178.
Cobbett, William, 186.
Coleridge, Hartley, 287.
Coleridge, S. T., 39, 45 *n.*, 115, 239, 240.
Colet, John, 36, 98 *n.*
Collins, F. Howard, *Practical Treatise of Midwifery*, 92, 113, 147.
Collins, William, 170.
Colman, George, the elder, 171.
Congreve, William, 163, 197.
Constable, John, 36, 120, 259, 260 and *n.*, 265.
Constitutional delicacy in early life, frequent among eminent persons, 118.
Consumption, 161, 162 and *n.*
Cook, James, 186, 194.
Cooley, C. H., 79.
Cooper, Anthony A., third Earl of Shaftesbury, 3.
Cotman, John S., 36, 170.
Cotton, Sir A. T., 156.
Counties, English, distribution of persons of genius among, 26 *ff.*; intellectual ability per square mile and per 100,000 inhabitants in, 28–32; apparent correlation between fertility in genius in, and other elements, 64, 65.
Counties, Scotch, distribution of genius among, 51–54.
Counties, Welsh, distribution of genius among, 51.
Cowley, Abraham, 121, 125, 137.
Cowper, William, 36, 170, 175.
Crabbe, George, 67 *n.*
'Craftsmen,' as fathers of men of genius, 70, 71; what the group includes, 71; predominant in parentage of artists, 73, 74.
Cranmer, Thomas, 36.
Criminals, generally spring from large families, 96; are often first-born children, 104.
Croker, John Wilson, 177.
Crome, John, 259.
Cromwell, Oliver, 170.
Cromwell, Thomas, 126.
Cullen, Dr., 166.
Cuneda, 50.
Curran, John P., 177.

Dalton, John, 137.
Dampier, William, 39, 194.
Dante Alighieri, 220.
Dark people. *See* Fair people.
Darwin, Charles, his double inheritance of genius, 82, 83; 41, 47, 59, 134, 163.
Darwin, Erasmus, 177.
Death, average age of eminent persons at, 153.
Decorative element in Celtic poetry, 220.
Dempster, Thomas, 98 *n.*
Denham, Sir John, 170.
Devonshire, quality of genius in, 44; and painters of tradition, 263.
Dexter, E., *High Grade Men in College and Out*, 130.
Diabetes, 169 *n.*
Dickens, Charles, 120.
Dictionary of National Biography, how utilized in this study, 1, 2; principle of selection from persons named in, 2 *ff.*; lack of biological data in, 14–16; men of genius named in Supplement to, 76, 77, 87, 88, 93, 144, 148, 267.
Dobson, William, the first genuinely English painter, 252, 253.
Doddridge, Philip, 98 *n.*
Dodgson, Charles L., 177.
Donne, John, 84.
Down, Langdon, *Mental Affec-*

tions of Childhood, 96, 103; 69, 116.
Doyle, Sir Conan, *Men of the Time*, 22, 33 *n.*, 35.
Drake, Sir F., 44.
Dream of Maxen Wledig, The, 217, 218.
Dryden, John, 197, 287.
Dublin, predominance of, in Ireland, 54.
Duckworth, Dyce, *A Plea for the Neurotic Theory of Gout*, 166.
Dugdale, Sir W., 104.
Duncan, Matthews, *Fecundity*, etc., 114; *Sterility in Women*, 119.
Dunstan, Saint, 39.
Dutch element in British genius, 24.

East Anglia, predominance of, in persons of genius, 34, 35, 36; characteristics of great men of, 42, 43 and *n.*, 60; has produced some of the worst men, 42 and *n.*
East Anglian focus, and painters of nature, 263.
Eddas, the, 224, 232.
Edinburgh, 52, 53.
Education. *See* University education.
Edward IV, 297.
Eichholz, Dr., *The Treatment of Feeble-Minded Children*, 179.
Eighteenth century, unusual number of persons of genius in, 11.
Eliot, George. *See* Evans, Mary Ann.
Elizabeth, Queen, 297.
Ellis, Havelock, *Evolution of English Painting*, 270 *n.*
Engelmann, Dr., 147.
England, all of the great foci of genius in southern part of, 41; northern part of, predominantly Anglo-Danish, 41, 42 and *n.*; eminent scientists in, 57 *ff.*; predominance of, in production of great sailors, 62; distribution of great actors in, 64; fusion of Celtic and Nordic spirit in, 232.
English, proportion of, among persons of genius, 21 *ff.*
Epilepsy, 176.
Erasmus, Desiderius, 248.
Evans, Mary Ann (George Eliot), 142.
Ewart, R. J., 115, 187.
Explorers, why generally dark, 303, 304.
Eyes, brilliancy of, 196, 197; colour of, strictly inherited, 298; 189 *ff.*, 289, 292–94.

Fair people, and dark people, distribution of, in Great Britain, 289; in different occupations, 290, 295; classes of, 292; divided into groups based on portraits in National Portrait Gallery, 293 *ff.*; in Norway, 305–07.
Families of persons of genius, size of, above the average of normal families, 91–95, 98 *n.*; marked predominance in ability of eldest and youngest children in, 101–05.
Faraday, Michael, 45 *n.*, 57 *n.*
Fathers, of eminent children, average age of, at their birth, 105–11, 117; average age of, at marriage, 138–40.
Faure, Élie, 262 *n.*
Féré, *Professional Neuroses*, 181.
Fergusson, Robert, 170.
Fielding, Henry, 39, 41, 47, 163.
Flaxman, John, 36, 267.
Flemish element in British genius, 24.
Fletcher, John, 36.
Fletcher, Joseph, 64.
Ford, John, 39, 169.
Foreign ancestry, and British. *See* Mixed ancestry.
Foreign countries, effect on emi-

nent persons of early residence in, 132–35.
Foreign universities, 128, 129.
Fox, Charles J., 39.
Fox, George, 170.
Foxe, John, 42.
French elements in British genius, 23.
French Revolution, the, 13.
Froude, J. A., 39.

Gainsborough, Thomas, 36, 254, 256, 257 and *n.*, 262 *n.*
Galt, John, 120.
Galton, Sir Francis, *English Men of Science*, 57, 58, 79, 88, 95, 103, 109, 110, 112, 148, 151, 157, 185; *Hereditary Genius*, 81, 94, 159, 160, 204, 205 and *n.*, 298.
Garrod, Alfred H., 165.
Genius, intellectual, tendency of, to run in families, 81; instances of relationships between eminent persons, 82, 83; factors of, 212. And *see* Talent.
Genius-producing classes, comparison of, with ordinary population, 77–79.
Geoffrey of Monmouth, 232.
George I, 297, 298.
George II, 298.
Gibbon, Edward, 163.
Gilbert, Sir Humphrey, 44.
Gilbert, William, 9, 36, 60.
Gildas, 48 and *n.*
Gillray, James, 170.
Gini, Signor, 105.
Giraldus Cambrensis, 55.
Girls. *See* Boys and girls.
Girtin, Thomas, 161.
Gladstone, W. E., 279 *n.*, 291.
Glisson, Dr., 61.
Godwin, William, 287.
Goidelic-Iberian centre. *See* South-western focus.
Goidels, in Wales, 50; in Ireland, 54.
Goldsmith, Oliver, 125.
Goodhart, Dr., 181.
Gout, marked association of, with persons of eminent ability, 162–68.
Gower, John, 29.
Grandparents of eminent persons, importance of origins of, 19, 20.
Grasset, Prof., *La supériorité intellectuelle et la névrose*, 209, 210.
Great Britain, evolution of painting in, 248 *ff.*
Gregory, Isabella A. Persse, Lady, *Cuchulain of Muirthemne*, 55, 214 *n.*
Gresham, Sir Thomas, 36, 70.
Grocyn, William, 39.
Grosseteste, Robert, 36.
Guest, Lady C., her translation of the *Mabinogion*, 214 *n.*
Günther, Hans, *Die Sexual-proportionen*, 101.
Guppy, *Homes of Family Names*, 40.
Gwynn, Stephen, 241.

Hair, colour of, 189, 191, 193, 289, 292, 294.
Hales, John, 46.
Hales, Stephen, 36, 61, 200.
Hall, G. Stanley, 285.
Hall, Marshall, 178.
Hall, Robert, 8.
Hamilton, Emma, Lady, 5.
Hamilton, Sir W. R., 125, 163, 176, 177.
Handwriting, illegible, tendency to, among men of genius, 180, 181.
Hansen, A. M., 306.
Hartwell, E. M., 178, 179.
Harvey, William, 30, 48, 60, 163.
Hastings, Warren, 41.
Hawkins, Sir John, 39, 44.
Hawthorne, Nathaniel, a pure example of the Celtic spirit in literature, 242; *The House of the Seven Gables* and the *Mabinogion*, 242.
Haydon, B. R., 170.
Health of eminent persons, divers particulars concerning, 118 *ff.*;

ill-health, in various categories, 159 *ff.*
Height. *See* Stature.
Henrietta Maria, Queen, 197.
Henriette d'Angleterre, sister of Charles I, 293 *n.*
Henry VIII, 297.
Herbert, Edward, Lord Herbert of Cherbury, 41, 176.
Herbert, George, 41.
Heredity of intellectual genius, 81 *ff.*; 'sexual partition' of, equal, 84 *ff.*
Hill, G., *English Dioceses*, 26 *n.*
Historical periods, distribution of persons of genius according to, 10–12.
Hobbes, Thomas, 39, 46, 118, 120.
Hogarth, William, 253, 255.
Holbein, Hans, 248, 249.
Holway, R. S., *The Age of Parents*, 113.
Homer, 9, 220.
Hook, William, 180.
Hooker, Richard, 39, 46, 197.
Huguenot element in British genius, 23, 24.
Huguenots in Ireland, 55.
Hull, Eleanor, 214 *n.*
Hume, David, 123.
Humphrey, Sir G., *The Human Skeleton*, 287.
Humphrey, Sir J., 104.
Hunt, Holman, 261.
Hunter, William, 163.
Hutchinson, Woods, *The Meaning of Uric Acid and the Urates*, 165, 166.
Hutton, James, 4.
Huxley, Thomas H., 39, 46, 61, 89 *n.*

Ill-health. *See* Health.
Imbecility, congenital, affinity of genius with, 206, 207.
Imprisonment, effect of, on genius, 201.
Inchbald, Elizabeth S., 177.
Industrial progress, and the production of eminent men, 79, 80.
Insane persons, high fertility of families from which they spring, 96.
Insanity, relationship of genius with, 169 *ff.*, 205 *ff.*; in forbears or descendants of eminent persons, 172, 173; and in their wives or husbands, 173, 174; significance of, 175, 176.
Intellectual activity in Great Britain, effect of great religious, social, and political movements on, 12–14.
Ireland, W. W., *The Mental Affections of Children*, 182, 183.
Ireland, distribution of genius in, 54, 55; Celtic tradition in, 214; Celtic literature in, 240–42.
Irish, proportion of, among persons of genius, 21 *ff.*; hampered by circumstances, 21.

James I, 297.
James II, 297.
Jastrow, J., 121 *n.*
Jeffreys, George, Lord, 8.
John of Salisbury, 39.
Johnson, Samuel, 163, 180.
Jonson, Ben, 235.
Jordan, Mrs., 170.
Joule, James P., 70.
Jutes, 49.

Kant, Immanuel, 286.
Kauffmann, Angelica, and Reynolds, 137.
Kean, Edmund, 170.
Keats, John, 39, 45 *n.*, 56, 118, 126, 161, 239, 240, 287.
Keble, John, 41.
Kemble, Charles, 41.
Kemble, John P., 41.
Kemble, Sarah, 41. And *see* Siddons.
Kent (county), fluctuation in genius-producing power of, 29–31, 34; affiliations of great men of, 47, 48.
Kiernan, Dr., 57 *n.*
Kingsley, Charles, 39, 177, 180.

Kingsley, Henry, 39.
Kneller, Sir G., 253.
Knox, John, 53, 301.
Körösi, 116.
Kretschmer, *Physique and Character*, 199 *n.*, 287 *n.*

Lamb, Charles, 36, 170, 177.
Landor, W. S., 41, 47, 125, 163, 234.
Landseer, Sir Edwin, 170.
Lawrence, Sir Thomas, 41.
Lawyers, eminent, longevity of, 154, 155.
Laycock, Dr., 166.
Lee, Nathaniel, 170.
Leinster, 54.
Lely, Sir Peter, 253.
Leslie, Charles, 106, 115.
Letulle, Maurice, 162 *n.*
Lever, Charles, 170.
Lewes, George H., 142.
Linacre, Thomas, 30.
Liquor-dealers, as fathers of men of genius, 70.
Locke, John, 39, 46, 118.
Lombroso, Cesare, *Man of Genius*, 110; 177, 205, 277.
London, as birthplace of men of genius, ignored, and why, 36, 37.
Longevity of men of genius, 153 *ff.*
Lowe, Robert, Viscount Sherbrooke, 305.
Lyell, Sir Charles, 134.
Lyly, John, 30.
Lytton, Edward G. B. E. Bulwer, Baron, 36.
Lytton, Edward R. L. Bulwer, Earl, 36.

Mabinogion, the, quoted, 215; the true expression of Celtic genius, 216 *n.*; 232, 242.
Macaulay, T. B., Lord, 41, 47, 182.
MacColl, D. S., 170 *n.*
MacDonald, Arthur, 188.
Macfarlane, 33 *n.*
Mackintosh, Sir James, 49.
Maclean, H. H., *Where We Get Our Best Men*, 21, 22; 78, 129, 130.
Macleod, Fiona. *See* Sharp, William.
Macpherson, James, 8.
Maginn, William, 177.
Magri, Prof., *Le Famiglie*, etc., 96.
Malory, Sir Thomas, *Morte d'Arthur*, 233.
Map, Walter, 41.
Marandon de Montyel, 96.
Marlborough, Duke of. *See* Churchill.
Marlowe, Christopher, 30.
Marriage of eminent persons, conditions with respect to, studied, 136 *ff.*; their average age at, 139–43. And *see* Sterility.
Marro, on the age of fathers of eminent persons, 110, 111; and of their mothers, 113; on disparity of ages of parents, 116, 117; 167, 194.
Marsh, Herbert, 171.
Marshall, J., 180.
Martineau, Harriet, 36, 173 *n.*
Martineau, James, 36.
Mary I, 297.
Mary II, 297.
Mary of Modena, queen of James II, 297.
Maudsley, H., 171, 172 *n.*
Maurice, F. D., 278 *n.*
Mediterranean, the primary centre of painting, 244, 245–48.
Melancholy, 199 *ff.*
Men, and women, comparative standard of ability of, 9.
Middlesex, aboriginal ability in, 36, 37.
Middleton, J. H., *Biographica Evangelica*, 159.
Mill, John Stuart, 125, 127, 180.
Millais, J. E., 261, 268, 291.
Milton, John, 56, 72, 163, 220, 240.
Mitchell, Sir A., 103.
Mixed ancestry, proportion of, among eminent persons, 21, 22–25.

Möbius, August F., 84.
Modesty. *See* Shyness.
Monmouthshire, why excluded from consideration, 40, 41.
Montagu, Elizabeth R., 9.
Moore, Thomas, 241, 242.
More, Hannah, 9, 173 *n.*
More, Sir Thomas, 36.
Moreau de Tours, *Psychologie morbide*, etc., 209, 210.
Morland, Henry R., 258.
Morris, William, 41, 209, 240.
Mothers of eminent children, age of, at their birth, 111–15, 117; as second or third wives, 115.
Müller, Max, *Autobiography*, 84.
Munden, Joseph S., 193.
Munster, 54.
Murchison, Sir R. J., 127.
Musical genius, rarely inherited, 84, 85.

Napier, John, of Merchiston, 106.
Napoleon III, 9.
Natality in families of eminent persons and in genius-producing families, 150–52.
National Portrait Gallery, index of pigmentation of various groups, based on portraits in, 290 *ff.*; 16, 189, 194, 195.
Nationality and race, not identical terms, 18.
Nature, painters of. *See* Painters.
Neilson, L. Adelaide, 63 *n.*
Nelson, Horatio, Lord, 36.
Newman, Francis W., 36.
Newman, John Henry, Cardinal, 36.
Newton, Sir Isaac, 9, 42, 59, 118, 126, 163, 171.
Nineteenth century, county distribution of persons of genius born in, 29 *ff.*
Nobility, hereditary, as such, excluded from consideration, 2, 3; few persons excluded by this rule, 3. And *see* Aristocracy.
Nordic spirit in literature, where first manifested, 224; compared with Celtic spirit, 225 *ff.*; predominance of emotion in, 225–27; fusion of, with Celtic spirit, 232 *ff.*
Norfolk (county), persons of genius in, 34, 35.
Norway, pigmentation of people of, 305–07.
Nottinghamshire, great artists in, 62, 63.

Oates, Titus, 5.
Occupational heredity, 72 *ff.*
Odin, *Genèse des Grands Hommes*, 79.
Offa, King of Mercia, 40.
Oliphant, Laurence, 171.
Organic inaptitude. *See* Imbecility.
Otway, Thomas, 278 *n.*
Oxford, and Cambridge, respective influences of, 128, 129, 130.

Painters, eminent, geographical distribution of, 262 *ff.*, 266; those influenced by nature and by tradition respectively, 263 *ff.*, 268, 269. And *see* England, Water-colour painters.
Painting, two primary and two secondary centres of, in Europe, 244–48; in Great Britain, 248 *ff.*
Paley, William, 180.
Papillault, M., 187, 188.
Parents of men of genius, social status of, 66 *ff.*; do their occupations influence the mental aptitudes of their sons? 72 *ff.*; importance of moral and emotional qualities of, 89, 90; lack of effectiveness in, 90, 91; boy-producing, 98; disparity of ages in male and female, 115–17. And *see* Fathers, Mothers.
Paris, Gaston, 229.
Pater, Walter, 36.
Paterson, William, 170.
Patrick, Saint, 134.
Pearson, J., 171.

Pearson, Karl, *The Chances of Death*, 92 and *n.*, 94; 147, 150.
Penn, Thomas, 41.
Penn, William, 41.
Perkins, William, 127.
Permewan, Dr., 180.
Pigmentation, of eminent persons, index of, 190–93; index of, based on portraits in the National Portrait Gallery, 295; and conclusions drawn therefrom, 296 *ff.*
Pitt, William, Earl Chatham, 39, 163, 170.
Pitt, William, 39, 163.
Pitt-Rivers, *Excavations in Cranborne Chase*, 38.
Poets, distribution of, 56; heredity of, 84; longevity among, less marked than among other groups, 154.
Popham, Sir John, 98.
Porson, Richard, 36.
Portraits painted and written, discrepancies between, 291.
Powell, Edgar, *The Rising in East Anglia in 1381*, 28 *n.*
Precocity of persons of genius, 121 *ff.*
Pre-Raphaelite movement, the, 260, 261, 262 *n.*, 267, 268.
Priestley, Joseph, 161, 177, 182.
Pugin, A. W. N., 170.
Purcell, Henry, 41, 47, 161.
Pusey, Edward B., 36.
Pym, John, 39.

Race, vagueness of term as applied to population of Great Britain, 18, 19.
Raleigh, Sir Walter, 39, 44, 45, 115.
Ranke, Johannes, 288.
Rauber, A., *Der Ueberschuss*, etc., 101.
Ray, John, 36, 60, 134.
Rayleigh, Lord. *See* Strutt.
Relationships between persons of genius, 82, 83.
Renaissance, English, in Kent, 29–31.
Renan, Ernest, 216 *n.*, 218.
Reveillé-Parise, 199, 210.
Reynolds, Sir Joshua, 39, 44, 137, 254, 255, 256, 257 and *n.*, 264, 265.
Rheumatism, 168.
Rhine, the primary centre of painting, 244, 245–48, 253, 269.
Rhys, and Brynmor-Jones, *The Welsh People*, 40 *n.*, 51 and *n.*
Rich, Lady Penelope, 137.
Ripley, William Z., *The Races of Europe*, 18 *n.*
Ritson, Joseph, 170.
Rivers, W. C., 105.
Robertson, J., *Essays and Notes*, 114.
Rodney, George B., Baron, 39, 170.
Romano, Julio, 249.
Romilly, Sir Samuel, 23.
Romney, George, 170.
Rossetti, Dante G., 170, 261, 268, 273.
Rossetti, William M., 268 *n.*, 273.
Royal family of Great Britain, pigmentation of, 296–98.
Royalty, excluded from consideration, 2, 3.
Rubens, Peter P., 250.
Ruskin, John, 170.

Sabine, Sir E., 171.
Sailors, great, in Devon and Somerset, 44, 45; distribution of, 62.
Saint-Hilaire, Geoffrey, 288.
Saxon, English, mental mediocrity of, 49.
Scientists, distribution of, 56–61.
Scotch, proportion of, among persons of genius, 21 *ff.*; intellectual ability especially marked among, 21.
Scotch universities, 128, 129, 130.
Scotland, distribution of genius in, 51–54; contrast between

Highlands and Lowlands in this respect, 52, 53; element of complexion in, 53; eminent scientists in, 56.
Scott, Clement, 63 *n.*
Scott, Sir Walter, 53, 123, 196.
Scott, William, Lord Stowell, 120.
Scottish National Portraits, 189 *n.*
Selection of subjects, principles of, 2 *ff.*
Seneca, 209.
'Sexual partition.' *See* Heredity.
Seymour, Lady Jane, 297.
Shaftesbury, Earl of. *See* Cooper.
Shakespeare, William, *The Tempest*, 236, 237; 30, 41, 47, 56, 72, 235, 249.
Sharp, William, 219 *n.*, 273.
Sheil, Richard L., 178.
Shelley, Percy B., 56, 182.
Sherbrooke, Lord. *See* Lowe.
Short persons. *See* Stature, Tall persons.
Shortsightedness, 181.
Shuttleworth, 103, 104.
Shyness, 197, 198.
Siddons, Sarah (Kemble), 47.
Sidgwick, Henry, 178.
Sidgwick, Mrs. Henry, *Health Statistics*, 94, 95, 143.
Sidney, Sir Philip, 84, 137.
Simpson, J. Y., on sterile marriages, 147.
Simpson, W. G., 119.
Smart, Christopher, 118, 170, 175.
Smith, Adam, 121.
Smith, Sir Thomas, 36.
Soldiers, great, distribution of, 61, 62.
Somersetshire, quality of genius in, 45, 46.
Somerville, Mary F., 9, 10.
Southall, *Wales and her Language*, 40 *n.*
Southey, Robert, 171.
South-western focus of genius, counties comprised in, 37, 38; characteristics of great men of, 38, 44–46, 60, 61; and painters of tradition, 263.
Spain, secondary centre of painting, 245.
Spasmodic movements, 180.
Spenser, Edmund, *Faërie Queene*, 234, 235; 56.
Stahl, Dr., 166.
Stammering, 177–80.
Stanhope, Philip D., Earl of Chesterfield, 289.
Starbuck, Prof., 104, 113.
Stature of eminent persons, 184 *ff.*, 271 *ff.*; final result of statistics concerning, 283 *ff.*
Stephen, Sir James F., 171.
Sterility, percentage of, among eminent persons, 145–48; in the United States and New Zealand, 147.
Sterne, Laurence, 118.
Stevens, Alfred, 39.
Stone (calculus), 168.
Story, A. T., *Life of W. Blake*, 45 *n.*
Stowell, Lord. *See* Scott, William.
Strutt, J. W., Lord Rayleigh, 118.
Suffolk, persons of genius in, 34.
Sully, Prof., *Genius and Precocity*, 121 *n.*; *The Education of Genius*, 131, 132.
Sutton, Sir J. B., 182.
Swift, Jonathan, 121, 169, 171, 278 *n.*
Sydenham, Thomas, *De Podagra*, 163; 39, 61.

Talent, and genius, difference in inheritability of, 81 *n.*, 85; difficulty of distinguishing between, 85.
Tall persons, predominance of, over short ones, 185, 186. And *see* Stature.
Temperament of genius, elements of, tend to resemble each other, 204 *ff.*
Tennyson, Alfred, Lord, 236 *n.*, 240.
Thirlwall, Connop, 125.
Thurlow, Edward, Lord, 126.
Tillotson, John, 170.
Timidity, 198, 199.

Toulouse, Dr., *Causes de la Folie*, 96, 151, 271.
Tradesmen, as fathers of men of genius, 69, 70; what the group includes, 70.
Tradition, painters of. *See* Painters.
Traherne, Thomas, 238.
Transsabrina, the, 40 *n.*
Trevithick, Richard, 39, 186.
Trinity College, Dublin, 128, 129, 130.
Trollope, Sir H., 170.
Turner, J. M. W., 258, 259, 265.
Tyndale, William, 41.
Tyndall, John, 57.

Ulster, 54, 55.
United States, college education in, 130; stature and intellectual ability in, 187, 188.
University education, of eminent men, 127 *ff.*; significance of, 130–32.
Unskilled workers, as fathers of men of genius, 71.
'Upper class' fathers of men of genius, 67, 68.

Vaerting, 113.
Vandyke, Sir Anthony, 25 and *n.*, 252.
Varigny, H. de, *Croissance*, 186 *n.*
Vaughan, Henry, 238.
Velasquez, Diego, 245.
Venice, secondary centre of painting, 245, 253.
Veres, the, 36.
Victorian History of Northamptonshire, 42 *n.*
Volsunga Saga, quoted, 226; 228.

Wagner, Richard, 231.
Wales, distribution of intellectual genius in, 49–51; a Goidelic country, 50; Celtic tradition in, 214; the home of the Arthurian legend, 232.
Walker, Robert, 252, 253.
Wall, A. J., 100.
Walloon element in British genius, 24.
Walpole, Sir Robert, 36, 43.
Walsingham, Sir Francis, 36.
Wansdyke and Bokerley Dyke, 38.
Warburton, William, 171.
Ward, S., 171.
Wasse, Joseph, 274 *n.*
Water-colour painters in England, 257, 259.
Wedgwood, Josiah, 41.
Wells, G. S., *A Study of the Order of the Birth of Children*, 104.
Wells, Sir S., 166.
Welsh, proportion of, among persons of genius, 21, 22; different language of, 21, 40 and *n.*
Welsh Border focus of genius, 39 and *n.*; 40, 41, 50, 51; counties included in, 39, 40; Welsh language in, 40 and *n.*; characteristics of great men of, 46, 47, 50, 51; scientists in, 60.
Wesley, Charles, 41, 118.
Wesley, John, 41, 163.
Whitbread, Samuel, 170.
William III, 297.
Williams, Sir Charles H., 170.
Williams, H., 48 *n.*
Wilson, Richard, 254, 267.
Winter, L., 104.
Wiseman, N. P. S., Cardinal, 125.
Wolsey, Thomas, Cardinal, 36, 43.
Women, standard of ability among, compared with that among men, 9, 10; greater proportion of, among persons of genius of mixed race, 24, 25; on county basis, 33 and *n.*; rarity of genius in, and the heredity of genius, 84 *ff.*
Word Portraits of Famous Writers, 282 *n.*
Wordsworth, W., 56.
World, the, effect of attitude of, toward eminent persons, 201.
Worms, Dr., 169.
Wren, Sir Christopher, 41, 125.

Wright, T., 171.
Writer's cramp, 181.
Wycherley, William, 41.
Wyllie, *Disorders of Speech*, 178, 179.

Yeats, W. B., 45 *n.*, 222.
Yeo, Burney, 166, 167.
Yeomen, as fathers of men of genius, 67 and *n.*
Yoder, A. H., *Boyhood of Great Men*, 95, 103; 100, 109, 110, 112, 113, 119.
Young, Thomas, 39, 46, 51, 125.

Zola, Émile, 271.